Copyright © International Sculpture Center, 2008
PRINTED IN USA

A collection of articles on sculpture parks and gardens drawn in part from *Sculpture* magazine.

Sculpture magazine and ISC Press are programs of the International Sculpture Center, a 501(c)3 nonprofit corporation.

All rights reserved. No part of this publication may be reproduced or transmitted in any form or by any means, electronic or mechanical, including photocopying, recording, or any information storage or retrieval system, without permission in writing from the publisher.

isc Press

19 Fairgrounds Rd., Suite B
Hamilton, NJ 08619, USA
www.sculpture.org

Distributed by
University of Washington Press
PO Box 50096
Seattle, WA 98145-5096
www.washington.edu/uwpress

Library of Congress Cataloging-in-Publication Data

Landscapes for Art: Contemporary Sculpture Parks
Edited by Glenn Harper and Twylene Moyer. — 1st ed.

p. cm. — (Perspectives on contemporary sculpture)
ISBN 978-0-295-98861-0 (pbk. : alk. paper)
1. Sculpture parks. I. Harper, Glenn, 1946– II. Moyer, Twylene, 1966–.
NB1278.L36 2008
730.74 — dc22   2008029362

Design and production by Eileen Schramm visual communication.
Printed on acid-free paper.

COVER: Tony Cragg, *Bulb*, 2001. Stone, 330 x 180 x 180 cm. View of work at Goodwood, U.K.

Publication of this book was made possible in part by generous support from the Atlantic Foundation and the National Endowment for the Arts.

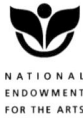

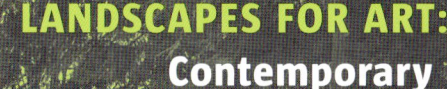

LANDSCAPES FOR ART:
Contemporary Sculpture Parks

Edited by Glenn Harper
and Twylene Moyer

Table of Contents

- 6 Foreword by Glenn Harper and Twylene Moyer
- 8 Art, Nature, People: The Sculpture Park Experience by Debra N. Lehane
- 14 Sculpture Parks as Outdoor Museums by Brooke Barrie
- 22 Planning the Museum Park at the North Carolina Museum of Art by Daniel P. Gottlieb
- 27 The National Gallery of Art Sculpture Garden by Sarah Tanguy
- 33 Making the Minneapolis Sculpture Garden: A Conversation with Martin Friedman by Carol Sterling
- 39 A Garden for Latin American Sculpture by Collette Chattopadhyay
- 42 DeCordova Museum and Sculpture Park: Staying on the Edge by Marty Carlock
- 46 Creating a Sculpture Garden in New Orleans: A Conversation with Sydney Besthoff by Robert Preece
- 51 Olympic Sculpture Park: Icons and Monuments by Matthew Kangas
- 55 Designing Sculpture Parks: The Full-Body Experience by Barbara Swift
- 61 Three Ideas of the Sculpture Garden: The Israel Museum, The Fields, and Grounds For Sculpture by Margaret Sheffield
- 68 Made For Each Other: Storm King's Vistas and Sculpture by Jan Garden Castro
- 72 Middelheim Open Air Museum of Sculpture: A Conversation with Menno Meewis by Robert Preece
- 75 Hakone Open-Air Museum: Sculpture in the Mountains of Japan by Ken Scarlett
- 80 Yorkshire Sculpture Park at 30 by Oliver Lowenstein
- 85 The Kröller-Müller Sculpture Park by Ken Scarlett
- 89 Laumeier Sculpture Park by Jan Garden Castro
- 93 Emerging Art at The Fields by Jan Garden Castro
- 96 Grounds For Sculpture: Present and Past by Patricia Summers
- 99 Australia's McClelland Gallery and Sculpture Park by Ken Scarlett
- 103 The Sculpture Park at Goodwood by John K. Grande
- 106 Frederik Meijer Gardens and Sculpture Park by Gerry Craig
- 110 Into the Woods: The Carell Woodland Sculpture Trail by Susan W. Knowles

- 114 **The Ephemeral Sculpture Garden** by John K. Grande
- 120 **TICKON and Sculpture in Nature's Eyes: A Conversation with Alfio Bonanno** by John K. Grande
- 126 **The Tree Museum, Canada** by Gil McElroy
- 129 **The Forest of Dean Sculpture Trail** by John K. Grande
- 132 **Sculpture in Woodland** by Robert Preece
- 135 **Wave Hill: Sculpture in the Garden** by Jonathan Goodman
- 139 **The Garden-Book: Environmental Art at La Marrana** by Andrea Bellini
- 144 **The Wanås Foundation: Patronage and Partnership** by Gregory Volk
- 149 **Site-Specific Sculpture at Fattoria di Celle** by Paula Bortolotti
- 152 **Collecting Experience: A Conversation with Steven Oliver** by Donna Brookman
- 158 **Sculpture in the Pines: The NMAC Foundation** by Cécile Bourne-Farrell
- 161 **The World Sculpture Park at Changchun** by Ken Scarlett
- 165 **The Open-Air Art Museum at Pedvale** by Allison Hunter
- 169 **The Cullen Sculpture Garden: A Conversation with Isamu Noguchi** by Tsipi Ben-Haim
- 172 **Hic Terminus Haeret: Daniel Spoerri's Garden** by John O'Brien
- 176 **Little Sparta: Ian Hamilton Finlay's Garden** by Anne Barclay Morgan
- 180 **Robert Irwin's *Central Garden* at the Getty** by Collette Chattopadhyay
- 184 **Nek Chand's *Rock Garden*** by Minhazz Majumdar
- 190 **Alternative Outdoor Spaces: Socrates Sculpture Park as a Case Study** by Alyson Baker
- 196 **Europos Parkas** by Joyce Ellen Weinstein
- 201 **Franconia Sculpture Park** by Ann Klefstad
- 204 **Salem Art Works** by Jacqueline Keren
- 208 **Toronto Sculpture Garden** by Gil McElroy
- 212 **Finland's Pirkkala Sculpture Park** by Allison Hunter
- 215 **Buffalo Bayou ArtPark and Community** by Kevin Jeffries

Foreword

When the International Sculpture Center first published a directory of sculpture parks and gardens in 1987, the pamphlet listed 97 parks. Nine years later, an updated edition featured 195 listings. Today, the field is too large and changing too quickly for a single book to capture it as a whole (the ISC is planning an on-line directory that will evolve along with the field). This book, then, is not a directory or an encyclopedia of sculpture parks and gardens. It is, rather, a survey of institutions that primarily exhibit contemporary artists (defined loosely as those active since about 1980, the start date for the two previous anthologies in the ISC's "Perspectives on Sculpture" series, *A Sculpture Reader* and *Conversations on Sculpture*).

As *Landscapes for Art* makes clear, there is no unique model for the contemporary sculpture park: typological and organizational possibilities abound, and we attempt to do justice to these variations in mission and strategy. But there is a common thread of purpose. These venues may be sprawling or intimate, woodland sanctuaries or urban hotspots; they may house major collections or install temporary interventions—but regardless of approach, they all fuse three normally distinct entities into a single, integrated experience. In a sculpture park, the artwork, the environment, and the history or aura of the place blend together almost seamlessly. As in a well-crafted garden, the line between the created and the inherited is blurred, or as curator Lisa Corrin says, a sense of inevitability is established so that "somehow these things grew up there and could never be anywhere else—it's as natural as breathing."

Reading the essays in order is not necessary, although the book's organization does imply a journey. Color indicators loosely group the featured parks and gardens into generalized families that move from familiar museum venues to established museum-style institutions like Storm King and Middelheim, to parks that focus on environmental and site-specific approaches (perhaps the sculpture park wave of the near future), to alternative and private sites such as Wanås, to gardens as sculpture and artist-designed parks, and finally to venues that offer artist residencies and serve as incubators for experimentation and risk-taking. Some of the sections include an introductory article, and others flow directly from the preceding category— a fluidity that reflects the flexibility and responsiveness of many smaller sculpture parks.

The articles, which take a variety of approaches, represent the viewpoints of critics, artists, landscape architects and planners, park founders and administrators. Moving from the visitor's perspective to the everyday realities behind the idyllic vistas, they offer behind-the-scenes glimpses of obstacles overcome, visions made tangible, and ideas never realized. Some pieces address directly sculptural aspects of sculpture parks and gardens, examining collections and their underlying philosophies, while others explore larger questions of design, planning, and maintenance, as well as the role of politics and the dynamics of cultural tourism. Some of the articles were newly commissioned for this publication, and others are reprinted from *Sculpture* magazine, a publication of the ISC. We have not included articles on public or private parks that occasionally display sculpture, concentrating, instead, on those for which art is a primary mission. We have also omitted a number of excellent public art programs with a park (or university campus) aspect, choosing to set them aside for discussion in a future volume that will deal with public art more broadly. The range of this anthology is limited primarily to sculpture parks in North America, Europe, Australia, and Japan, where the field's most substantial growth, over the longest period, has taken place. The ISC's on-line directory will survey a wider territory, both in terms of geography and the historical scope of artists featured in the parks.

Choosing to cover only parks that feature primarily contemporary artists has meant that we have left out several important institutions, including the Hirshhorn Museum and Sculpture Garden in Washington, DC, and the sculpture garden of the Museum of Modern Art in New York. Both are distinctive and vital examples of sculpture parks, but they focus on artists from Modernism to Minimalism, from Rodin to the 1970s (though MoMA recently turned its garden over to an exhibition of the recent work of Richard Serra, and the Hirshhorn garden and grounds feature sculpture by Mark di Suvero, Kenneth Snelson, Dan Graham, and Juan Muñoz, among others). There are also a number of excellent parks that are referred to in various articles, such as the groundbreaking PepsiCo collection and the Noguchi Museum's sculpture garden, which are not individually profiled.

We would like to thank the writers for their contributions to *Landscapes for Art*; for those articles that originally appeared in *Sculpture*, we also thank them for their permission to reprint their work. We also thank Beth Wilson and Elizabeth Lynch (editorial assistants for *Sculpture*), Johannah Hutchison (Executive Director of the International Sculpture Center), Eileen Schramm (the designer of this volume and of *Sculpture*), the Board of Directors of the ISC, J. Seward Johnson and the Atlantic Foundation and the National Endowment for the Arts (for their generous support of this publication and the ISC), and the staff of the ISC (past and present) who have made both this book and the magazine possible.

—*Glenn Harper & Twylene Moyer*

Art, Nature, People: The Sculpture Park Experience

by Debra N. Lehane

Sculpture parks and gardens proliferated across the world in the 20th century, and they continue to rise in popularity.[1] Brookgreen Gardens in South Carolina, established by artist Anna Hyatt Huntington in 1931, was the first independent sculpture park in America. In 1939, Philip Johnson designed the first American museum sculpture garden at the Museum of Modern Art in New York City. It would be another 21 years, however, before sculpture parks began to multiply in the U.S., starting with the opening of Storm King Art Center in upstate New York in 1960. Sculpture parks caught on a bit earlier in Europe: Belgium's Middelheim Open Air Museum of Sculpture dates back to 1950. In Asia, Japan's Hakone Open-Air Museum opened in 1969. Today, millions of people visit sculpture parks and gardens every year. New parks continue to open; and others are under construction, including the San Francisco Museum of Modern Art's 14,000-square-foot rooftop sculpture garden and the Indianapolis Museum of Art's much-anticipated Fairbanks Art and Nature Park.

Sculpture parks are, as Leslie Kaufman, director and founder of the Burlington County College Sculpture Garden in Pemberton, New Jersey, states, "being redefined as more than just galleries of outside art but as planned destinations with cultural offerings for the community."[2] They are also as varied as the sculpture they exhibit. These venues offer an informal environment in which visitors can engage with art while enjoying nature in communal open-air spaces.

The human interest in gardens is an ancient one, glimpsed through archaeological evidence, surviving artworks, and mythology. In more recent times, cultures across the world developed distinctive garden styles. The best known include the Renaissance and Baroque grotto, the Japanese tea garden, the French formal garden, and the English cottage garden. Elisabeth B. MacDougall, in her introduction to Sidney Lawrence and George Foy's *Music in Stone: Great Sculpture Gardens of the World*, states that "the impulse to place statues in an ornamental setting is as old as civilization itself."[3] This may be true, but as William Howard Adams, senior fellow of the Garden History Library at Dumbarton Oaks, Washington, DC, notes, "The sculpture garden as an outdoor gallery is a phenomenon of the 20th century."[4]

As might be expected, the forces behind the rise of the sculpture park are historic, economic, and cultural. Nick Capasso, curator of the DeCordova Museum and Sculpture Park in Lincoln, Massachusetts, believes that sculpture parks and gardens owe something to the general tendency toward museum expansion in the 1990s — every museum plan called for a garden, if it did not already have one.[5] Tim Burgard, curator at the Fine Arts Museums, San Francisco, identifies the recently designed garden spaces at the de Young Museum as a "front porch" for the museum, creating family-oriented, transitional spaces.[6] Peter Lundberg's experience suggests another reason for the proliferation of parks and gardens. A sculptor and former assistant to Mark di Suvero, Lundberg has started several small parks on the East Coast. As a maker of large works, he found storage and exhibition space a problem. To solve this dilemma, he rented a field from farmers in his hometown of Bomoseen, Vermont, and invited fellow sculptors to install some of their works.

Many writers identify Modernism as the catalyst behind the rise of outdoor sculpture.[7] As Mark Treib states, "Sculpture in the modern era—especially since the late 1950s—moved outdoors for a variety of reasons. Modern architecture, stripped of ornamentation and figuration, relegated art to the role of the disparate piece set on a plaza in front of a building."[8] As the size of buildings increased, sculptors sought design balance by working larger, and as contemporary sculpture "outgrew interior spaces, it was forced to move outdoors."[9] Sculptors were aware of the advantages offered by placing their work outside the controlled gallery space, but at the same time, they sensed an aesthetic struggle between the art, the architecture, and the urban plaza. In the 1960s, Land artists emphasized the viewer's direct experience with art. Viewers became part of the work. This sensibility of directly experiencing a work of sculpture outdoors carried over into the sculpture park and garden experience. Although Land Art itself is not prominent in sculpture parks, site-specific works began to appear as artists responded to place. A popular contemporary example is Andy Goldsworthy's *Storm King Wall*.

By the 1960s, the U.S. economy was thriving. Philanthropy was on the rise. In the 1970s, the National Endowment for the Arts developed its Art in Public Places program. Public art programs began to appear in cities around the country, but artists were dissatisfied with the limitations placed on them by the public process. This situation may have helped to reinforce the development and importance of the private sculpture park where artists had more freedom to create works of their choosing.[10]

Storm King was the first outdoor museum dedicated solely to the exhibition of sculpture. It is most noted for its displays of monumental artworks in a bucolic landscape. Irving Lavin, professor emeritus of the history of art at the Institute for Advanced Study in Princeton, New Jersey, frames the basic elements that he believes have contributed to Storm King's success as "physical (scale), aesthetic (relationship between objects and setting), intellectual (program and meaning), and social (relationship between patron and audience)."[11] Although Lavin lists the intellectual element, or vision, as third on his list, the importance of a founding vision is evident from the earliest sculpture parks. For example, for Alfred H. Barr, Jr., founding director of the Museum of Modern Art, "MoMA was a cause, an educational mission, and all its activities, buildings, and acquisitions were part of a continuous and integrated didactic program: the presentation of modern art. The sculpture gardens were clearly seen as an integral part of the curatorial and exhibition realm."[12]

The vision for many newer sculpture parks focuses on the artistic process. For example, in Shafer, Minnesota, Franconia Sculpture Park (founded in 1996) "nurture[s] artistic growth, creativity, and interaction between emerging, mid-career, and established sculptors in an outdoor, rural setting," according to its Web site. Salem Art Works in Salem, New York, and the Djerassi Resident Artists Program in Woodside, California, are primarily interested in supporting artists and the creative process. Their sculpture collections are by-products of their programs.

Each park or garden has a unique design. Just as an artist responds to an individual site, the landscape architect or architect analyzes the strengths and weaknesses of the entire space, whether it is 500 acres or only one. The designer of a sculpture park begins with space, using flora, sky, light, and topography to create contrast, movement, shape, color, and texture. The challenge is finding the right balance between nature and art to produce a successful composition. There are two primary ways to approach the sculpture garden: the master design can be informal, with the art sitting within a naturally appearing landscape, or it can be a formal arrangement of "rooms" or galleries created for the display of art.[13] Several parks combine the two. In every model, however, time, scale, and siting are paramount. Barry Thalden, landscape architect with Thalden Corporation, when creating a master plan for Laumeier Sculpture Park, saw his responsibility as "establishing a coherent and dynamic spatial sequence that would exist independently of the sculpture."[14]

Aesthetically, an outdoor setting is appreciated for its variable natural light, which creates a constantly changing viewing experience, influenced by weather conditions and seasonal variations. A visual dialogue takes place between the art and nature. British sculptor Henry Moore's appreciation of these changing conditions is seminal in regard to subsequent interest in siting large-scale sculpture outdoors and in nature. As Moore stated, "Out of doors the light is always changing, with the hour of the day and with the seasons, and at night. Moonlight magnifies." He also noted, "There is no background to sculpture better than the sky, because you are contrasting solid form with its opposite space."[15]

Other natural elements also enhance the display of sculpture. Treib notes, "Large tracts of forest and meadow provide sufficient space for large works," but he also warns, "The degree of success varies: often too many pieces share too small a space. The tendency of designers to create support walls and bases as objects in themselves, in competition with the sculpture garden, also undermines a clear viewing of the works."[16] For artists and sculpture park officials alike, the most important design element in a sculpture park or garden is how the sculpture is sited. Nick Capasso calls this the "marriage of landscape and sculpture."[17] Artists care deeply about the work they create and are often assets in the placement of sculpture, guiding the site selection to a location that enhances both the work and the park.

Successful parks take design, art, and nature into equal consideration. But there are additional concerns important to visitors. For instance, public parks and gardens in the U.S. must comply with Americans with Disabilities Act (ADA) standards. Maintenance is another practical consideration: "Every institutional property must be designed for the minimum maintenance it is likely to receive, for in a period of stringent budgets the outdoor maintenance is usually the first item to be cut."[18] Finally, sculpture parks and gardens must be designed for the totality of the visitor's experience.[19]

Visitor experience is addressed by a series of articles appearing in *The Public Garden*, a journal of the American Public Gardens Association. Most of the October 1992 issue is dedicated to "art in the garden." Written for public garden administrators, the articles address practical concerns like collection policies, exhibit programming, maintenance planning, and conservation of sculpture in the outdoor environment. The first essay is a philosophical discussion by Donald M. Kendall, the man behind the PepsiCo sculpture park in Purchase, New York. His first-hand account of the creation of PepsiCo's park echoes the vision behind Storm King, but for Kendall, the sculpture

Henry Moore, *Reclining Figure*, 1956. Bronze, view of work at the Donald M. Kendall Sculpture Gardens at PepsiCo, Purchase, New York.

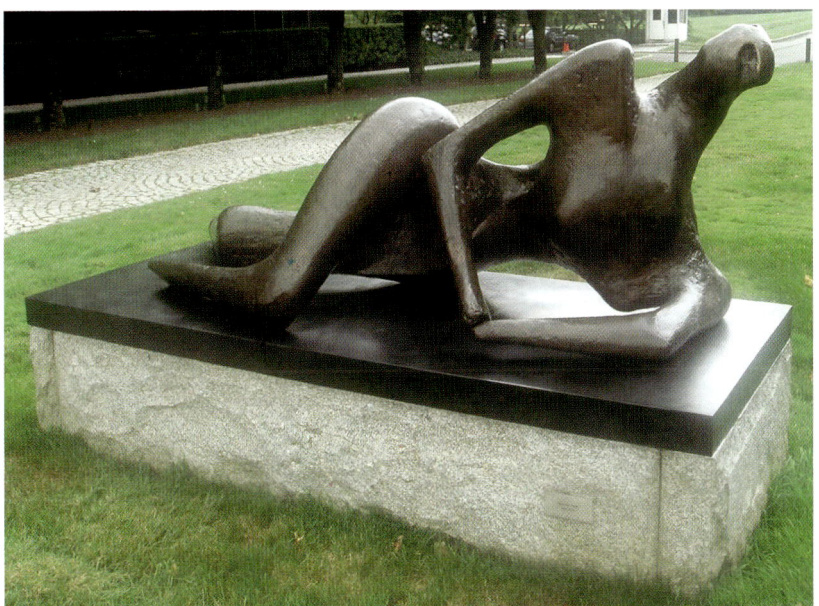

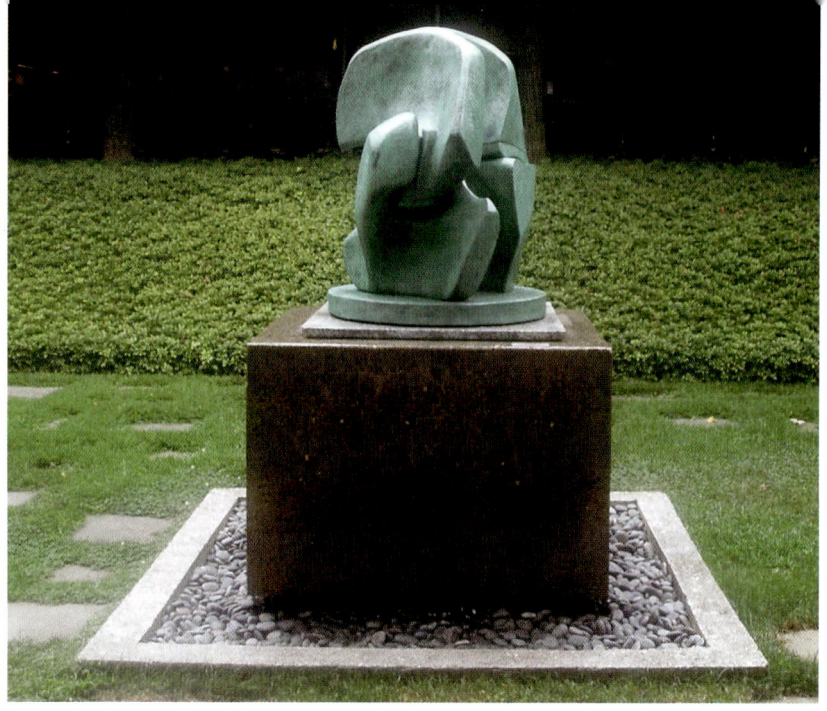

Henry Moore, *Locking Piece*, 1962. Bronze, view of work at the Donald M. Kendall Sculpture Gardens at PepsiCo, Purchase, New York.

became an offering to the community to allay concerns about the new corporate headquarters: the creation of the sculpture park was not only Kendall's personal project, but also a gift to the residents of Purchase intended to establish a connection with the community.[20]

According to Elisabeth Cornu, Objects Conservator at the Fine Arts Museum of San Francisco, the acquisition of sculpture has become the second most important category for contemporary collecting museums.[21] Combine this with the general popularity of three-dimensional art, and one can assume that the trend for museum sculpture gardens will continue well into the 21st century. Yet the future of some independent sculpture parks is not so certain. Capasso fears that the non-museological parks that sprang up in the 1990s will slowly close due to expenses associated with large sculpture and that these costs may cause the trend to "sharply de-accelerate": "One big dip in the economy and most of those smaller parks will disappear or become moribund."[22]

The rapid expansion of sculpture parks and gardens in the latter part of the 20th century speaks to the value of providing quiet settings for the display of sculpture and contemplation of nature, but it also raises many design issues, conservation concerns, collection development issues, and governance and funding challenges. By bringing the museum and sculpture park communities together and combining efforts, we can begin to address these issues. Sculpture parks and gardens are a creation and phenomenon of our modern society, offering both purpose and meaning. Large or small, they are retreats where earthly spirits are revived and creativity encouraged, focal points where art, nature, and people can intersect and coincide.

Notes

1. Three publications have helped to quantify the sculpture park phenomenon. In 1987, the International Sculpture Center published its first *Directory of Sculpture Parks and Gardens*. It contained 97 entries. By 1996, when the second edition was published, the number of entries had more than doubled to 195. Another directory, *A Guide to the Sculpture Parks and Gardens of America*, also published in 1996, reviewed 85 sculpture parks and gardens; 61 of the listed sites were created after 1970. See also Sidney Lawrence and George Foy, *Music in Stone: Great Sculpture Gardens of the World* (New York: Scala Books, 1984) and Jimena Blázquez Abascal, Valeria Varas, and Raul Rispa, *Sculpture Parks in Europe: A Guide to Art and Nature* (Basel: Birkhaüser, 2006).
2. Leslie Kaufman, "Sculpture Parks and Gardens Conference," <www.sculpture.org/documents/webspec/parks/sp&g.shtml>.
3. Elisabeth B. MacDougall, in Sidney Lawrence and George Foy, op. cit., p. 8.
4. William Howard Adams, *Nature Perfected: Gardens Through History* (New York: Abbeville Press, 1991), p. 330.
5. All quotations from Nick Capasso are from an interview with the author, April 11, 2006.
6. Tim Burgard, interview with the author, April 6, 2006.
7. See Margaret A. Robinette, *Outdoor Sculpture: Object and Environment* (New York: Whitney Library of Design, 1976), p. 16. Andrew Causey, *Sculpture Since 1945* (New York: Oxford University Press, 1998).
8. Marc Treib, "Sculpture and Garden: A Historical Overview," *Design Quarterly* 141 (1988): p. 50.
9. Ibid., p. 50.
10. See Peter Boswell, "Sculpture Gardens," *Public Art Review*, Fall/Winter 1991: p. 11.
11. Irving Lavin in Peter H. Stern, et. al., *Earth, Sky and Sculpture: Storm King Art Center* (New York: Storm King Art Center, 2000), p. 57.
12. Laurie D. Olin, "The Museum of Modern Art Garden: The Rise and Fall of a Modernist Landscape," *Journal of Garden History*, Summer 1997: p. 158.
13. See Treib, op. cit., p. 45.
14. Thalden, quoted in Jory Johnson, "Art and Amenities," *Landscape Architecture*, April 1989: p. 77.
15. Stephen Spender, *Henry Moore, Sculptures in Landscape* (New York, Clarkson N. Potter, Inc., 1979), pp. 32 and 9.
16. Treib, op. cit., pp. 54, 53.
17. Capasso, op. cit.
18. Robert Zion, "Save Some Green for Your Garden," *Museum News*, November 1972: p. 36.
19. See "Meeting the Needs of Museum Visitors," a chapter in *The Manual of Museum Planning*, edited by Gail Dexter Lord and Barry Lord, which focuses on what museum planners need to know about how visitors use and experience museums.
20. Another publication from the APGA, *Reaching out to the Garden Visitor: Informal Learning and Biodiversity*, provides excellent information on informal learning, which can be applied to sculpture parks. "Informal Learning in Public Gardens," by Barbara H. Butler and Beverly Serrell, both museum professionals with extensive experience in education and visitor studies, describes voluntary and self-directed learning. See also John H. Falk and Lynn D. Dierking, *Lessons Without Limit* (Walnut Creek, CA: AltaMira Press, 2002), p. 9.
21. Elisabeth Cornu, interview with the author, April 11, 2006.
22. Capasso, op. cit.

Sculpture Parks as Outdoor Museums

by Brooke Barrie

Does a museum have to be enclosed? The Hakone Open-Air Museum, the first of its kind in Japan, and at its inception only the second of its kind in the world, will be 40 years old in 2009. Located within the Fuji Hakone Izu National Park on the island of Honshu, 60 miles southwest of Tokyo, the museum exhibits its collection of over 100 contemporary sculptures outdoors. The collection includes works by Henry Moore, Constantin Brancusi, Niki de Saint Phalle, Barry Flanagan, and Marisol, among others.[1] Famous for its deep-green forests and soaring, snow-capped mountains (Mt. Fuji is nearby), Hakone is the perfect spot for the realization of the Open-Air Museum's mission: to create harmony and balance between art and nature. The hot springs, which bubble up into a 20-meter-long footbath where you can soothe your weary feet while appreciating the sculptures, also contribute to this harmony. What traditional museum can claim such an amenity? But the fundamental concept behind this organization is to place sculpture *and* visitors in the landscape so that both are in close contact with nature.

In describing the origins of the Hakone Open-Air Museum, its founder, Nobutaka Shikanai, said in an interview: "Although I was aware that modern sculpture often existed in a garden setting, there were no open-air museums as such…I planned to build outside in the open air and to organize exhibition areas around sculpture primarily. I would then proceed to add buildings for paintings and smaller sculpture, which reversed the usual process."[2]

The term "open-air museum" breathes life into the word "museum" and evocatively describes the type of sculpture park whose mission is museum-like in character—a museum in which landscape and sky take the place of walls, floor, and ceiling.[3] One of the most important open-air museums is Storm King Art Center, located in Mountainville, New York, a small town next to Storm King Mountain and the Hudson River. After Brookgreen Gardens in South Carolina, Storm King is the second oldest large-scale sculpture park in the country.[4] It is a museum that, as its Web site suggests, "celebrates the relationship between sculpture and nature." Founded in 1960, Storm King encompasses 500 acres of diverse landscape including fields of native alfalfa, buckwheat, and oats, wildflowers, woodlands, and mountains. It provides a site for over 230 contemporary American and European sculptures from the 1960s to the present. A core group of 13 sculptures by David Smith is surrounded by monumental, mostly abstract works from other world-renowned sculptors such as Magdalena Abakanowicz, Alexander Calder, Mark di Suvero, and Isamu Noguchi. Driving along the New York State Thruway, many people have experienced a glimpse of di Suvero's immense, bright orange, I-beam constructions or Andy Goldsworthy's fieldstone wall winding through the trees and up a rise toward the highway.

Like Hakone, Storm King has a building containing exhibition galleries, a museum shop, and offices. Built in 1935 and designed by Maxwell Kimball, the original Normandy-style residence now houses nine galleries for changing exhibitions. But, true to the nature of this plein-air museum, Storm King's primary purpose is to acquire and place works outdoors "as part of a visual fabric that includes its immediate surroundings and the distant landscape scene—expanding the context for viewing far beyond traditional garden confines."

Laumeier Sculpture Park in St. Louis, Missouri, is another well-established sculpture park. It was created in 1968 via a gift of Mrs. Henry Laumeier's 72-acre estate to the people of St. Louis County and the greater metropolitan area. This initial donation was followed in 1975 by a gift from Ernest Trova of 40 sculptures to begin the sculpture park. Recently celebrating its 30th anniversary, Laumeier has grown to become an internationally recognized, open-air museum of more than 100 acres, showcasing over 75 works from its collection.

Glen Gentele, director of Laumeier, characterizes its concept and mission: "The conceptual framework for Laumeier Sculpture Park underscores the idea of overlapping systems and communities converging—literally, programmatically, and

View of Hakone grounds with (left) Henry Moore, *Two-Piece Reclining Figure: Cut*, 1979–81, and (right) Jean Dubuffet, *Arborescence*, 1971–80.

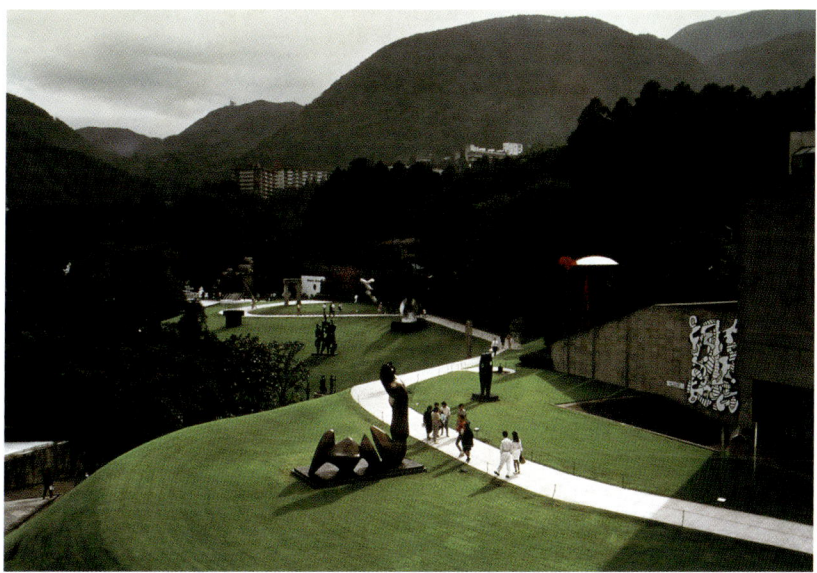

metaphorically. Laumeier Sculpture Park effects positive change in communities and individuals by expanding the context of contemporary sculpture beyond the traditional confines of a museum." Like its more traditional cousins, Laumeier offers extensive education and outreach programs, as well as frequently changing indoor exhibitions. In addition, concerts are held in an outdoor amphitheater, and art fairs, lectures, and special events are enjoyed by the public. To that end, Pugh + Scarpa of Santa Monica, California, has recently been selected as the architect for a new Fine Arts and Education Center. The museum's galleries, gift shop, and administrative offices are currently housed in an early 20th-century stone house, the former Laumeier residence.

One feature sets Laumeier apart from other sculpture parks: its emphasis on adding site-specific and environmental sculptures to the collection. From 1980 to 1990, 10 artists participated in a unique program: "Their work, incorporating various philosophic and aesthetic attitudes, made Laumeier shed the role of passive art park to become a laboratory for risk-taking and achievement."[5] A prime example is Beverly Pepper's first site-specific earthwork *Cromlech Glen* (1985–90), an earthen amphitheater formed by a mammoth, steep-sided circular mound. Stone steps at the ends of the embankments lead up to a slate path that runs along the rim. Site-specific works and environmental constructions by Vito Acconci, Mary Miss, and David Nash can also be found on the grounds.

Like Laumeier, the Nasher Sculpture Center in Dallas, Texas, located on a 2.5-acre site in the heart of the downtown arts district, began with a substantial gift. Founder Raymond D. Nasher donated $70 million and more than 340 pieces from the Raymond and Patsy Nasher Collection of Modern and Contemporary Sculpture. Pritzker Prize-winning architect Renzo Piano designed the 55,000-square-foot Sculpture Center in five, equal-sized, parallel pavilions. Glass façades allow the interior galleries to extend visibly into the outdoor garden. Even the indoor spaces were designed to create a flowing transition from inside to outside. Landscape architect Peter Walker's award-winning, 1.5-acre sculpture garden features rotating exhibitions of approximately 25 large outdoor pieces. In this case, the collection had a tremendous bearing on the design of the building and grounds, and a distinct integration of building and garden was the result.

Opened in 2003, the Nasher Sculpture Center houses one of the world's premiere collections. Assembled by the Nashers beginning in the 1960s, it features works by Alberto Giacometti, Barbara Hepworth, Anish Kapoor, and Claes Oldenburg. Richard Serra's 50-ton *My Curves Are Not Mad* (1987) was the first sculpture installed in the garden. A notable recent purchase is Jonathan Borofsky's *Walking to the Sky* (2004), a 100-foot-tall, stainless steel and painted fiberglass sculpture that depicts seven life-size figures walking into the sky along a tilted pole, while three figures on

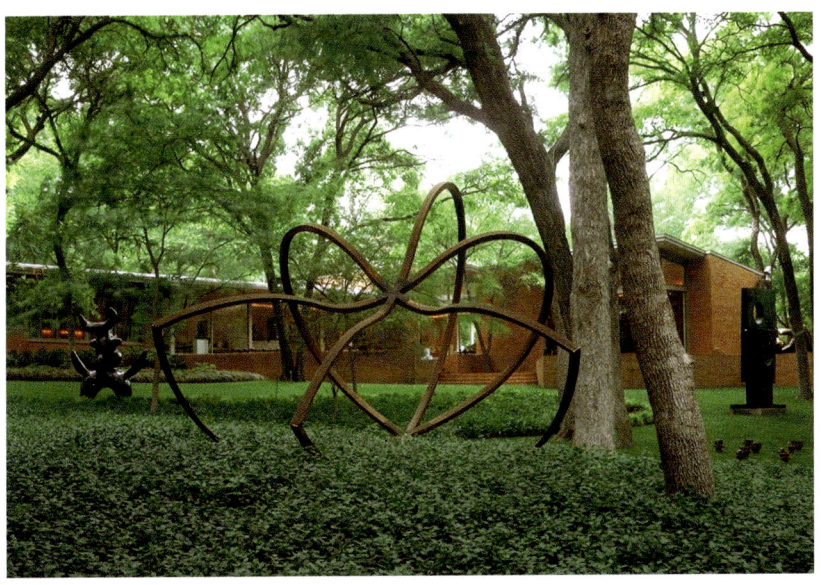

Richard Deacon, *Like a Bird*, 1984. Laminated wood, 121 x 208 x 205 in. View of work at the Nasher Sculpture Center, Dallas.

the ground observe their ascent. Unlike Laumeier, the Nasher has commissioned only one site-specific work as part of the garden: James Turrell's *Tending, (Blue)* (2003). This "skyspace," an austere room inside a terraced, landscaped berm, features a beveled cut-out in the roof that frames the light and colors of a continually changing sky.

Steven Nash, the Nasher's founding director, says, "The primary mission for the Nasher was to create a serene oasis for art and culture within the heart of a busy city. Contributing to urban life and redevelopment was an important part of the agenda." The Nasher's success is fittingly expressed by Marcel Krenz: "Between the garden, alive with oak trees, cedars, pines, weeping willows, and magnolias, and the light-flooded interior spaces filled with works by Donald Judd, Joel Shapiro, Antony Gormley, and Mark di Suvero, visitors get to stroll around the sculptures, seeing them in what seems to be their natural habitat."[6] Raymond Nasher insisted from the beginning that the landscape was as important as the building, and his approach was resonant of Nobutaka Shikanai's at Hakone. Nasher died in March 2007 after realizing his vision "to create an outdoor 'roof-less' museum that will serve as a peaceful retreat for reflection of art and nature and a public home for his collection of 20th-century sculpture."

While these sculpture parks each offer buildings for changing exhibitions and/or permanent collections, Millennium Park, 24.5 acres located in the heart of downtown

Chicago, does not. It does, however, have Frank Gehry's Jay Pritzker Pavilion, an outdoor performing arts venue and centerpiece for the park. Enormous billowing ribbons of stainless steel lie atop the 120-foot-high pavilion, and an overhead trellis supporting an innovative sound system extends outward, covering an elliptical lawn. The pavilion, with its 4,000 fixed seats (the lawn accommodates another 7,000), is home to free concerts and events throughout the year.

Millennium Park, which opened in 2004, is a relative newcomer to the field. Like both the Nasher and Laumeier, Millennium Park is an urban retreat in striking contrast to the pastoral settings of Storm King and Hakone. But of all these examples, Millennium Park is the most all-encompassing in its approach, with an unprecedented combination of art, music, architecture, and landscape design. In addition to the Pritzker Pavilion, it contains the Joan W. and Irving B. Harris Theater for Music and Dance, the Exelon Pavilions where the welcome center is located, the McCormick Tribune Ice Rink, and McDonald's Cycle Center — a 300-space, heated indoor bicycle

Anish Kapoor, *Cloud Gate*, 2005. Stainless steel, 1006 x 2012 x 1280 cm. View of work at Millennium Park, Chicago.

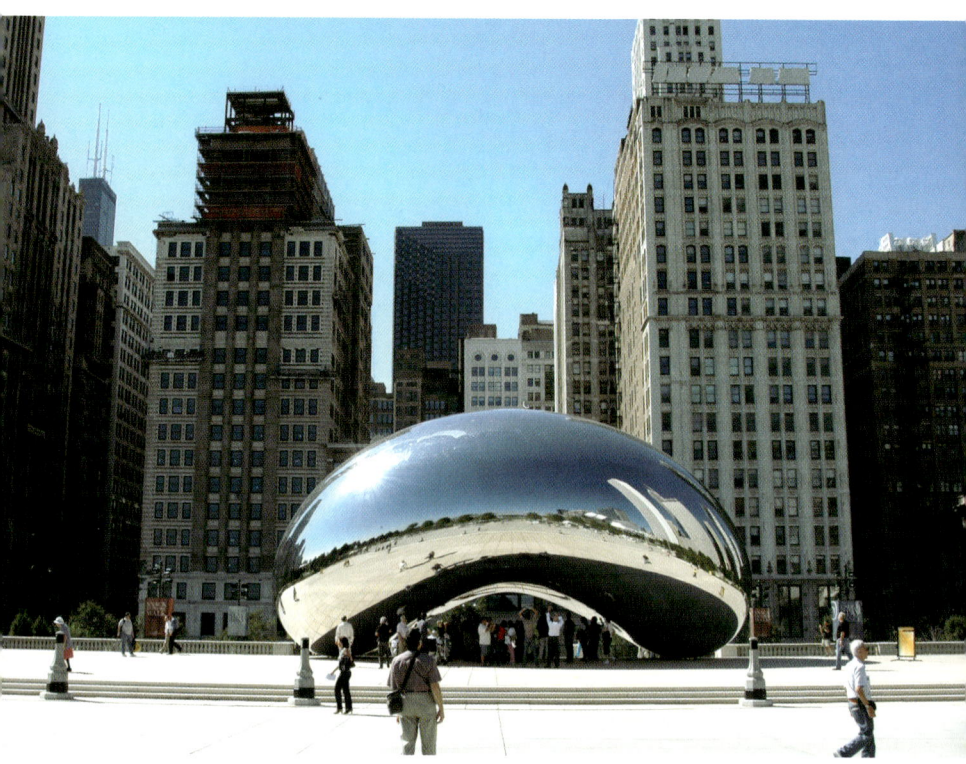

parking facility with lockers, showers, a snack bar with outdoor summer seating, bike repair, bike rental, and other amenities designed to encourage biking to the park and other downtown locations. These extraordinary facilities allow not only for significant arts programming, but also for fitness and family-oriented events and festivals.

Millennium Park was created for the enjoyment of the people of Chicago and the city's visitors. The names given to its facilities underscore the fact that the park is the result of a unique partnership between the City of Chicago and the philanthropic community. Its history and mission, quite different from those of the sculpture parks previously discussed, are stated on its Web site: "In 1997 Mayor Richard M. Daley directed his staff to develop plans for a new music venue to be built over the active tracks and surface parking lot. What is now Millennium Park was first conceived in 1998 as a way of creating new parkland in Grant Park to transform the unsightly railroad tracks and parking lots that had long dotted the lakefront. Over time, with Richard M. Daley's vision and Frank Gehry's involvement, the project evolved into the most ambitious public undertaking in Chicago's history."[7] A measure of its success can be found in an on-line interview with Edward Uhlir, director of design, architecture, and landscape for Millennium Park, in the June 2007 edition of *The Planning Report*: "In 2005, Priceline.com determined that Millennium Park was the 35th most popular tourist destination in the country, and in 2006 it jumped to number one, beating the Las Vegas strip and Central Park."

Millennium Park's other architectural and landscape elements include the BP Bridge, a 925-foot-long bridge designed by Frank Gehry, which connects the park to the Daley Bicentennial Plaza and provides an acoustic buffer from traffic noise; the Chase Promenade, a tree-lined walkway through the center of the park; the Boeing Galleries, two formally designed outdoor exhibition spaces consisting of nearly 34,000 square feet, which hosted five Mark di Suvero sculptures for most of 2007 and 2008; the contemporary Lurie Garden, paying homage to the city's motto, "Urbs in Horto" (City in a Garden), designed by the team of Kathryn Gustafson, Piet Oudolf, and Robert Israel; and finally, Wrigley Square and the Millennium Monument, an inviting, open space with a replica of the original peristyle (a series of columns enclosing a court) that stood on the same location from 1917 to 1953.

Two of Millennium Park's most prominent features are sculptures: the interactive *Crown Fountain* (2004) by Jaume Plensa and Anish Kapoor's *Cloud Gate* (2005), his first public outdoor work in the U.S. Both pieces were specifically commissioned for the park, and the artists were selected by donors. Plensa's fountain consists of two 50-foot-high, glass block towers situated at either end of a 232-foot-long reflecting pool. The towers project video images on LED screens of the faces of 1,000 Chicago residents; arcs of water spout out of their mouths. Phyllis Tuchman, referring to Kapoor's piece, says, "*Cloud Gate*...perfectly reflects blue cloud-filled skies, towering buildings along Michigan Avenue, and the smiling faces of countless fans studying their own images."[8] Inspired by the properties of liquid mercury, *Cloud Gate* is seamlessly constructed from 168 highly polished stainless steel plates. The sculpture—66 feet long, 42 feet wide, and 33 feet high—is among the largest in the world.

There are many corporate art museums and galleries, but major corporate sculpture gardens are uncommon. The Hakone Open-Air Museum was created by Fujisankei Communications Group (a major Japanese media conglomerate that now has a foundation to operate the museum) as a result of its founder's passion for contemporary sculpture. A similar example in the U.S. is the critically acclaimed Donald M. Kendall Sculpture Gardens at PepsiCo, opened in 1970 and founded by the company's chief executive. Kendall, who began the collection in 1965, "sought to create an atmosphere of stability, creativity, and experimentation. He envisioned as essential to that ambience a museum without walls, where works of art could be enjoyed by employees, the community, and the public."[9] He also sought to integrate architecture, landscape, and contemporary sculpture. Today, the 144-acre gardens are home to 45 masterworks of the 20th century, representing Max Ernst, Alberto Giacometti, Joan Miró, George Segal, and Kenneth Snelson, among others.

Located on the grounds of the former Blind Brook Polo Club, the park was designed by landscape architect Edward Durell Stone, Jr. His father, renowned architect Edward Durell Stone, designed the seven concrete and glass headquarters buildings. In 1980, British landscape architect Russell Page was hired to extend the gardens and plan them specifically around Kendall's sculptures. Copper beeches were planted around Louise Nevelson's *Celebration II* (1976), and blue-gray spruce trees were placed around Alexander Calder's soaring, bright red sculpture, *Hats Off* (1969). Groves of birch trees were planted, and ponds, fountains, and paths were constructed to provide settings for the artworks and integrate them with the landscape. Many pieces from the collection are situated along the "Golden Path," a yellow stone walkway that winds through the grounds. Smaller sculptures can be viewed in more intimately scaled areas like courtyards and sunken gardens; large-scale works are given long vistas and expansive green lawns.

What do these institutions have in common with traditional museums? Almost everything. They "procure, care, study, and display objects"; they "acquire, conserve, research, communicate, and exhibit." They are all "nonprofit, permanent institutions in the service of society." These sculpture parks have created a new tradition, one in which the outdoors is equally if not more important than the indoors.

In a 1985 letter to the director of the Hakone Open-Air Museum, Henry Moore expressed his pleasure at having his sculptures publicly accessible in an outdoor environment: "When you are out in the open air in the sun, rain, and clouds…it helps people appreciate that sculpture is part of life."[10] Hear, hear!

Notes

1 In fact, the Hakone Open-Air Museum is "the third largest repository of Moore sculptures in the world, after the Hirshhorn Museum and Sculpture Garden in Washington, DC, and the artist's estate in Hertfordshire in England." See Sam Hunter, *In the Mountains of Japan* (New York: Abbeville Press, 1988), p. 13.

2 Ibid., p. 28.

3 In his introduction, Hunter states that as a sculpture park, the Hakone Open-Air Museum "was preceded only by the much smaller Middelheim Open Air Museum of Sculpture in the Belgian port city of Arnheim, founded in 1950." Hunter, op. cit., p. 12.

4 Jane McCarthy and Laurily K. Epstein, *A Guide to the Sculpture Parks and Gardens of America* (New York: Michael Kesend Publishing, Ltd., 1996), p. 84.

5 Beej Nierengarten-Smith, *Laumeier Sculpture Park, Ten Sites: Works, Artists, Years* (Missouri: Laumeier Sculpture Park, 1992), p. 4.

6 Marcel Krenz, "Revisiting the Nasher Sculpture Center," *Sculpture*, November 2005, p. 21.

7 From Millennium Park's Web site: "From the 1850s through the late 20th century, the site that is now occupied by Millennium Park was controlled by the Illinois Central Railroad. In Daniel Burnham's 1909 Plan of Chicago, he considered the railroad property to be so untouchable that he developed the Grant Park portion of the plan around it. Construction began on Grant Park in 1917...With the completion of Grant Park, the railroad area remained a blight in its corner."

8 Phyllis Tuchman, "Chicago's Cloud," *Town & Country*, August 2006, p. 71.

9 Rachel A. Antman, "Modern Sculptures, Outdoors and Free," *The New York Times*, September 29, 2006, p. 7(F).

10 Hunter, op. cit., p. 86.

Planning the Museum Park at the North Carolina Museum of Art

by Daniel P. Gottlieb

The North Carolina Museum of Art sits on 164 acres in a rapidly growing region rich with major universities and colleges, high-tech companies, and the state capital. The Museum Park, also known as the Preserve, is on the site of a former state prison adjacent to the museum building. Since the land was conveyed to NCMA in 2000, it has undergone a radical transformation into an art park that serves as a laboratory for the intersection of art, recreation, and environmental management. With the construction of an innovative new day-lit gallery building, sculpture gardens, and education center, the completed museum campus will integrate formal and informal experiences of art, indoors and out.

Bounded by major urban arteries with rolling fields, forests, and creeks, the site was grazed by cattle and horses until its conveyance to the museum. Since then, a greenway has been constructed that connects the museum and park to the community, via a 650-foot-long pedestrian bridge that serves as the recreational "spine" of the 100-acre natural area. The bridge spans a major interstate, connecting to the university district and east to downtown Raleigh. Heading west, the trail connects to a large state park and trails beyond, making the museum a cultural pearl in a necklace that links many regional destinations. A network of natural trails brings visitors to quieter zones where sculpture projects engage with the environment.

The park has been planned and is managed by defined zones: uses are either active or reflective; development is built or natural; art experiences are formal or informal. Certain zones are protected for environmental restoration, whereas others are designated for festivals or development (building expansion and parking). These zones are intended to give museum visitors a variety of outdoor experiences that complement the galleries and connect with the community. The NCMA zoning model was first suggested by a 1988 conceptual site plan, titled Imperfect Utopia: A Park for the New World. Conceived by the collaborative team of artist Barbara Kruger, architects Henry Smith-Miller and Laurie Hawkinson, and landscape architect Nicholas Quennell, the plan highlighted the opportunity for the museum to break new ground in treating the site as an integral part of its facilities and expanding access to a wider public. By developing the grounds with varied experiential zones, NCMA would take advantage of the appeal generated by recreational areas and parks. Imperfect Utopia also suggested board-regulated zone protection and an emphasis on artist collaborations: both are enduring principles in designing and managing the Museum Park.

The Museum Park plan is a synthesis of conditions and constraints (the new museum building, major highways, and old prison site), the Imperfect Utopia plan,

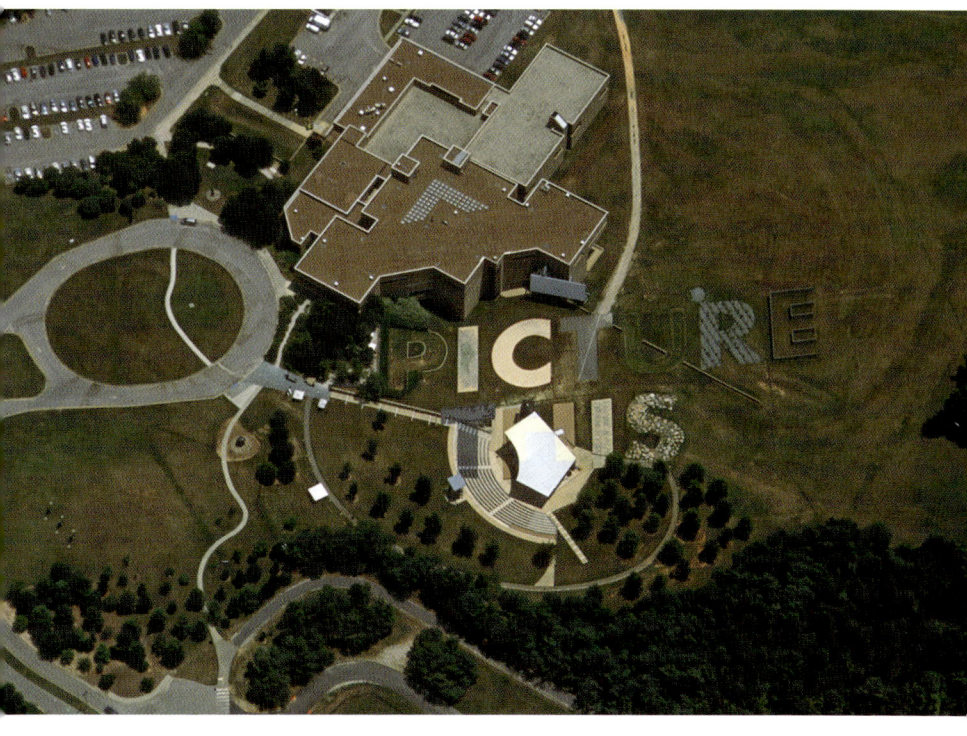

Barbara Kruger, Henry Smith-Miller, Laurie Hawkinson, and Nicholas Quennell, *PICTURE THIS*, 1992–97. Mixed media, 80 ft. long.

and observations I made as NCMA's director for museum planning and design during visits to sculpture parks in the U.S., Europe, and Japan. Early on, I assembled an interdisciplinary planning group, consisting of a curator, a museum educator, a landscape architect, a park manager, and an ecologist, to develop a master plan for the site, which established the museum's curatorial point of view: site-specificity, engagement with natural conditions, and the park itself as inspiration for artworks. The art plan outlined a program of potential artists to consider for commissions over time and to estimate costs for temporary, permanent, and art-in-service projects. Educational and environmental management plans followed. The planning group also had invaluable input from the City of Raleigh's greenway planner and the North Carolina Department of Transportation in developing the greenway project. This plan has been updated recently to incorporate the new building design and final trail configuration. A primary goal of the updated plan is to stitch together the major components and ideas of the museum campus: new gallery building, renovated building for exhibitions and education, and the Museum Park, with its various zones and aesthetic attributes.

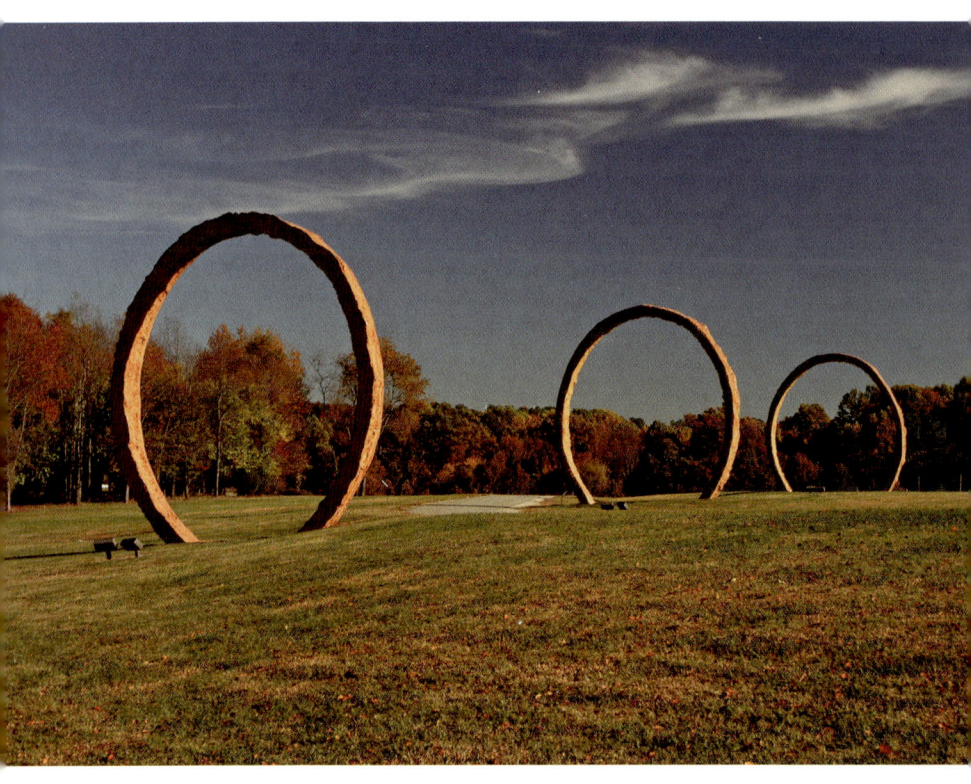

Thomas Sayre, *Gyre*, 1999. Concrete, iron oxide, and steel, 3 elements, 150 ft. long.

    The Kröller-Müller Museum, in the Netherlands, offered us an interesting model: it is a major museum that combines a great art collection with a formal sculpture garden and large forested area programmed with art. The forest, just beyond the garden gates, is punctuated with miles of trails and well-curated sculpture. Walking or riding one of the 900 white bicycles maintained by the museum, visitors can spend a delightful day discovering art by major artists in the relaxed outdoor environment and within its day-lit galleries. The Kröller-Müller's three major zones of building (formal art setting), gardens (transitional space), and woods (informal art and recreational environment) directly express the qualities we were developing at the Museum Park.

    Discovery of art through recreation and active participation was a consistent feature of the sculpture parks I visited, whether in England's forest sculpture programs or in the urban setting of Skulptur Projekte Münster. The act of discovery is a powerful social experience. In Münster, culture tourists experience a kind of Easter-egg hunt, following maps on foot or bikes around the city to locate site-specific works that engage the history and culture of Münster. Visitors to the once-a-decade event ride around in this "city of bicycles" and enjoy the experience of challenging and humorous contemporary sculpture, checking maps and exchanging observations with one another. By developing physically active opportunities, and by introducing artworks and artists' interventions into parks, a broader slice of the public is likely to encounter art and become engaged in the contemporary art dialogue.

At the North Carolina Museum of Art, we face the challenge of using the Museum Park to draw visitors into the galleries (and vice-versa) through programs and information designed to work in both directions. Over time, we project that as many people will come for the park as for the collections and exhibitions in the museum buildings. To reinforce the integration of programs, as well as to protect sensitive environmental zones, it is critical to design well-defined ribbons of circulation that connect zones of use. Trails are designed as primary (paved), secondary (crushed stone), or tertiary (earth or mulch). Artworks are located in relation to the greenway or woodland trails. A specially designed secondary trail is being constructed through all of the zones to connect the majority of artworks and make a one-mile walking loop.

The Forest of Dean sculpture program, on the English/Welsh border, offers an important case study in how the relationships of art, park trails, and visitors can evolve and what management issues can arise from those interactions. At Dean, the problem was one of precedence: Which comes first, art or trails? Artists invited to make projects in 1988 wanted the experience to be a kind of pilgrimage through the forest; they believed that a contrived circulation pattern would restrict conditions for future artists. As a result, 18 works were sited without connecting trails: visitors were left to find them on their own, without maps or guidance. The immediate popularity of the project quickly put too much demand on the landscape, which became overrun by confused art-seeking tourists who trampled the forest and created management crises. Ultimately, a pamphlet was produced and a trail constructed to connect most of the works, thereby relieving visitor frustration and slowing further damage. Dean's chief forester said, "I never would have imagined the power of art." To rectify the situation, the Forest Commission and arts organizers formed a partnership called the Sculpture Trust. The Forest Commission agrees to maintain the works in the forest, after the Sculpture Trust selects and pays for each installation of art. Before a new work is installed, both parties meet to review the proposal in detail for feasibility, public safety, and future maintenance. Together, they develop a collaborative management plan.

The Forest of Dean Sculpture Trust served as a rich model for the Museum Park management structure. I initiated a cooperative park management group, called the Partnership for Art and Ecology, with the neighboring College of Natural Resources at North Carolina State University. Park experts and restoration ecologists work with museum staff to review all improvements and projects in the park and write management policies and plans. The partnership functions like the zoning board originally envisioned in Imperfect Utopia. Throughout the planning process, the partnership served as a creative forum for balancing environmental issues with appropriate public access to sculpture.

Sculpture is commissioned for the Museum Park as temporary, permanent, or art-in-service (where it serves a functional purpose). An artwork in the park may be considered for the permanent collection after one year's exposure to the elements and visitors. Sculpture not accessioned is deemed temporary and must eventually be removed. A continuing concern for museum conservators is the inevitable degradation of work in the elements, particularly those constructed of organic materials. Conventional museum standards obviously can't be applied to the preservation of many outdoor contemporary artworks. In the woodland, a marvelous accessioned work by Chris Drury, *Cloud Chamber* (2003), is built of logs, stone, and concrete. More about the visitor's experience than the object itself, this walk-in camera obscura projects an image of the trees and sky above onto the walls and floor within. The work requires regular maintenance, and repairs are reviewed to ensure that they do not compromise the integrity of Drury's intent.

The art-in-service program includes artist-designed infrastructure elements, such as signage structures, benches made from recycled prison bars, and a park pavilion for education. The museum's most ambitious art-in-service project is a two-acre pond rehabilitation by Mary Miss that creates a large-scale stormwater demonstration and environmental artwork from an unsightly and poorly functional sediment control pond. Working with a water-quality engineer and landscape architect, Miss produced a plan for the pond that deconstructs the process of cleaning runoff by using a series of terraces and paths. The work will demonstrate to visitors how surface water runoff can be managed in an environmentally responsible and aesthetic way by creating a series of ponds culminating in a large pool, which will also function as a permanent art and environmental education venue. By 2010, all major elements of the integrated museum campus plan will be completed. The new building, designed by Thomas Phifer, the renovated special exhibitions and education center, and the Museum Park will transform a very good traditional museum into a multifaceted art, education, and recreational destination for the next generation to enjoy.

<www.ncartmuseum.org>

The National Gallery of Art Sculpture Garden

by Sarah Tanguy

More than 30 years in the making, the National Gallery Sculpture Garden opened in 1999. From the outside, it looks like a picturesque garden restrained by a neoclassical girdle. Once inside, the striking contrast between nature, architecture, and the 17 sculptures—a riotous mix of contemporary works placed at irregular intervals—reveals itself in full force.

Although the concept for a sculpture garden originated in the '60s, the museum (under then-director J. Carter Brown) only secured the 6.1-acre lot in 1991; when Rusty Powell succeeded Carter Brown as director a year later, he initiated the design phase. But it took a $10 million gift from the Morris and Gwendolyn Cafritz Foundation to turn the dream into a reality. As the design took shape, Powell wanted to avoid the "starter kit" look common to many new constructions.[1] The Olin Partnership responded with a graded landscape, old plantings, and meandering pathways around a revamped fountain and a double ring of linden trees.

Marla Prather, former curator of 20th-century art, outlined the curatorial vision: "We never set out thinking that it would be predominantly a garden filled with work by American contemporary artists. I think it naturally progressed that way because living American artists are making some of the greatest sculptures around."[2] Another reason was the multi-million-dollar price tags on early Modernist works, which would have "exhausted [the] acquisition budget fairly quickly." Prather also acknowledged the conservation risks and maintenance issues associated with placing such masterworks, even those from the gallery's own collection, in an outdoor setting.

The sculptures range in date from 1973 to 1999. These dates can be deceiving, however, as many of the more recent works are by artists who established themselves years earlier or who are now deceased. The Americans include Louise Bourgeois, Scott Burton, Alexander Calder, Mark di Suvero, Ellsworth Kelly, Sol LeWitt, Roy Lichtenstein, Isamu Noguchi, Claes Oldenburg and Coosje van Bruggen, George Rickey, Lucas Samaras, Joel Shapiro, David Smith, and Tony Smith. The Europeans are Barry Flanagan, Joan Miró, and Magdalena Abakanowicz.

Because of this concentration on contemporary sculpture, Prather sees a "kind of integrity" in the garden "in terms of the connection between objects and the continuity of the whole." But what is striking is just the opposite. The selection's greatest virtue lies in its open embrace of stylistic diversity. Rich in texture and varied in scale, many of the works are idea-driven, appealing to the mind more than to the emotions. Regrettably, none of them are site-specific or commissioned. As a result, they cannot escape appearing as so many objects placed in a garden, no matter how well sited they are.

Off the central east entrance, Tony Smith's intriguing, 17-foot-high *Moondog* plays hide-and-seek through intervening trees. Conceived in 1964 and made posthumously in 1998–99, the aluminum work consists of 15 octahedrons and 10 tetrahedrons. Standing on three legs and painted black, the multifaceted work instills a sense of awe tempered by a zany tilt and interpenetrating geometry, which frames views of the garden and beyond. Prather recalls the reaction of Jane Smith, the artist's widow, to the site: "In one direction, I see the dome of the U.S. Capitol and in the other direction, I see the Washington Monument, and then I see my husband's sculpture; you can't not be conscious of where you are."

Claes Oldenburg and Coosje van Bruggen deliver once again as master magicians who make the small large, the soft hard, the inanimate animate, and the ordinary extraordinary. The nearly 20-foot-high *Typewriter Eraser, Scale X* commands its site with a bold torque, bright palette, and bristles reaching up to the sky. Prather comments: "I love the sense of chaos and order. The object is wonderfully coherent and coming apart at the same time...Those bristles feel as though a breeze has just moved through them."[3] There is also a touching irony about this piece that appears so up-to-date but whose original function is now virtually forgotten. Prather continues: "Claes Oldenburg sent me a cartoon about the sculpture where the child is saying to his mother, 'What's a typewriter eraser?' She explains, and he says, 'Mommy, what's a typewriter?'"

Roy Lichtenstein's *House I* also abounds in playful intelligence. The brightly colored, two-sided house is actually concave, with the chimney extending farthest. For Prather, it offers a "cartoon in the middle of the garden," and as Lichtenstein's widow, Dorothy, explained, it gave the National Gallery a chance to circumvent a restriction on adding an architectural element in the garden.[4] A tour de force in overturning design precepts, *House I* ingeniously deconstructs traditional perspective and compresses two dimensions and three dimensions into a single composition while maintaining its Euclidean lines.

This sense of disorientation contrasts with Scott Burton's *Six-Part Seating*, installed diagonally across the garden. The subtle composition celebrates the harmonious relationship between man and nature through a functional yet cosmic Minimalism. Six polished red granite chairs, each bearing the same solid, hard-edged geometry, center around an open void. Under the shade of trees, visitors can enjoy this intimate resting spot and are invited to contemplate the potential of Minimalism itself as well as more everyday issues.

A differing approach to geometric abstraction informs Ellsworth Kelly's *Stele II*. A uniform slab of one-inch weathering steel, the sculpture approximates a 10.5-foot square with rounded corners. Close inspection reveals an old patina made up of myriad sparkling flashes. "Most of my sculpture has been planar; I want the frontality of it, and I think that the shape, how it relates to everything around it, is what I'm interested in," Kelly explains.[5] In this case, he wanted the work set against the sky and the buildings across the street. *Stele II*'s distilled geometry masks its inspiration in nature. In particular, it recalls the negative shape that Kelly found in a grouping of trees in his backyard: "The shape itself is a kind of memory of other things and therefore a metaphor for something else. When people look at it, I want them to think that it does belong in some way, but they don't know where or how—it's mysterious."

Louise Bourgeois's silvery bronze *Spider* provides a much-needed relief from the preponderance of geometry. A stunning example of a craggy arabesque, its deceptively spindly legs support a 24-foot span, with one leg sensually curving upward. Surreal in its proportions and in its transformation of everyday perceptions, the creature changes with each vantage point. At times, it lurks inside a ring of low shrubs, awaiting the unwitting visitor; at other times, it is clearly visible and looks like a rocket from planet Arachne. Playful and disturbing like much of Bourgeois's work, for her, the spider has long symbolized the complex nature of womanhood, deadly in its mission to protect and nurture.

The most haunting work by far in the garden is Magdalena Abakanowicz's *Puellae (Girls)*, an outdoor variant on her well-known indoor groupings of adult figures. Here, the viewer encounters 30 anonymous figures, only three feet high, standing under the

Scott Burton, *Six-Part Seating*, 1985/98. Polished granite, each element, 95.25 x 44.45 x 100.33 cm.

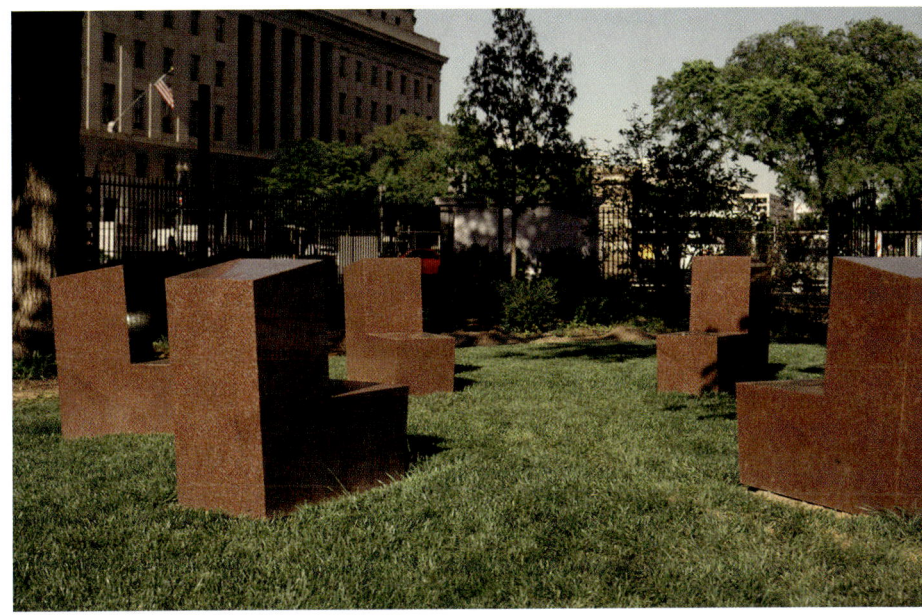

cover of the lindens. The artist spent a day and a half adjusting the exact placement of the figures in relation to the site and to each other. In discussing her subject, she explains: "I was fascinated by the body of a child with its soft bone structure, soft junctions, and deriving out of it, movements impossible to be performed."[6] Stiff and headless, they only begin to hint at the tragic memory that inspired them. Abakanowicz recalls being told that in the winter of 1942, hundreds of Polish children froze to death in unheated cattle trucks en route to Germany. Each of the figures is a unique cast from a burlap original. "[My] sculptures are records of my movements, thoughts, and feelings. None of this is repeatable. I waited about 30 years for *Puellae* to ripen in my mind and intuition and to become a reality." Prather comments, "If you look at the feet, the arms, if you look at the way these delicate pre-adolescent torsos are formed, it's a very beautiful and moving work...[that] strikes a different emotional note. It's good to have a counterpoint."

Some of the works fare less well. A few appear lost. Sol LeWitt's *Four-Sided Pyramid* and Barry Flanagan's *Thinker on a Rock* are helped by their dialogue with the history of art, the former with ancient Near Eastern buildings and the latter with Rodin's *Thinker*. Although LeWitt's faceted structure benefits by engaging with the architecture outside the garden, the impenetrability of its white surface lacks the airy elegance of his linear three-dimensional work. (This lack is made up by Lucas Samaras's adjacent blue-patinated bronze *Chair Transformation Number 20B*, whose diagonal stacking of a signature motif appears to defy gravity.) Flanagan's cast-bronze sculpture, on the other hand, begins and ends as a one-liner, but it no doubt amuses the public with its Disney-esque, oversized animal subject.

The integration of the garden with the museum's East and West Buildings, the Mall, and the urban setting meets with varying success. Despite attempts to construct the marble portions of the garden with the same stone (from the same quarry) as that used for the East and West Buildings, only enough was available for the benches and fountain. The change in materials is most strongly felt in the stone wall posts, a lack compounded by their molding profiles, which are less complex and deeply carved than those of the garden's Neoclassical neighbors. As a result, the wall sections read as stage sets and appear weak next to the boldly articulated iron fencing. By contrast, the gentle swellings in the land gracefully echo the curvilinear rhythm established by the benches around the fountain. Another area of sustained delight is offered by the changing frames of the sculptures as they engage in dialogue with the sites beyond the fence.

The undisputed triumph, however, is the fountain, which (as part of a deal with Congress) continues to serve as an ice-skating rink in the winter. Besides providing a central focus, the fountain is a mesmerizing kinetic artwork in its own right. For Prather, the presence of water and sound makes for "a more dynamic and refreshing space." She adds,

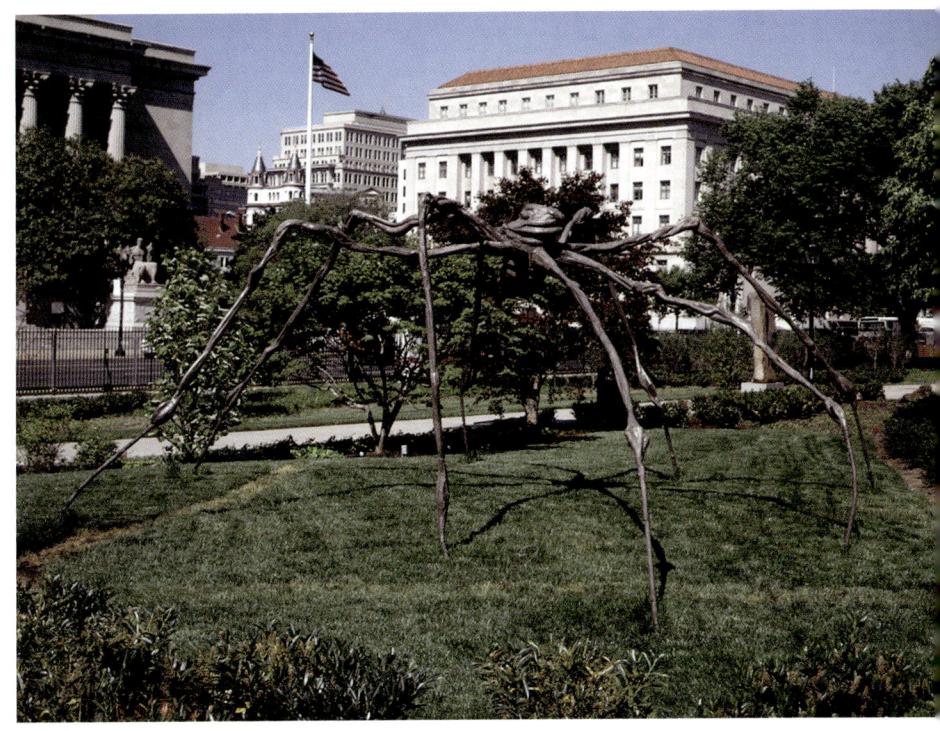

Louise Bourgeois, *Spider*, 1996/97. Bronze with silver nitrate patina, 458.15 x 1012.19 x 970.92 cm.

"It's a very beautiful form. As the jets of water meet, they form a wonderful tree shape in the middle." A proposed augmentation would commission James Turrell to create an immaterial sculpture by coloring the water with fiber-optic lighting.

A discussion of the NGA garden would be incomplete without comparing it to the Hirshhorn's Sculpture Garden directly across the Mall. As the two collections now stand, they enjoy a complementary relationship. The Hirshhorn collection is rich in early Modernist works, and with Rodin's *Burghers of Calais* and Matisse's *Backs*, it "has the figurative tradition very powerfully represented," Prather explains. While the circular pool at the National Gallery garden echoes the shape of the Hirshhorn's building, the settings differ markedly, with the former reading as an enclosed street-level campus and the latter as a sunken plaza. More noticeable still are the National Gallery's changing palette and textural variation in contrast to the Hirshhorn's strong showing of cast bronzes.

Prather points out that she has enjoyed working with living artists and describes the entire process as a magical one whose rewards have been ongoing. Especially memorable was a meeting in the spring of 1998: "We had been looking at the plan.

All of a sudden, we had maquettes, and we could see the relative scale and the relationship to the trees and the relationship of the sculptures to one another. That's when it became a kind of reality…Once it became three-dimensional, we all sat there and marveled." The excitement grew with the installation of each new work: "The constantly shifting landscape is by far the most exhilarating experience in contrast to the white gallery where everything is stable."

The finished garden continues this theme of progressive change. While it will "always have an organic quality," before adding new work or organizing special exhibitions, Prather cautions: "We need to learn about the space, to see how the works relate to the nature that will grow up around." A couple of possibilities are mounting exhibitions that juxtapose indoor and outdoor works by the same artist or that compare drawings inside the galleries with sculpture in the garden.

In a city filled with equestrian statues and monuments, the National Gallery Sculpture Garden is a welcome addition. Visitors have embraced it, and for them, it offers "another way to think about what public sculpture is and can be. And that's what a lot of these artists, particularly Oldenburg, have really addressed," Prather concludes. Its Mall location, moreover, guarantees a certain immortality, as Ellsworth Kelly points out: "It's a glorious feeling to have my work there in Washington."

Notes

1. Powell quoted from the May 17, 1999 press conference at the National Gallery.
2. Unless otherwise noted, all quotations are from an April 27, 1999 interview with Marla Prather at the National Gallery.
3. Prather quoted from the May 17, 1999 video produced by the National Gallery.
4. Prather quoted from the May 17, 1999 press conference at the National Gallery.
5. All quotations are from a telephone interview with Ellsworth Kelly on May 24, 1999.
6. All quotations are taken from written responses submitted on June 10, 1999 to my questions.

<www.nga.gov>

Making the Minneapolis Sculpture Garden: A Conversation with Martin Friedman

by Carol Sterling

During Martin Friedman's 32-year association with Minneapolis's Walker Art Center (30 as director), he transformed a regional arts institution into a major cultural resource. Under his leadership, the Walker became internationally renowned for its exhibitions, collection, publications, and programs in design, architecture, and the performing arts. Since retiring from the Walker in 1990, Friedman has served as a consultant to the Nelson-Atkins Museum of Art and the Hallmark Family Foundation and worked on the development of the Kansas City Sculpture Park. He is also an advisor to the Socrates Sculpture Park in Long Island City.

In September 1988, Friedman oversaw the opening of the Minneapolis Sculpture Garden. A joint venture with the City of Minneapolis Parks and Recreation Board, this 10-acre site was the impetus for the Walker to acquire many large-scale outdoor pieces. In addition, a number of artists were commissioned to create new works, including Martin Puryear, Claes Oldenburg and Coosje van Bruggen, Jackie Ferrara, Frank Gehry, Judith Shea, Brower Hatcher, and Siah Armajani. More recent commissions have brought works by Sol LeWitt, Mario Merz, Dan Graham, Atelier van Lieshout, and Sarah Sze to the garden.

Carol Sterling: In 1988, you realized your dream of creating the Minneapolis Sculpture Garden, at the time the nation's largest urban sculpture garden. How did that come about?

Martin Friedman: First, there was the unused land directly opposite the Walker. In the early part of the century, it was the site of an armory and was used for marching, drilling, and band playing. All sorts of events took place there — concerts, boxing matches, automobile shows, and, I think, marathon dancing. The land was largely fill, and it was on an ancient river bed. Little by little, the land's history caught up with the armory, and the building began sinking into the fill. After many futile attempts to stabilize it, it was blown up in 1933. When we began eyeing it, the land was, and still is, under the jurisdiction of the Minneapolis Parks and Recreation Board. Not much was happening there. A big chunk had been sawed off to accommodate an interstate highway, which erased the formal gardens that once bordered the armory. Occasionally someone would fly a kite or do a little dog training out there, but there was little public use. I kept looking at it longingly, but it was difficult at that time to convince the Park Board that we should be able to use it on a regular basis. They had allowed us to install a Mark di Suvero sculpture for the opening of the new Walker building in 1971. Even though our new building had three roof terraces to accommodate works of art, that really wasn't much outdoor space. Of course I began lusting for the Park Board's space and thinking of ways to be able to use it.

It turned out that a member of the Park Board, a public-minded citizen, had also been thinking seriously about this space as the ideal spot for a ball-shaped fountain that he was planning to donate to the city. I was informed that the former armory site was reserved for the fountain. In other words, we should just forget about it. It took some determined politicking to have the proposed fountain relocated to another park, and no one involved came out feeling too great after that bruising experience. But then what?

We realized that the Walker had to come up with a more positive approach to the Park Board and to the city in general. We began thinking about the land as a public garden where great works of art would be seen in ideal park-like surroundings. Further, we even had the guarantee of some serious initial funding to get the process moving: thanks to a few generous supporters, we could raise substantial funds to

Dan Graham, *Two-way Punched Steel Hedge Labyrinth*, 1994–96. Stainless steel, glass, and arborvitae, 506 x 207 x 90 in.

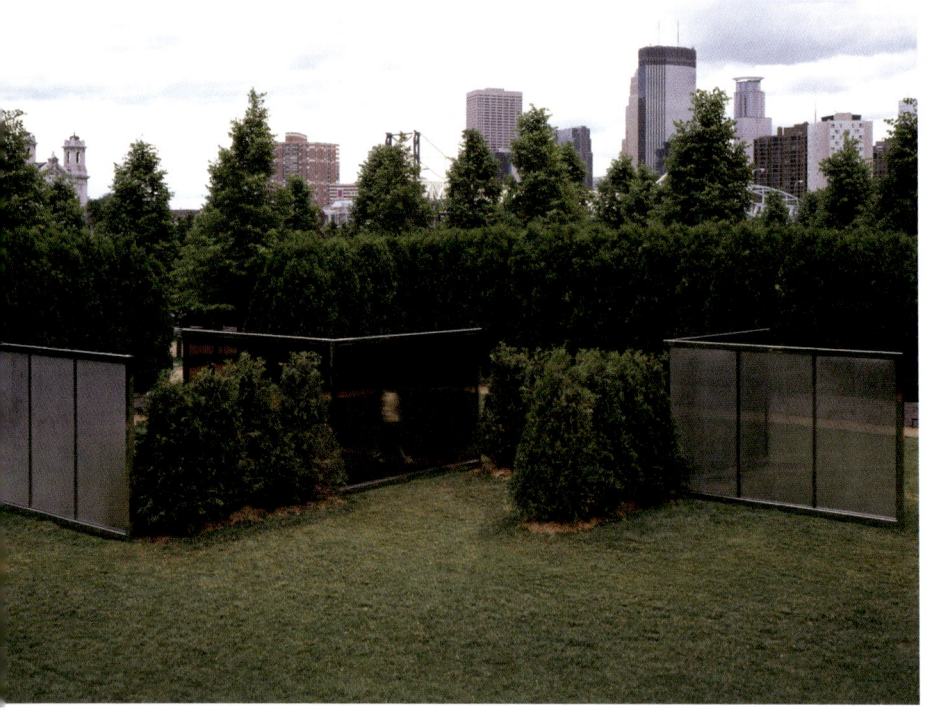

create a sculpture park that would be designed by Edward Larrabee Barnes. In effect, it would be an outdoor extension of the museum's building.

Suddenly we got lucky. I met David Fisher, the new superintendent, who had taken over the city's system of parks and lakes. He was as interested in how that DMZ acreage might be put to public use as I was, and he was fascinated by the idea of a sculpture park. Soon, we became partners in the big venture. The Walker Art Center would be responsible for all artistic programs and the selection of artworks, and the Minneapolis Parks and Recreation Board would be in charge of the garden's maintenance and security. Once that agreement became official, things really began to move, and major support for construction and for gifts of works of art began to come in.

The Minneapolis Sculpture Garden turned out to be more of a success with the public than anyone could possibly have imagined. It became a wonderful welcome mat for the museum and for its next-door neighbor, the Guthrie Theater. Soon, one of several commissioned works in the garden, *Spoonbridge and Cherry*, took on special significance as the unofficial symbol of the city, a kind of Eiffel Tower of Minneapolis. From the outset, the garden has had extensive use, in winter as well as summer, and it continues to be a popular destination for locals and out-of-town visitors. It's been a great attraction on its own, and at the same time, it has enabled the Walker to attract broad new audiences.

CS: What does such a garden mean to the life of the community?

MF: It becomes part of the urban fabric. People visit the Minneapolis Sculpture Garden not only to enjoy sculptures in a verdant setting; many walk through it daily on their way to and from work. It's connected to downtown Minneapolis by the *Irene Hixon Whitney Bridge*, designed by Siah Armajani. Joggers and cyclists use the bridge constantly, and groups of nursery-school kids are always being led across it. The garden is central to the city. I can't imagine Minneapolis without it.

CS: What did it do, and what does it still do, for the museum?

MF: Everything. It's perceived as an inviting space, supportive of the museum. It attracts a great number of first-time and repeat visitors. Many who respond positively to the sculptures then decide to see what's on view in the Walker itself. The garden encourages them to come in and look around.

CS: What made the sculpture garden so successful? Could you pinpoint a few key factors?

MF: Its location—not just because of its proximity to the Walker, but because it's on the edge of downtown. Then, there's the Midwestern passion for nature. The idea of bringing art and nature together this way has generated great response, just like the variety and quality of the sculptures. There is a great range of objects, from the most descriptive to the most abstract. There's a lot for everyone. There are many areas to explore and many places to sit (on benches designed by artists) and look at art. The

Cowles Conservatory has changing displays of flowering plants and, in the center, a shallow pool surrounded by tall palms. In the middle of the pool is Frank Gehry's huge *Standing Glass Fish*. And the Armajani bridge doesn't just span 16 lanes of fast-moving highway traffic, it also provides a series of viewing platforms at different levels overlooking the garden. The spaces are large but not daunting. Everything is approachable. I think it has human scale.

CS: Did you have any special challenges in commissioning site-specific works for the garden?

MF: Many of them. For one thing, the sculptures that we commissioned were intended as permanent works: Martin Puryear's tapered granite columns at the entrance, Jackie Ferrara's wooden-deck seating area, the Oldenburg/van Bruggen fountain, and the Armajani bridge were to be there for the long haul. This meant that the Walker had special concerns, such as the durability of materials and maintenance issues, especially considering Minnesota's long mega-winters. In fact, it soon became clear that installing sculptures outdoors requires quite a different mindset than placing them in the galleries. When you work outside the building, on public land, you soon realize that you are only one of many other specialists, all of whom have pretty good ideas about what can or cannot be done on that land. Lots of discussions with city and state officials are necessary in order to arrive at constructive collaborative approaches.

Fortunately, the Walker's partnership with the Park Board has worked out well, and the Minneapolis Sculpture Garden is perceived by the public as an ongoing joint venture. There were other important partnerships. I attended numerous evening meetings with concerned community groups, each with its own idea of what the garden should or should not look like, and, in some cases, whether there should even be a garden. Often, the next morning, I would arrive bleary-eyed for a 7:00 breakfast meeting (such meetings are a crucial ritual of business and civic life in the Midwest). Aside from the regulars from the Walker and the Park Board, there was a constantly changing cast of characters munching away: city and state representatives, city engineers, sidewalk and zoning specialists, all with definite ideas of their own and the authority to back them up. It was pretty territorial stuff. As I quickly learned, they were not obstructionists, in any sense, but simply wanted to know in full detail what we had in mind for the garden and bridge. They explained why some of our proposals were achievable, while others were not—but the atmosphere was always positive. Things moved along systematically, but it was a long process, a series of negotiations. There were so many agencies whose approval was needed for clearances and variances. When you work as long and as closely as the Walker did with city, state, and park officials, you can expect to be constantly involved in such deliberations. But these were highly productive sessions during which it became clear that the Minneapolis Sculpture Garden project had considerable moral as well as technical

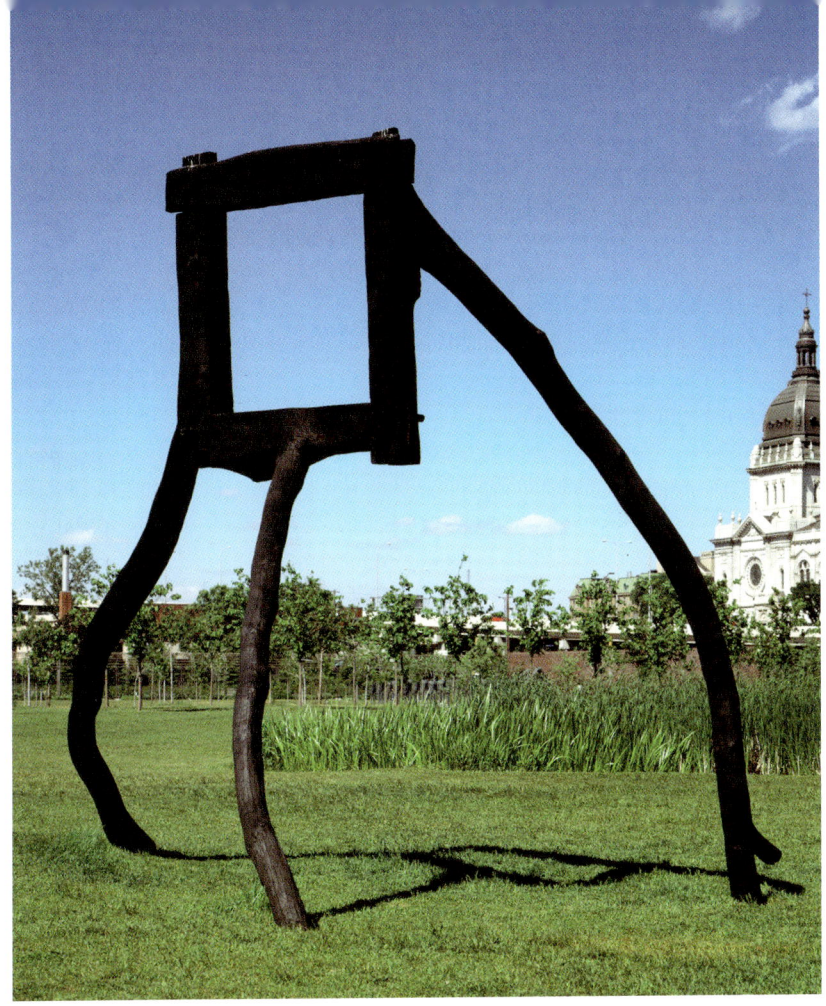

David Nash, *Standing Frame*, 1987. Charred white oak, 172 x 209.75 x 209.5 in.

support from these various agencies. In effect, they bought into the idea and helped make it happen.

CS: It is clear that you were a successful fundraiser. What did you bring to the situation that led people to trust you with their resources?

MF: I think that the idea of the sculpture garden largely sold itself. As to attracting substantial funding from private, corporate, and foundation sources, the Walker's record of artistic accomplishments and the positive public response to them were the key factors. Of course, the notion of a sculpture garden as a public space had a particularly strong appeal. Many people who contributed substantially to its realization couldn't have cared less about sculpture but saw the garden as a great new civic resource. Others were more interested in the park concept—a handsome tree-filled space near the center of town. Still others were interested in the garden as a place that would offer a variety of special programs and activities for various constituencies—young people, the elderly, and others. We gave potential donors the option of supporting the construction, helping the Walker acquire important sculptures for display, or sponsoring specific programs ranging from education activities to special exhibitions. Happily, a number of sponsors wanted to help the Walker acquire important sculptures for the garden, either through purchase of existing works or by commissioning new ones.

CS: Was the support mostly local?

MF: Yes, primarily. It was a broadly based local effort, with lots of generous support from individuals, corporations, and foundations—it was quite an expression of faith in the effort and reflected a strong sense of regional ownership of the garden. This sense of ownership was especially evident once the bulldozers arrived. As construction proceeded, it was fun to see how many people were attracted to the site, not just from the immediate neighborhood but from all over town. Things really got interesting once the works of art were being installed. Every sculpture was scrutinized and debated. Everyone had an opinion. There were visitors to the site at all hours of the day and well into the evening. The garden was claimed by the community. It was theirs. It will always be theirs.

<www.walkerart.org>

A Garden for Latin American Sculpture

by Collette Chattopadhyay

In fall 2005, the Museum of Latin American Art in Long Beach, California, opened its Robert Gumbiner Sculpture and Events Garden, the first North American, outdoor collection devoted exclusively to contemporary Latin American sculpture. Some of the pivotal works, including Fernando de Szyszlo's *Sol negro 2* (1995), Guillermo Trujillo's *El Nucho de MoLAA* (2005), and Luis Efe Vélez's *Rhada*, come from the collection of Robert Gumbiner, a physician who founded the museum nine years ago. His vision and art-world connections, along with those of the museum's director, Gregorio Luke, guided the selection of works, many of which arrived by air and sea transport in the weeks preceding the garden's unveiling.

The newly terraced, 5,000-square-foot sculpture court sits adjacent to the museum and was designed by Chris Brown of the California-based firm Architectus. The courtyard, which features multi-terraced platforms, uses the square as its primary architectural motif. Evoking ancient Meso-American urban complexes such as Tenochtitlan and Teotihuacán, the garden's format reinforces the vision that contemporary Latin American art and identity are in part the conceptual heirs to pre-Columbian cultures.

While most of the sculptures date from the last 10 years, some are by seminal early 20th-century pioneers now in their 70s and 80s, while others are by emerging artists in their 30s. The resulting mix of idioms includes essentialist, Cubist, Surrealist, and magic realist emphases. The artists include Pérez Celis and Gustavo López Armentia from Argentina; Amparo Garzón and Luis Efe Vélez from Colombia; Carlos Luna from Cuba; Max Leiva from Guatemala; Alberto Vargas Aguirre, Marco Aldaco, Heriberto Juárez, Noé Katz, and Jorge Marin from Mexico; Guillermo Trujillo from Panama; Benito Rosas and Fernando de Szyszlo from Peru; Luis Torruella and Jorge Zeno from Puerto Rico; Cecilia Miguez from Los Angeles and Uruguay; and William Barbosa and Gaudi Esté from Venezuela. Together, these works provide a glimpse into the complexities of contemporary Latin American art.

Rather than imitating European or North American art directions, Fernando de Szyszlo decided in the 1940s to construct a new understanding of South American identity, one moored in both the present and the pre-Columbian past. One of the first to evolve such a post-colonial perspective in South America, de Szyszlo created art that defined his own circumstances, rather than "leaving its justification in the hands of another," to adapt a comment by Jean-Paul Sartre. Building an alternate conceptual framework that looked to Inca culture as a touchstone for the present, de Szyszlo created works such as *Sol negro 2*, a disk with a hole in its center. Endowed with an obdurate materiality similar to that of Inca foundation stones, which were re-used in the construction of cathedrals in Cuzco, *Sol negro* evokes rituals of the sun and moon, ancient torture, and gravestones, constructing a metaphor of contemporary artistic identity from the past.

Noé Katz adopts comparable conceptual strategies. Though made of iron painted with polyurethane, his cubic column *The Secret Voyage* (2005) resembles incised stone, evoking the ancient Zapotec danzante figures from Monte Alban in Oaxaca, Mexico. More playful than de Szyszlo, Katz adopts the leitmotif of a journey, combining narratives from his own explorations with those of his father's migration to Mexico and the family's inheritance of ancient Zapotec history.

Carlos Luna, the youngest artist here, uses portraiture to narrate the story of his transition from poverty in Cuba to success in Mexico. The result is a colossal bronze, *War-Giro* (2005). One side of the sculpture, alluding to the past, features an abstract skeletal figure outlined against pants, a jacket, and hat. On the obverse, the figure appears as a dashingly clad bourgeois. "There are two characteristic personages in my

Carlos Luna, *War-Giro*, 2005. Bronze, 249 cm. high.

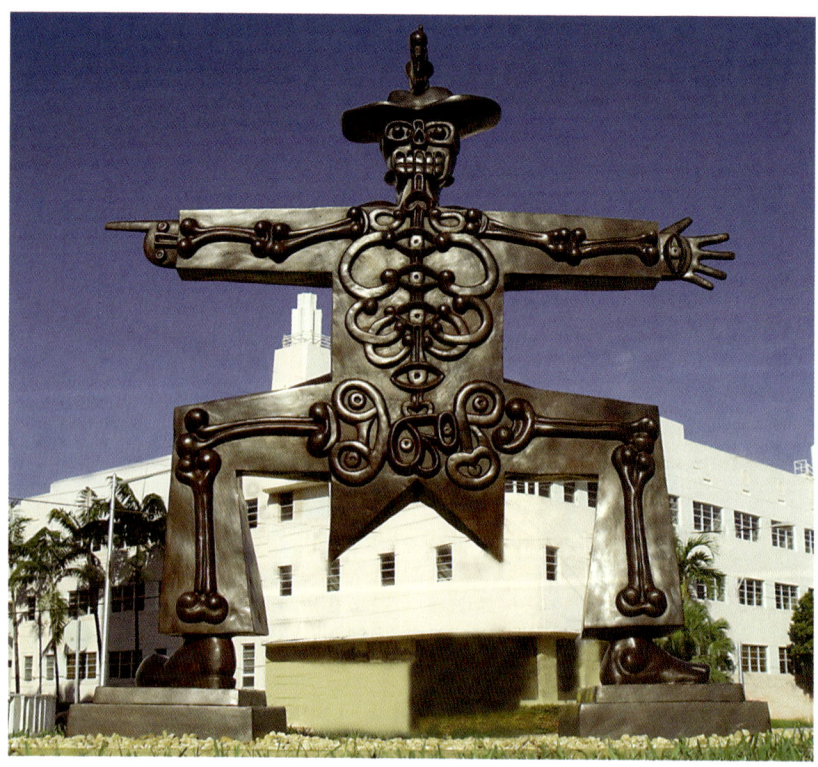

Noé Katz, *The Secret Voyage*, 2005. Polyurethane on iron, 86.5 x 39.25 in.

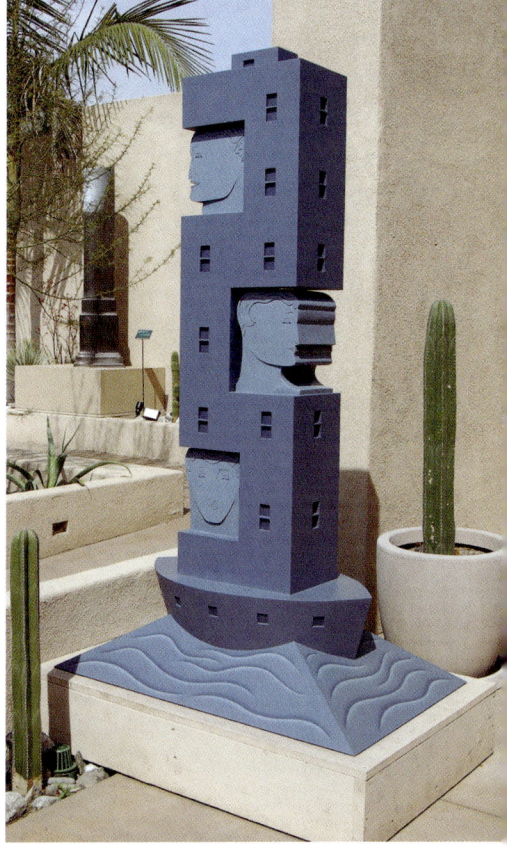

work," Luna remarks, "El Guajiro, who is a peasant and, in my opinion, the true hero of Cuban national life, and El Hombre-Gallo (The Rooster-Man), the magical, mythical animal side of this Guajiro." Infused with a magic realist sensibility, Luna's work links the past to the present, invoking lore and narrative.

By comparison, Cecilia Miguez's *Time Traveler* (2005) turns from the past to the future. Stranded in an unknown space, the lone figure stands as a mythic priestess, motionless and meditative in a realm beyond the known reaches of time. Suggesting that fantasy plays as large a part in explaining ourselves to others as reality, Miguez's work, like the writings of Latin American magic realist authors, presents a world infused with ambiguities and possibilities.

While the assembled works demonstrate significant contemporary sculptural developments in the Central and Southern hemispheres, there are some gaps. Artists who have been feted with major gallery or museum exhibitions in California during the last decade are ironically missing. These include Gabriel Orozco, Helen Escobedo, Kcho, Fernando Botero, Tunga, Caldus, Jesús Rafael Soto, and Gego, among others who have done much to define directions in contemporary Latin American art. Despite their absence, the new garden provides a welcome resource for the ongoing appreciation and study of contemporary Latin American sculpture.

<www.molaa.org>

DeCordova Museum and Sculpture Park: Staying on the Edge

by Marty Carlock

In 1989, the DeCordova and Dana Museum in Lincoln, Massachusetts, legally changed its name to the more descriptive DeCordova Museum and Sculpture Park. The intent was to emphasize its outdoor display of three-dimensional work. The only permanent sculpture park in New England, DeCordova has assembled some 80 pieces of sculpture, including work by such 20th-century giants as George Rickey, Alexander Liberman, Mark di Suvero, and Jim Dine, on 35 acres. Naming names here is misleading. Some of the most impressive creations are borrowed and could depart at any time—although loan periods can be nebulous. di Suvero's *Sunflowers for Vincent* was centered on the front lawn in 1988 and is still there.

"We take pride in maintaining a *contemporary* sculpture park," said Nick Capasso, the park's curator. "One of the things that's different here is the rotating program. Most of the work is on loan; it goes back, and new things come. That way, we're always contemporary. Otherwise we'd be the museum of the '80s and '90s." Only about a quarter of the works on the grounds are permanent, and they are judiciously selected for their art historical significance.

A legacy to the town of Lincoln, the DeCordova and Dana Museum came with 28 rural acres overlooking Sandy Pond, the town reservoir. (The trustees subsequently added seven more acres.) Since 1950 it has been a museum focusing on 20th-century and now 21st-century art. From time to time, the museum would display sculpture on the lawn. "It wasn't an organized program," says museum spokesman Corey Cronin. But the summer of 1966 marked the inauguration of a groundbreaking series of outdoor sculpture exhibitions; 47 sculptors from the Northeastern U.S. and Europe lent pieces. The catalogue for the show noted that artworks too large to be exhibited easily indoors frequently go unseen: "This exhibition brings to the attention of the public works which embody the artist's quest for monumentality and his artistic solution."

According to Capasso, "We were one of the first places in the country to show sculpture in any systematic way. Some of the artists were so thrilled they gave pieces to the museum." Even so, the program remained fairly informal. Outdoor shows occurred irregularly every few years in the '60s and '70s. It wasn't until a new director, Paul Master-Karnik, came on board in 1984 that the sculpture park became a major focus for the museum: "Paul saw the potential."

In the late 1980s, the DeCordova won a $75,000 National Endowment for the Arts grant for a sculpture park initiative. "That was a great impetus," said Rachel Rosenfeld Lafo, a curator since 1983 and now director of curatorial affairs. "It took us to another level." She and Master-Karnik developed a three-part policy: finding and commissioning site-specific works, borrowing the majority of the works on a temporary basis, and severely restricting what came into the permanent collection to work by major artists. "It gives the collection a critical and art historical backbone," Capasso explains.

Activity fluctuates from year to year, along with the budget. "We do things on a shoestring," Capasso says. "We've just invested a lot of money in a master plan, and we're trying to keep things vital." Lafo estimated that sculpture park activities cost approximately $50,000 in 2007, cautioning that labor costs are hard to estimate. Five new works were sited in the park during the year, three others left, and two were scheduled to be removed. The curators are looking at six artists for inclusion in the spring, but that will depend on funding. The museum prints a new four-color map each time the park changes—"There were three printings last year," she said, "and that cost $20,000." The park relies heavily on grant money.

Choosing new works keeps Capasso and Lafo traveling. Both are curators and make the necessary studio visits, then bring their collaborative recommendations to

Ilan Averbuch, *Skirts and Pants (after Duchamp)*, 2000. Etched glass and wood, 10 x 20 x 20 ft.

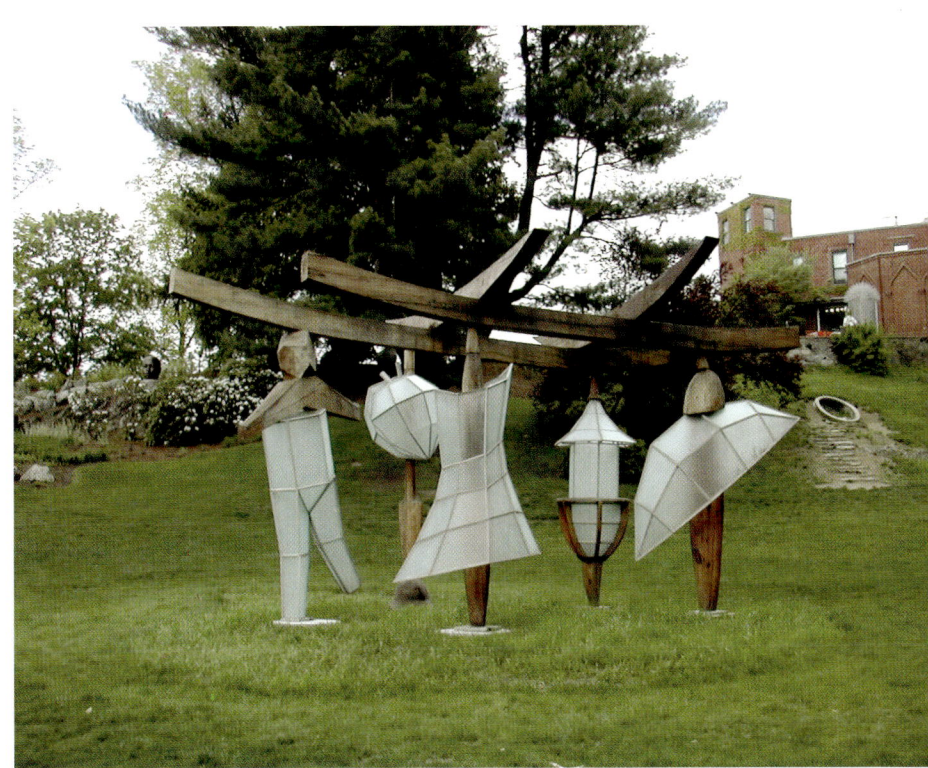

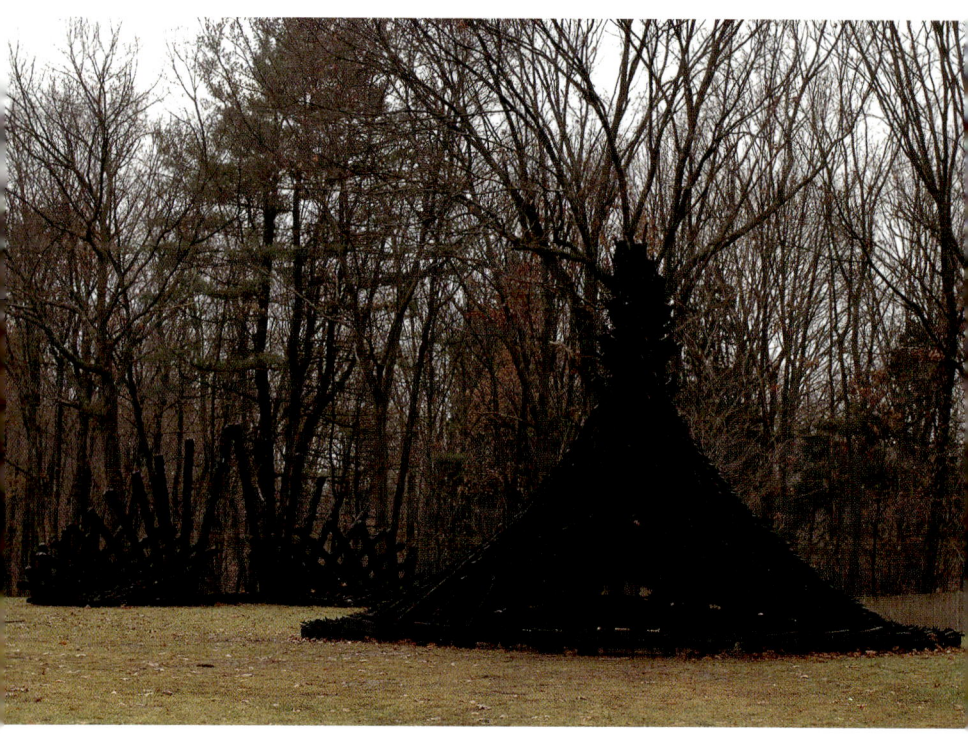

Chakaia Booker, (foreground) *No More Milk and Cookies*, 2003, rubber tires and wood, 14.5 x 28 x 19 ft.; (background) *The Conversationalist*, 1997, rubber tires and wood, 20 x 21 x 12 ft.

the director, and the three hash out final choices together. "We select work based on the quality of the sculpture, not on the heft of the artist's résumé," Capasso says. "We've borrowed right out of people's MFA thesis shows."

"When we're out in the field, we're as mindful of the landscape as we are of the sculpture we choose. Often a site really needs a sculpture, and we go looking for an appropriate piece. But sometimes we see a sculpture that we just have to show, and if necessary we create a place for it." Capasso was hired in 1990. His dissertation was on public art, and he admits that the sculpture park is his first love: "We're the only museum in New England that has a curator permanently dedicated to the sculpture park."

"One of the wonderful things we enjoy is a lot of micro-environments," Capasso says. "We have pine woodlands and deciduous woodlands, lawn and the slope to the pond. And the roof." The flat roof of one section of the museum building currently hosts a figure about to throw her own head over the edge. An elevator allows visitors to go up and find out why—and to enjoy a scenic view westward. Among the micro-environments is Alice's Garden, which was developed as a place to show smaller-scale work. Capasso explains that if some of these works were "plopped out on a lawn [they would] just disappear. We needed a landscaped architectural context. For now, Alice's Garden is reserved for bronzes. It's a rock garden, so stone sculpture doesn't show up well. It's also a natural landscape with flowers, lots of color, May to October. So we didn't want brightly colored work there—no plastic, no painted metal. And it's an educational tool to have all these bronzes juxtaposed: you get a stylistic conversation across symbolic, representational, and abstract work, with references to the natural landscape."

Capasso believes that one of the great things about putting work outdoors is being able to manipulate ways of seeing it. Two gigantic hearts by Jim Dine mark the far edge of one glen: "From the driveway those things don't look that big. But if you approach them, you find they're huge, and you're rewarded with all these details. It intensifies the viewer's experience of the work." He takes satisfaction in how sculpture is sited here: "Every sculpture should be placed in an optimum way, where it not only looks its best but means its most. For example, the Marianna Pineda figure at the edge of Alice's Garden. It's extending a gift but also holding up a hand as if in warning. That gesture works best at the entrance to a place."

Two phases of a $4 million master plan developed by the Halverson Group of Boston have been completed: first, redirecting the driveway, creating a visitor station, and regrading and replanting the grounds; then redesigning the entrance plaza to the museum and opening up spaces. The third phase will be to clear some other acreage. "We have a few acres we've not yet put sculpture into," Capasso says. "We plan to create a Sculpture Zoo, with contemporary, family-friendly animal sculpture—a few permanent pieces, some Tom Otterness works, for instance." DeCordova's curators strive for mix and variety. Capasso says, "Our mission is to educate the public about the various ways artists are working. And we are blessed with these 35 beautiful acres, so people can go from sculpture to sculpture to sculpture and place to place to place."

<www.decordova.org>

Creating a Sculpture Garden in New Orleans: A Conversation with Sydney Besthoff

by Robert Preece

Since the 1970s, Sydney and Walda Besthoff have specialized in collecting modern and contemporary sculpture, in addition to photorealist painting. In November 2003, the five-acre Sydney and Walda Besthoff Sculpture Garden opened at the New Orleans Museum of Art. It features 57 sculptures, 44 of them donated by the Besthoffs' foundation, including works by Arman, Botero, Bourgeois, Burton, Chadwick, Chia, Hepworth, Lipchitz, McCollum, Moore, Pomodoro, Rickey, Segal, Shapiro, and Zadkine. (The remaining 13 were museum purchases or gifts from other donors.)

Previously, most of the Besthoff collection was on view at K&B Plaza, a seven-story office building in downtown New Orleans, which Sydney Besthoff purchased in 1973. The building, designed by Skidmore, Owings and Merrill in 1960–62 and featuring an 18-foot granite sculptural fountain designed by Isamu Noguchi, became the headquarters of K&B Incorporated, a family-owned drugstore chain founded by Besthoff's grandfather. Besthoff served as chairman and CEO of K&B until 1997, when he sold it to the Rite Aid Corporation. He still owns the building, though, and even after the donation, it contains a sizable art collection.

Besthoff has served on the boards of numerous business and arts organizations. He was a founder of the Contemporary Arts Center of New Orleans and past president of its board of directors. He also serves on the board of the New Orleans Museum of Art. Walda Besthoff, who is committed to the performing arts, particularly theater and dance, served on the board of the Contemporary Arts Center in the 1980s, chairing the Capital Campaign for its expansion. She is currently a trustee of the New Orleans Museum of Art.

The Besthoff Sculpture Garden has taken advantage of its lush Southern setting to place the sculptures within a mature landscape. The site includes two distinct areas: a grove of 200-year-old live oaks and a grove of 100-year-old pines interspersed with magnolias. A lagoon, traversed by three footbridges, bisects the space. While the understated detailing of the design elements defers to the sculptures, it also emphasizes the unique natural context. In the 10 years since this sculpture garden was conceived, Besthoff has traveled to dozens of sculpture parks. He and NOMA director E. John Bullard agreed that the totality of the experience makes for success—a sculpture garden is more than the sum of its parts. Besthoff told the *Times-Picayune*, "It's the location, the pieces they have, the landscape, how [the works] are situated."

The design team for the Besthoff Garden took an ensemble approach, attempting to strike a balance between art and nature. Meandering pathways guide visitors through a series of outdoor galleries. Obvious design elements are limited to two small pavilions at the main entrance, benches and an overlook terrace, low walls, and a small waterfall. While the plantings are still recovering from Katrina's devastation, only one sculpture—Kenneth Snelson's *Virlane Tower*—was damaged by the storm. The artist repaired the work, and it has since been returned to the garden.

Robert Preece: What attracted you to 20th-century sculpture?

Sydney Besthoff: Originally, we were very interested in antique furniture. However, after you fill up the house, there's not much you can do. We wanted something else to collect. And I particularly wanted to collect something within my size range, that I could get my arms around, that wasn't too vast. And so we selected a very abstruse form of art known as photorealism and went into it in the late '60s/early '70s, when it was just starting to become hot. After that, we became very interested in other forms of art.

We had an office building in downtown New Orleans, with a 20,000-square-foot plaza. We commissioned our first work, which happened to be by George Rickey.

Arman, *Pablo Casal's Obelisk*, 1983. Bronze, 240 x 84 x 60 in.

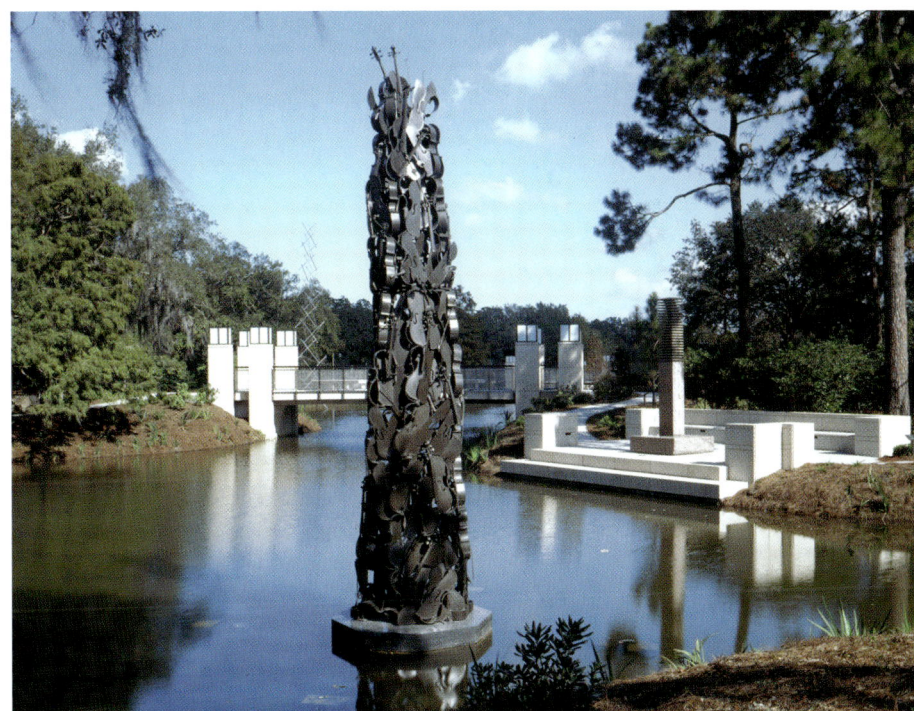

George was really delighted with the commission and came here to install the piece. I worked with him on the installation—in the sense that I was around. I got really interested, and that got me started. From there, we commissioned a few pieces, bought a few pieces. As the years went on and on, we had a lot of stuff.

RP: Forty-four major works is a huge gift. What conditions did you require? What concerns did you have?

SB: I did put some conditions on the gift. The garden was to be named after my wife and myself. A portion of the group has to be shown on a continuing basis. For a certain period of time, the works cannot be alienated—sold, mortgaged, transferred, or gifted. Those were the basic conditions. And the garden had to be open to the public. I didn't want to have the museum lock the garden up—not allow access or open it only to members. It has happened in the past with gifts.

RP: Why did you do this?

SB: We had already set up a foundation, and all of the pieces given to the museum were part of the foundation. So, there was no tax benefit in giving the sculptures to the museum. We wanted to donate the works because it would be good for the city of New Orleans, certainly good for the museum, and it would simplify my estate. What are my kids going to do with the pieces when I die? The sculpture garden was in the planning stages for about 10 years. As with all nonprofit entities, everything had to be done by consensus, and it took a long time to work out the details.

RP: I understand that you were intimately involved in the practical aspects of installing the sculptures in the garden. Could you explain how this worked?

SB: For the general garden design, Lee Ledbetter, the architect, and the landscape architect, based in New York, laid out the overall site. I provided input about the paths and spaces for the garden. Then we placed the sculptures. We sited each work where we thought it was best—a four-way mutual discussion—myself, the museum director, the architect, and the landscape architect. We had some arguments: for example, the architect sometimes wanted one thing, and we were looking for another, and the museum was looking for another concept. As it turns out, most of the "more sedate" pieces are in the pine grove as you first come in, and the more contemporary pieces are on the far side.

When it came to the installation, we had to discuss how the sculptures were to be mounted, and that required a fair amount of discussion. Some pieces were already on plinths when they were at the K&B Plaza. Some were re-used, but a lot of times we had to design bases. Other sculptures didn't need bases because they sit directly on the ground. I was involved in the discussions, and I have a lot of practical experience on how to do it. You're moving a 2,000-pound sculpture, and it has to fit between trees and branches, and it has to come down on the right spot—and it needs a plinth that is going to weigh 2,000 pounds and needs to be bolted together.

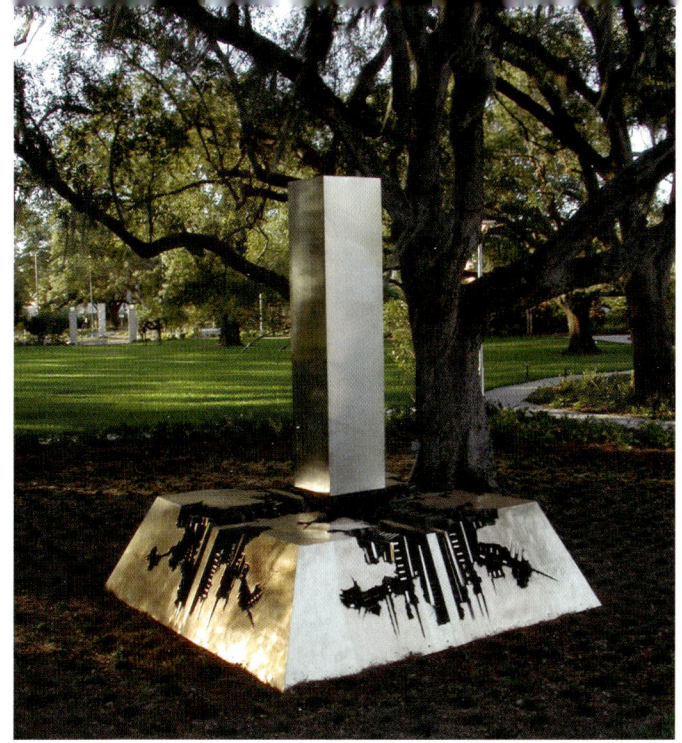

Arnaldo Pomodoro, *Una Battaglia*, 1971. Bronze and stainless steel, 149 x 149 x 141 in.

RP: For me, the garden was rather intense. There are many layers to the design: the architecture, the paths, the integration with water, the greenery, and the various kinds of staging. Sometimes it's dramatic.

SB: That's a very astute observation. One of the things that makes the garden relatively unique is that it has all of these different concepts built in. The architectural concept has no straight lines, everything is curved. It's a real English countryside garden, in the style of Capability Brown. We specifically wanted to get away from the Italian Renaissance and the French formal look, which most sculpture gardens adopt for some reason. Another thing is that because New Orleans is built on an alluvial plain, and there are no hills, the highest elevation is two feet above the next highest elevation.

RP: That's amazing, because it feels a bit hilly.

SB: That's because you're looking at the sides of the lagoon, which is really only nine inches deep. In the garden, we inherited 100-year-old pines and 200-year-old oaks. We took out about 60 diseased trees and put in 125. In another 25 years, they'll be gorgeous. The sculptures are among them. We specifically wanted to have the three bridges and the walks, to have different views of the sculptures. You get various views, including the two in the lagoon itself. You see the sculptures in a complete "surround" basis. And there are no "keep off the grass" signs.

We knew that if we didn't enclose the space or fence it, we would have vandalism problems, but the landscape architect designed it so that you wouldn't have views beyond the fence. There's a lot of shrubbery, and the fence will be covered in five years.

RP: I understand that the International Sculpture Center conference held in New Orleans in 1976 inspired you and your wife.

SB: We had just bought the K&B building a couple of years before. The Noguchi at the time was inoperative—and I had to get it to work. At that time, I had already commissioned the Rickey and I had some experience with that. The ISC had a conference here, and I went. I enjoyed it, went to several other meetings, and I've been a member ever since.

RP: What goals would you and Mrs. Besthoff like to achieve with the sculpture garden in the future?

SB: We'd like to add a few pieces. I think we can add as many as 25 pieces to the garden. My wife thinks we can add 10. Of course, anything that we'd do would have to be in conjunction with the museum.

RP: Do you have other collecting goals?

SB: I certainly am interested in doing something for the museum on a continuing basis. We'll have to find some categories and concepts that they feel they would like to have. On a personal basis, I now have a fairly empty plaza.

<www.noma.org>

Olympic Sculpture Park: Icons and Monuments

by Matthew Kangas

The Seattle Art Museum's Olympic Sculpture Park is important for a number of reasons, not the least of which is that it provides Seattle with the downtown park it never had. That, and the fact that landscape architecture plays a greater role than in many other urban sculpture parks, suggests that, while OSP extends SAM's profile across the downtown corridor onto a publicly accessible waterfront, the long-term success of the park will hinge on two things: the maturation over time of Weiss/Manfredi's plantings and the addition of more sculptures—both permanent and temporary—to supplement the core collection of 17 Modernist sculptures and five postmodern commissions. Neither factor should present a problem, though both will require patience. OSP's programming, as originally conceived by Lisa Corrin (SAM's deputy director and Jon and Mary Shirley Curator of Modern and Contemporary Art from 2001 to 2005), is intended to be flexible, with loans, commissions, and temporary installations creating a constantly evolving experience.

As we stroll through the Z-shaped $65 million site (with another $20 million from Jon and Mary Shirley for upkeep and free public admission) bisected by railroad tracks and street transportation on lower levels, an emerging hybrid of an art park, ex-toxic waste Superfund clean-up site, and stage for dramatic vistas begins to offer a setting for the enshrinement of sculptural icons and monuments. The entire project helps to meet the goal of creating a more viable downtown living environment, one hospitable to the display, with proper respect, of valuable cultural properties.

The land itself, the site of a former Union Oil of California storage tank facility, first had to be healed by a mixture of federal, state, county, city, and private environmental foundation monies. After an international search, Weiss/Manfredi Architecture/Landscape/Urbanism of New York was selected to design a multi-level park, employing an ingenious set of pathways and trails, all offering views of the Olympic Mountains to the north, across Elliott Bay on Puget Sound to the west, Seattle's radically expanded skyline to the south (with over 30 new high-rises), and the Burlington Northern Santa Fe railroad tracks and bustling street traffic on Broad and Western to the east and south. Weiss/Manfredi designed the park to include meadows of native grasses and wildflowers, three garden zones that represent Northwest landscapes, and a valley and shore with evergreen and deciduous forests typical of the region. Marion Weiss says, "We aspired to create a sculpture park at the intersection of the city and the water, and to define a new model for bringing art to the public."

Louise Bourgeois's swooshing fountain *Father and Son* (2004–05) features two stainless steel figures that appear and disappear with rising and falling water levels, their movements accompanied by the hourly tolling of a bronze bell. Nearby, Bourgeois's black marble *Eye Benches I, II,* and *III* (1996–97), a signature image since 1984), mark the park entrance near the water level on Alaskan Way. *Father and Son* announces one of two sculptural categories within OSP: icons and monuments. It is a monument. Monuments are mostly outdoor sculptures that dominate a site with their size, scale, or tone. Icons, like Ellsworth Kelly's *Curve XXIV* (1981), placed on a wall at the entry to the PACCAR Pavilion at the park's southeast corner, operate less three-dimensionally and are often flat, or read as flat, like paintings. Flat or linear, rather than rounded or bulky, icons at OSP also include Mark di Suvero's *Schubert Sonata* (1992) and Alexander Calder's *Eagle* (1971), along with Anthony Caro's *Riviera* (1971–74). Visitors from Philadelphia will remember how long *Eagle* stood in front of the Philadelphia Museum of Art before Microsoft co-founder Jon Shirley and his wife, Mary, brought it to Seattle through their purchase and gift to SAM.

Besides monuments and icons, OSP also presents a fascinating interface between function and the autonomous sculptural object. Far from an art/craft issue, this connection deals with the intersection of designers and architects in the art world. Local furniture designer Roy McMakin's *Love & Loss* (2005) is one of the new commissions: benches, trees, and tables spelling out the letters of the title allude to deaths from AIDS. Another functional commission, Teresita Fernández's *Seattle Cloud Cover* (2006), a pedestrian bridge made of "laminated glass with photographic design interlay," has already been damaged and repaired once.

Mark Dion's *Neukom Vivarium* (2004–06), the largest of the functional works, takes the form of a hands-on science center: its custom-designed greenhouse encloses a giant 60-foot-long dead tree. Like Buster Simpson's *Host Analog* (1991) at the Oregon Convention Center in Portland, *Neukom Vivarium* stretches the outer limit of art as an independent object: it is completely dependent on its ecological context and environment. Decorative tiles surround the horizontal mummy-like tree. The entire installation has a creepy, ghoulish character: nature may be dying all around us, but we can keep it on life-support here indefinitely.

Among the monuments, none is bigger than Richard Serra's *Wake* (2004), 10 plates of weathering steel that were vandalized (and cleaned) within the first weekend of the park's opening in January 2007. Meant to be framed by a graded evergreen forest on two sides, *Wake* is another art/nature match that will take five to 10 years to mature. Meanwhile, considering that Serra's first public commission anywhere (*Wright's Triangle*, 1979–80) was subjected to student graffiti when it was unveiled at Western Washington University in Bellingham, *Wake* has fared well thus far. Virginia and Bagley Wright (about whom Serra said to me, "The Wrights? They invented me!") commissioned Serra's Bellingham debut and were also instrumental in bringing *Wake* to Seattle, along with Costco founder Jeff Brotman and his wife, Susan.

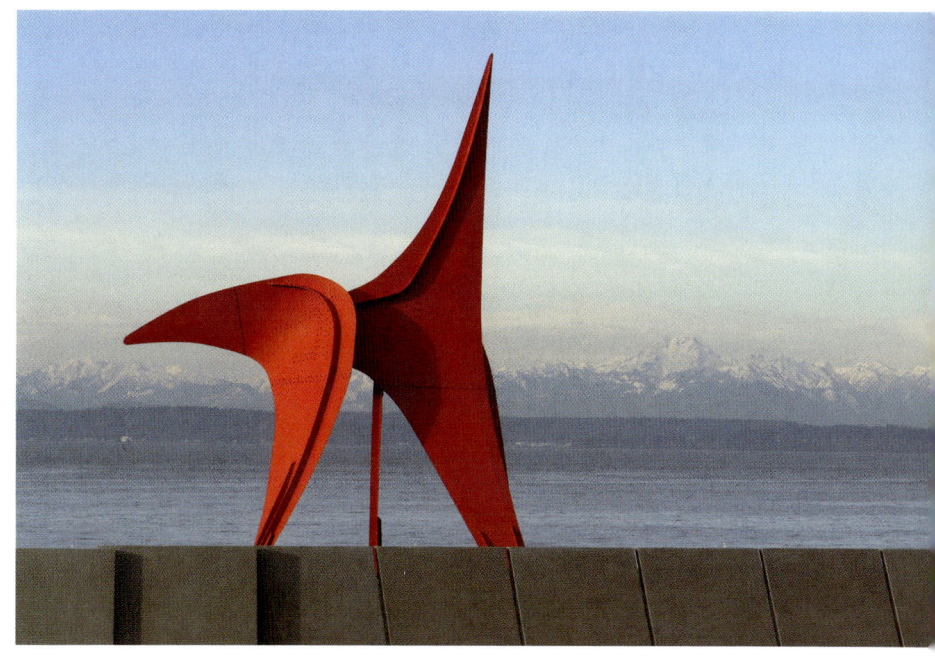

Alexander Calder, *Eagle*, 1971. Painted steel, 38.75 x 32.5 x 32.5 ft.

Tony Smith's *Stinger* (1967/1999) will look better when its own grove matures. A regrettable pathway, though, cuts directly through Smith's five-unit, black-painted steel *Wandering Rocks* (1967). Beverly Pepper's *Persephone Unbound* (1999) and Perre's *Ventaglio III* (1967), the latter a brilliantly reflective stainless steel stack of "drawers," are backed up against retaining walls, too summarily "planted."

When outdoor sculpture cannot be walked around and seen from all sides, something is lost. This doesn't matter with Louise Nevelson's *Sky Landscape I*—its back isn't developed. But Oldenburg and van Bruggen's 20-foot-high *Typewriter Eraser, Scale X* is installed on a steeply inclined hill rolling down to Western Avenue. There is no way for viewers to approach it safely. Here, a monument has been turned into an icon, made graphic, and removed from accessibility.

Another di Suvero work, *Bunyon's Chess* (1965, his first commission, again from the Wrights), suffers the same reduction. Originally a backyard play piece for the Wrights' four children and their neighborhood pals, *Bunyon's Chess* was made off limits after a few years at the artist's request due to his fears of the children injuring themselves. Instead, a rope was attached to the balcony off the Wrights' dining room so visitors could pull it, activating movable elements. Its site at OSP— on a hill near the shoreline—is highly visible, but the work seems smaller than

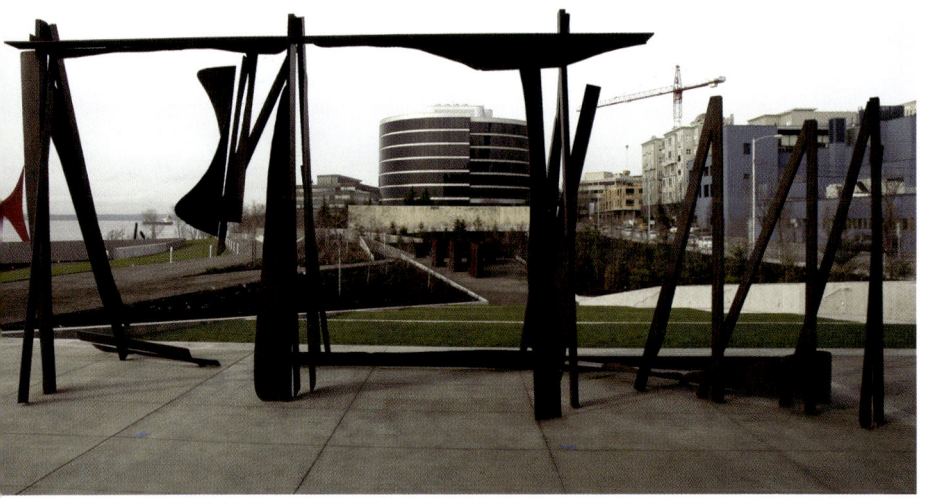

Anthony Caro, *Riviera*, 1971–74. Rusted and varnished steel, 10 x 27 x 10 ft.

before, losing much of its monumentality while gaining an iconic, linear character that suggests a Franz Kline painting.

Olympic Sculpture Park may be the latest jewel in Seattle's vaunted civic and corporate art in public places programs, but it is neither the earliest nor the last. As a central park with art, it is unique to the region. With a thicker mane of trees, shrubs, and underbrush, it will provide an enhanced setting for works of art that are important because they suggest rather than preach. They honor the viewer's intelligence rather than dead politicians, historical figures, or social causes, which, to paraphrase Yeats, are sculptures for old men. OSP welcomes young audiences, who have made it into their own summer playground (complete with rock concerts at the PACCAR Pavilion) and who will live to see its full maturity and development as a spectacular natural and urban matrix.

During January and February 2007, beginning at one of the museum's evening parties for the public, Iole Alessandrini's *Greener* (2006–07) laid down dozens of interactive ropes of laser lights on the long steps going down to the Gates Amphitheatre. The entire terrace was illuminated. People were able to walk on the glowing apparition and enjoy it. With this combination of ecology and technology, Alessandrini set the right note for future artworks to be commissioned by this remarkable haven for sculpture.

<www.seattleartmuseum.org>

Designing Sculpture Parks: The Full-Body Experience

by Barbara Swift

The development of a sculpture collection and the intentional placement of objects in a fabricated landscape have a long tradition. This discussion of two sculpture parks is intended to contrast very different site conditions and serve as a framework for considering the potential of the new Olympic Sculpture Park. The Japanese imperial villas of Katsura and Shugakuin, the Chinese gardens in Suzhou, and the grounds of Versailles and Stourhead are constructs in which the interaction of the object with the spatial organization of the landscape and the sequence of movement are carefully considered for a desired experience. Vistas, view corridors, landforms, and enclosures, coupled with the kinesthetic experience of moving through the landscape, structure the experience of place with a focus on the interaction of context and object. Rich ecosystems and the phenomenological characteristics of a specific landscape inextricably link the act of seeing with movement, smell, temperature, weather, seasons, and memory, resulting in a full-body experience of a specific time and place in the context of cultural references. This is the beautiful coupling of the sublime and the rational, of culture and biology.

Sculpture parks have a unique place in this tradition. The objective of creating an environment where heightened awareness is focused on the interaction of object and context demands exceptional understanding, with attention to the design and organization of the whole. The viewer is an essential part of this equation. The viewer's body is the tool of measurement and perception. Without an understanding of this rich interaction and a design that embodies an acute attention to the spectrum of influences, the effect is flawed, the interaction is weakened, and the result is a simplistic placement of objects. When it is done well, the experience is exceptional.

Two general organizing frameworks can be used separately or together. Each results in a different viewer experience. The first is exemplified by the Japanese landscape tradition in which the context is less overtly structured and participation occurs via movement and observation. The highest form is found in Zen temple gardens such as Kokedera, where the individual moves through the fabricated informal landscape and incrementally becomes more aware of the relationship of the body to place and time. The three-way relationship in this case links the viewer, the object, and the place. The second organizing framework, with its roots in the occidental Renaissance landscape tradition, structures the context to create a centralized focus. Viewers are implicitly aware of the intentional nature of the experience, the structure of the sequence created by others, and the playing out of a collective cultural contract between viewer and patron. The experience becomes a four-way relationship joining viewer, object, place, and authority/patron.

Context requires consideration, and the nature of the context is essential in creating the opportunity for this high degree of engagement. The level of sensory complexity and "noise" in relation to the subtlety or power of the object is central to creating an environment that supports the work and creates a resonance between object and place. The sensory complexity of an urban environment, with its diverse uses and issues of scale, is a very different situation from a sensuous bucolic landscape. With great sensitivity and awareness, both can be exceptional partners in creating a compelling experience.

Storm King Art Center and the Seattle Art Museum's Olympic Sculpture Park offer two extreme examples of the sculpture park form. One occupies an iconic landscape defined by magnificent temperate forest framing large rolling pastures. The experience is predominately a relationship of viewer, object, and place. The other, in the heart of a complex urban environment bisected by roads and train tracks, uses a site organization defining a four-way relationship of viewer, object, place, and patron. The organization, structure, and resultant experience in each park stem from the aggregate of artwork, context, and site design.

Storm King consists of 500 acres of restored farmlands (worked for over 200 years), located in the sublime landscape of the Hudson River Valley. The setting has the sense of an older inhabited landscape, now matured into a resolved sequence of interlocking pastures and woodlands. The form of the land suggests years of tilling, with eased transitions from level pasture to sloped hillside. Weather systems bring constantly changing light and texture to the grounds. The reintroduction of native long grasses has resulted in an elegant, informal ground plane framed by woodlands and allees of large deciduous trees. The entry sequence brings the visitor through the landscape, with artworks of heroic scale marking the entry corridor. Parking is located in groves along the drive to the museum, which stands on a hill overlooking the park.

This comparatively simple situation creates a consistent context, without the sensory complexity of a more urban environment or diverse ecosystem. The predominant sounds are bird calls, wind in the trees, occasional vehicles, and human voices. The simplicity and scale of the landscape enable a focus on the work, which is located within a spectrum of intimate and grand spaces. The artworks are sited throughout the grounds, with periodic groupings of work by individual artists. Richard Serra's *Schunnemunk Fork* sets layered landscape datums circumnavigated by a trail in a 10-acre rolling pastoral landscape. Andy Goldsworthy's *Storm King Wall* marks the edge of a woodland, and the trampled ground illustrates the role the wall plays in the landscape. Magdalena Abakanowicz's *Sarcophagi in Glass House* sits in the valley between two landforms, hunkering down in an oddly dark and animate manner. *Momo Taro* by Isamu Noguchi is carefully sited among large trees, spaced so that the sculpture functions as an equal element in the forest. Several works by Alexander Calder slip down the main hill and become playful emerging elements in the landscape as the visitor circumnavigates the hill or walks the slope.

The organizational structure allows the visitor to make choices. One can take paved walkways, follow mown grass paths, or roam freely through the grounds. This range of choice, coupled with the scale of the landscape and the extensive collection, gives the visitor a sense of freedom and generosity. The nature of the experience is the visitor's to create. As a result, the experience is personal, and the work is experienced in the "round."

The sense of emerging and shifting elements, combined with the freedom to select a route, produces an experience that intimately involves the individual with the work, place, and time. The experience of seeing the work from a distance and slowly moving toward it engages the visitor equally in the land and the work. This is a very personal process, without an overtly controlled landscape structure defining the nature of the experience or determining what one should conclude. While this experience is possible in a more complex environment, the simplicity and neutral character of the Storm King landscape, with its cultural roots in the English tradition, reduce

Mark di Suvero, *Pyramidian*, 1987–98. Steel, 65 ft. high. View of work at Storm King Art Center.

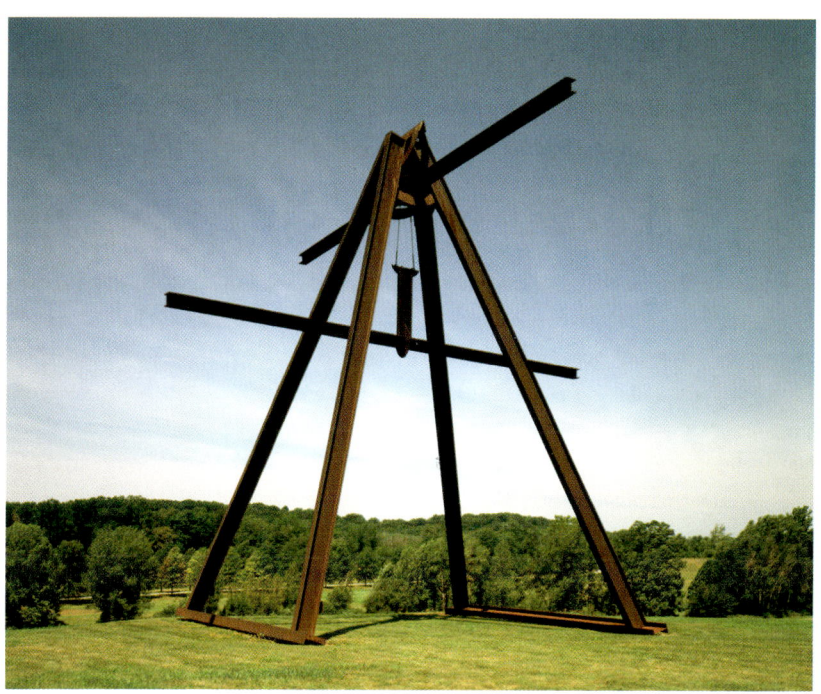

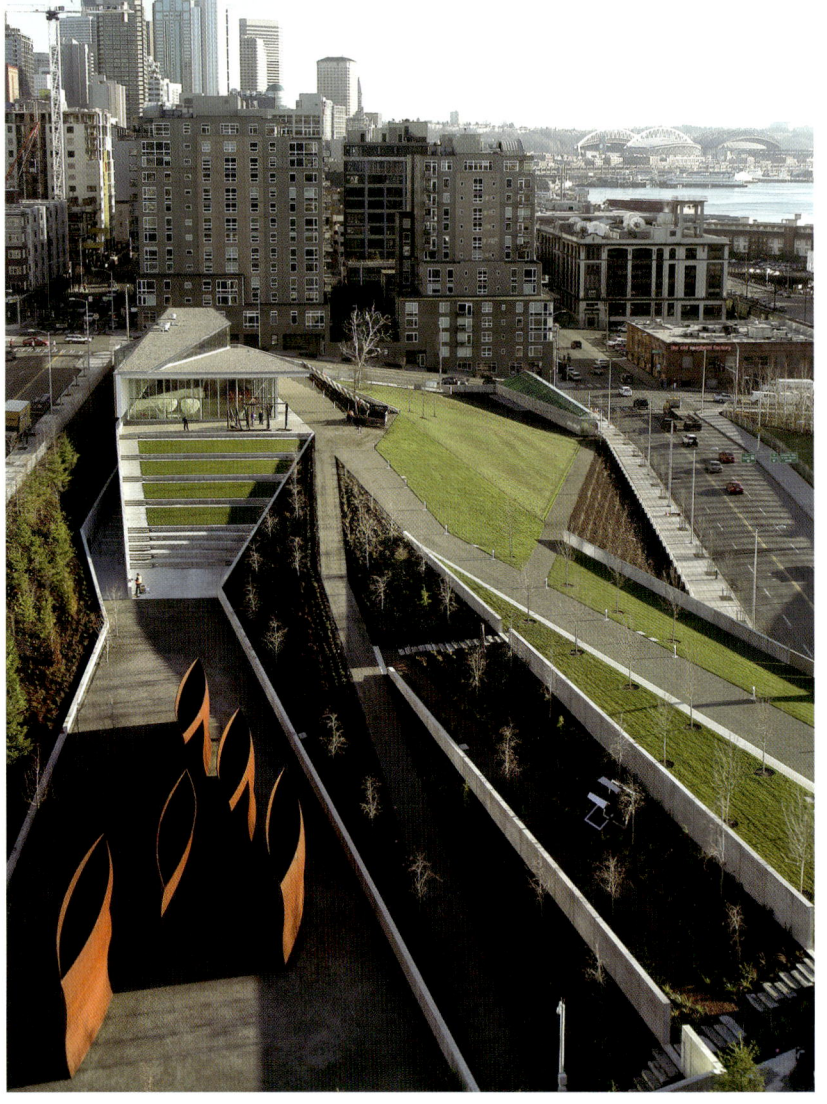

Aerial view of Olympic Sculpture Park, with Richard Serra, *Wake*, 2004.

the time spent interpreting the landscape. Instead, time is spent immersed in the full-body experience of place and work.

    Olympic Sculpture Park presents very different and challenging circumstances. Located on the downtown Seattle waterfront, the nine-acre park was constructed on hard-used sites with extensive brownfields. Set on a sloped hillside with 60 to 70 feet of grade change divided into three major parcels, and bisected by roads and train tracks, the park is surrounded on three sides by the cacophony of urban life. Its western edge, though, is defined by shoreline offering expansive views of Elliot Bay, islands, and the mountains beyond. Oriented to the west, the park is exposed to maritime storm systems, which bring cycles of wind, rain, and sun.

OSP, which opened in 2007, is the product of a desire for art outside the museum walls and a park in the city. Its defining aspirations include the development of a functioning ecosystem and the creation of a unique setting for outdoor sculpture and public recreation using a continuously constructed landform connecting the three land parcels. With multiple objectives and development partners, along with the often-challenging influences of a changing urban environment, the park produces a complex experience.

The essence of OSP is defined by the central conceptual strategy of linking the three site blocks with a continuous landform or zig-zag spine. This spine serves as the primary pedestrian promenade, turning north and then south like animal tracks on a steep hillside. At its edges, steep slopes spill away to arterials or rail lines. Where the spine is framed by walls, the high overlooks are majestic and orient views of the city and region beyond the park.

Topography and access define the site, projecting views outward and resulting in a highly energetic sense of walking a narrow ridge line. While an effective organizing tool, this approach segregates the site into three major experiential zones. The spine, the only largely level area in the park, serves as the dominant area for circulation, viewing, and gathering. The immediately adjacent sloped zone, which constitutes a significant portion of the site, impedes comfortable access. A third zone at the bottom of the walls and slopes includes the roads and railroad tracks. The latter two zones, while constituting over 50 percent of the park, permit only limited public use due to difficulty of access or safety concerns. The majority of the park experience, therefore, is exposed, with expansive commanding views.

Contained or internally focused spaces at OSP are limited and include the Valley inhabited by Richard Serra's *Wake* and the shoreline cove. With a new landscape, the future is an essential participant, and trees will eventually provide a significant spatial structure. While OSP is in its infancy, one can imagine *Wake* surrounded by a dark, richly textured forest frame rising 60 to 100 feet. The aspen grove creates a counterpoint to the steep West Meadow and Elliot Avenue, and nestled on a small level platform is Tony Smith's *Stinger*. In both cases, due to the sense of enclosure, the relation of art to context will resonate in the future and be whole. The contained form of the cove is defined by the curved, sloped beach and its responding water line. This site is begging for a compelling work.

As a result of the site design, the sequence and routes of travel are largely defined by someone other than the viewer. This places a great burden on the placement and scale of the artwork, which must create a compelling interaction with the viewer—the full-body experience. For the visitor directed along prescribed paths, there are two ways to experience the work. The first is a fully free sequence of moving in from a distance, where the artwork appears in a larger context, to the intimate tactile scale, where the artwork dominates the context. This is the full-body experience of place and work in which the visitor has a large degree of control over the sequence. The second is a truncated version, where intimate access to the artwork is available only to the interloper walking off path. In this case, the artwork must be carefully sited and of a power and scale to bridge the gap in experience and command the visitor at an intimate and personal level despite distance. *Bunyon's Chess*, *Split*, *Typewriter Eraser, Scale X*, and *Eagle* are all experienced from a distance, and of this group, Calder's *Eagle* and Roxy Paine's *Split* bridge the gap. *Typewriter Eraser, Scale X* marks Elliot Avenue like a highway billboard, a good combination of artwork and site. The others struggle in their efforts to command the viewer and place.

The Olympic Sculpture Park is urban and new, and it is very different from the eased forms and culturally familiar landscape of Storm King. One is an easily understood and simple bucolic landscape in which sculpture does not need to compete with context for its place. OSP combines a noisy urban environment, a complex site bisected by arterials, and multiple demanding aspirations. The park is visually and experientially complex and lacks a balance between enclosed, sheltered, simple spaces and framed expansive overlooks. The landscape, which is outwardly oriented in its basic design structure, plays an important civic and environmental role, but it has not yet fully established its place.

This park is and will always be a demanding circumstance, and it requires a different curatorial approach. There is great opportunity here, one that begs a shifted view of civic landscapes, the proud presentation of a community collection of artwork, and the personal experience of artwork and place. In this case, place is the dominant force in the relationship of visitor, object, patron, and place. The vital, "noisy" quality requires constant engagement, suggesting a philosophy of experimentation with temporary and permanent installations.

The challenge is to build on the power and inherent nature of the place, to integrate the spirit of the earlier rough-working waterfront at the edge of a fjord and engage the full site, accessible or not, with the vigorous presentation of commanding artworks. While larger is not always better, the scale and complexity of the park demand artwork with great presence. Olympic Sculpture Park has the potential to be a new form, where artworks are compellingly integrated into daily life, where the work leaves the confines of the landscape and moves into transportation arterials and addresses the ecosystem in a fundamental manner. This undomesticated, experimental experience can be as gripping and as palpable in memory as walking the fields of Storm King, with the body slipping through an environment of artwork, land, and time.

Three Ideas of the Sculpture Garden: The Israel Museum, The Fields, and Grounds For Sculpture

by Margaret Sheffield

Sculpture gardens are metaphors for many things besides a love of sculpture: they satisfy our need for repose and contemplation, and they express a sense of our relationship to nature. These are also the functions of a traditional garden, whether ancient or modern. Sculpture outdoors, formerly mythological or heroic statuary, goes back to Greek and Roman times. One thinks of Tiberius's garden on Capri and Hadrian's villa at Tivoli, for example. The piazzas of Rome and Florence cannot be imagined without great symbolic statues: the Campidoglio without Marcus Aurelius or the Piazza della Signoria without Michelangelo's *David* would be woefully incomplete. While not sculpture gardens, these public places have something in common with our urban sculpture parks.

Sculpture gardens, as we know them, came into being after World War II, with the development of the large-scale sculptural idioms of such artists as Picasso, Henry Moore, Alexander Calder, Isamu Noguchi, and David Smith. The most familiar sculpture gardens are urban, like those of the Museum of Modern Art in New York or the

Magdalena Abakanowicz, *Negev*, 1987. Limestone, 280 x 280 x 3500 cm. View of work at The Israel Museum.

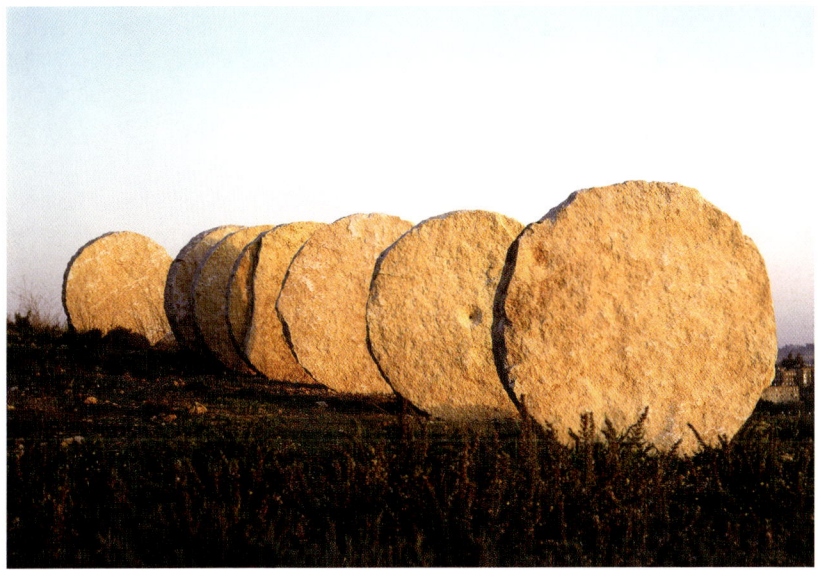

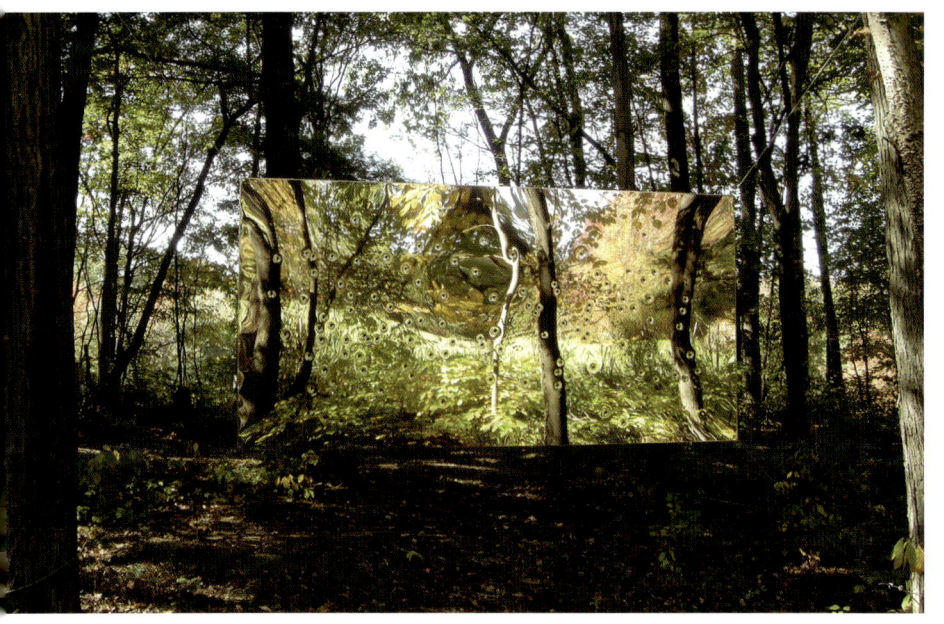

Margaret Evangeline, *Gunshot Landscape*, 2004. Stainless steel and aircraft cable, view of work installed at The Fields.

Hirshhorn Museum in Washington, DC. These venues are unabashedly academic. What strikes one is not so much the individual work, or the contemplative spirit of the garden, but the brisk, inexorable march of art history: Rodin, Maillol, Moore, Picasso, and David Smith. Such collections serve many people well, but they cannot compare to the grandeur of outdoor spaces where individual sculptures are given room, context, and freedom.

The most powerful outdoor sculptures are those created for specific spaces. Examples would surely include Noguchi's *Momo Taro* (1978) and Richard Serra's *Schunnemunk Fork* (1987) at Storm King, as well as Magdalena Abakanowicz's *Negev* (1987) and James Turrell's *Space that Sees* (1992) at the Israel Museum, Jerusalem. Unfortunately such works are the exceptions, since most sculpture gardens start with one person's private collection, transplanted to a new location. As Abakanowicz observes: "The sculpture park is very often like a zoological garden, the sculptures, created elsewhere and placed accidentally among flowers and bushes, watch the visitor like animals in their cages."

Sculpture gardens are invaluable as rare public places devoted to art and nature and their integration with humanity. There are at least three radically different ways of putting sculpture outdoors, and three different sculpture parks show the range of mission, site, and scale, as well as different views of nature: the Israel Museum, Noguchi's charismatic masterpiece fusing Japanese rock gardens with the austere landscape of Israel; The Fields Sculpture Park at Omi International Arts Center, 90 acres of sculpture on 300 acres of un-landscaped beauty in the Hudson River Valley; and Grounds For Sculpture in Hamilton, New Jersey, 35 acres of deft, lyrical landscaping by architect Brian Carey. The Israel Museum and Grounds For Sculpture represent artfully designed nature, while The Fields is naturally aesthetic but largely unadorned. All three maintain the poetry of a garden to some extent while operating as sculpture parks. All have one-person and group exhibitions, and all function as meeting places and civic centers for the arts.

The Israel Museum is magisterial, occupying a stark, numinous site with dramatic views of the Judean Hills. The garden was a gift of the impresario and collector Billy Rose, who selected Isamu Noguchi to design a setting to house his collection. Like all of Noguchi's gardens, this one has an existential as well as an aesthetic reality, for it reflects his motivation to integrate man with sculpture and nature. His vision of the museum is almost palpably symbolic. Noguchi said that he felt "homeless" both in Japan and in America, and he identified with the historic homelessness of the Jewish people. He hoped passionately that the garden would "bring a myth out of the world, and a sense of belonging out of our loneliness."

The Israel Museum garden demonstrates Noguchi's genius at expressive design, at fulfilling his ideal of sculpting a spatial unity. The word "ambulatory," which he used to describe the changing perspectives as viewers walk through the UNESCO gardens in Paris, applies to the Israel Museum as well. Here, Noguchi started out with ideas taken from traditional temple gardens in Japan. But he also created an endless labyrinth of perspectives for the viewer walking up and down the hillsides, always, as he insisted, "aware of the dialogue of earth and sky." Noguchi wanted the energy of the earth to be part of the viewer's apprehension of the sculptures, explaining that "inside the garden, the landscape surges and touches the horizon." For all the excruciatingly subtle art, the landscape both inside and outside the garden reads as wild and untamed. Noguchi spoke of respecting the "sanctity of the place itself," and he insisted that only Mediterranean trees and bushes—Jerusalem pines and rosemary—be allowed in the garden. He specified that only local Jerusalem stone be used, as well as local black basalt.

Noguchi's first great idea was to create five 30-foot-tall retaining walls that look like mounds in the landscape and visually echo the surrounding hills. A second stroke of genius was his creation of intimate outdoor and indoor exhibition areas for smaller sculptures, as well as spaces formed by concrete geometric partitions. This allows viewers to communicate with a single work, while not cutting them off from the other sculptures or, indeed, from the garden as a totality.

Since 1982, Suzanne Landau has been the Israel Museum's chief curator of contemporary art and curator of the museum garden. The original Billy Rose collection contains the work of Rodin, Maillol, Lipchitz, and Moore, but the presentation is so dynamic that it eliminates any hint of the didactic. As Landau said recently, "The really exciting work has been the addition of site-specific work by Richard Serra, Magdalena Abakanowicz, and James Turrell."

Two of the most beautiful additions to the garden, by Abakanowicz and Turrell, were contributed by the American Lewis Rudin. In 1987, Abakanowicz first thought of a figurative work, but when she came to Jerusalem and saw the stone, she saw that "stone is the vocabulary, the language of Israel." *Negev*, named after the desert where the artist found the limestone, is a magnificent work composed of seven stone disks that evoke wheels, shields, and the sun. The disks are irregularly circular, the limestone broken by local Bedouin stonecutters "the way the limestone wanted to be broken." Turrell's *Space that Sees* was 10 years in the making. He selected one of the garden's earth-filled terraces as his site. The contractor who made the piece first had to remove all the earth. The huge room is open to the sky: 10 meters at the base and seven meters high.

Israel Museum directors Martin Weyl (1975–95) and James S. Snyder (1997–present), together with Landau, have added contemporary sculptures while retaining the contemplative magic of the landscape, its indeterminate views, and the garden as a sculpted unity. Adjacent to what aims to be a comprehensive museum, going back to the origins of civilization, the works by Abakanowicz, Serra, and Turrell gain definition by contrast. The garden rests on an ancient site, in an ancient land, which adds the perspective of eternity to modern sculpture.

The Israel Museum is a masterpiece of unity, the integral unity of Noguchi's original design. Although The Fields does not have a sculpted unity, it does have an agricultural unity derived from green New England farmland, some of which continues to be worked. This landscape flows with little to stop its rhythms, and it is to the credit of curators Peter Franck and Kathleen Triem that sculptures have been made to fuse organically with the rhythms of the land.

The Fields' mission was recently defined by founder and chairman Francis Greenberger as twofold: "To show international artists and to be at the forefront of sculpture today." Two shows from the summer of 2002 fulfilled this mission. In June, The Fields installed its first one-person show, 10 monumental works by the French sculptor Bernar Venet. While Venet's *Arc*s, *Angle*s, *Diagonal*s, and *Indeterminate Line*s—varying in height from 14 to 55 feet—could be said to represent physical materiality at an extreme of mass and scale, the second exhibition, "Light in the Landscape," shifted the focus to ephemeral effects, breaking down preconceptions about outdoor sculpture.

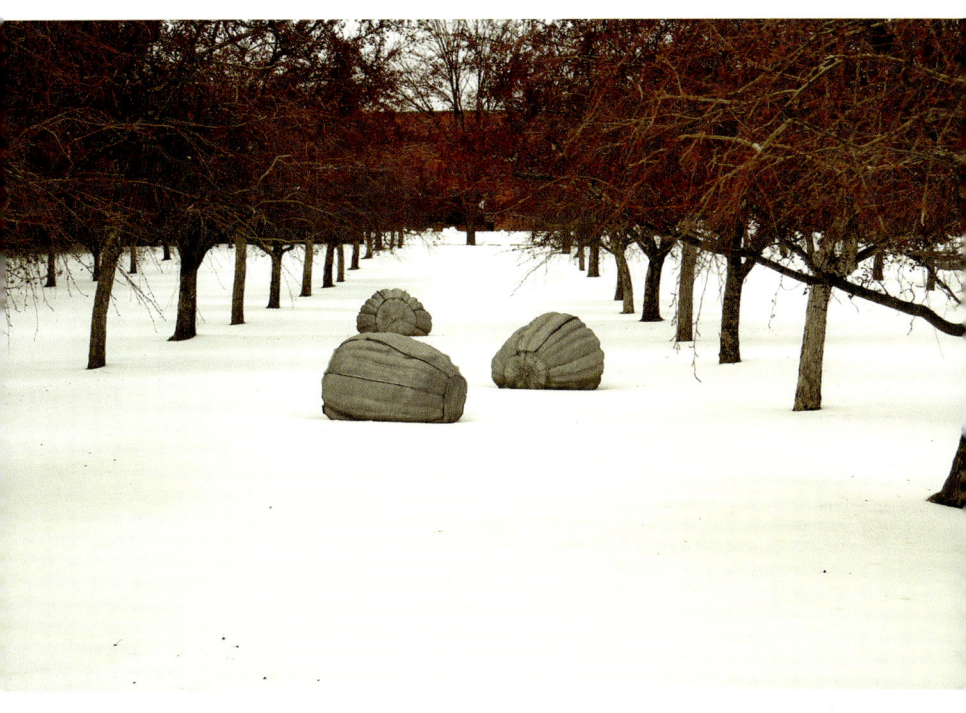

John Ruppert, *Pumpkins*, 1999. Cast aluminum, 5 elements, 29 x 43 x 42 in. each. View of work at Grounds For Sculpture.

The Fields is unique in its range of moods and styles, from the classical Modernism of Beverly Pepper, Alexander Liberman, and Venet to the minimal primal power of Jene Highstein and the anti-heroic irreverence of Donald Lipski. The latter has created two first-rate works at The Fields: *Dirt Ball*, two tons of rope rolled into a menacing 11-foot sphere, and *Sallie*, composed of old glass bottles lying on their sides in a wagon with wheels. *Sallie*'s idiosyncratic and surreal wit belies the somber theme of recycling. Its sharp angles set against a curvaceous hill add to the humor of disconnection.

Franck and Triem, as sculptor Robert Lobe has said, make every work seem site specific. An outstanding example is Highstein's *Inverted Cone*, which is sited by a pond, where it seems to have always been, its primitive aura like a geometric Delphic Oracle. Highstein reworked the surface so that the energy seems to rise up from the earth. The curators attribute their ability to site the works to the fact that they are architects. They said recently that "factors such as scale, sight-lines, progression from one sculpture to another, and conceptualizing the park as a totality are all considerations for choosing a site."

A year-round sculpture garden, The Fields is unique in creating a hands-on "everyday paradise." Its beauty equals that of Hudson River School paintings—no ugly parking lots detract from the view—and visitors may meander at leisure, even accompanied by a dog. The Fields began with a loan of more than a dozen sculptures from art dealer Andre Emmerich; because of this, the original emphasis was on abstract works from the 1960s and 1970s. But the curators have been adding other styles, movements, and works by less well-known sculptors who have had residencies at Art Omi. For example, Gary Quinonez's cast resin *Push Pins* was recently added to the collection. Greenberger's goal to make Art Omi a "fresh and flexible refuge, a meeting and work place, and an exhibition forum for creative minds" has already been fulfilled. The beauty and intellectual boldness of The Fields are new, but they are realized in a place that seems to have been there forever.

Like Noguchi's garden in Jerusalem, Grounds For Sculpture was designed by one man, architect Brian Carey. The design reflects the concerns of founder J. Seward Johnson, a populist about art, who wanted to promote contemporary sculpture. Unlike Noguchi's garden or The Fields, which had strongly defined landscapes, Grounds For Sculpture had to begin from scratch with the rubble left over from the New Jersey fairgrounds. Carey's idea was to create a landscape with enough historical and aesthetic variety, with references to many English and French garden styles, to enhance any kind of modern sculpture. For Robert Lobe and Beverly Pepper, Carey created a seamless transition from outdoor landscape to indoor viewing space. High ceilings and glass walls permit the installation of large-scale work indoors, for instance, Lobe's *Apollo and Daphne*. The nine-foot-tall anodized aluminum sculpture moves with energy and spatial exuberance to express Daphne's metamorphosis and escape from Apollo's embrace. Carey's design allows continuously changing views of such indoor works, from outside in. Pepper was also struck by seeing her 20-foot-high sculptures in an indoor space: "The works obtained a completely different relation to each other, and to the viewer, who is relatively controlled indoors. The ceiling also changed the perspective—a pressure expanding the space downward, instead of entering the infinity of outdoors."

Abakanowicz's 22-part stone composition, *Space of Stone*, installed in 2002, was, in the artist's words: "Created out of granite pieces, which had been broken in the quarry in a natural, accidental way, which shows the mysterious, strong texture of the stone. The texture is similar to that of a tree trunk, or a human muscle. This is nature's confession of her creative powers." This work, made of two kinds of granite—a darker granite from Foxhill, Pennsylvania, and a lighter granite from Barre, Vermont—ranks among the most imposing and spectacular of the site-specific works in the garden. Abakanowicz selected the granite elements because of their surface textures; she further developed the identity of each piece by flaming the surface with a torch.

In this and her other outdoor works, Abakanowicz confronts the human imagination with the imagination of nature. She sees sculpture as a metaphor to express what happens in this interaction, which words cannot express. There is a palpable sense of nature's cellular energy, which recalls Noguchi's vision of stone as a universal language. Abakanowicz spent several years with *Space of Stone*'s broken granite, learning about its nature, the relationship between the 22 forms, and the tension created in space. She has written that each of her works has been "born of the chosen space and the chosen material—ideas that would never be born in the artist's studio."

In today's fragmented cosmos, the sculpture garden's vocabulary of metaphor and rhythm is an existential reminder of unity. The placing of art in an outdoor natural setting is the most ennobling way we can "use" art and also nature—a far cry from the common practice of turning landscapes into shopping malls. Outdoor sculpture should change the space that surrounds it. At its best, the lines and volumes of sculpture create, in and through a partnership with nature, a new space with altered rhythms and lines.

Made For Each Other: Storm King's Vistas and Sculpture

by Jan Garden Castro

Pyramidian, a massive, 65-foot sculpture, begins to take on its final shape, towering over a valley at Storm King Art Center in Mountainville, New York. Mark di Suvero and his trusted two-man crew have just attached a second horizontal I-beam to a central inner circle so that the two beams form an inverted T near the top of a metal pyramid. Created from four steel beams, *Pyramidian* points to earth and sky, west and east, north and south—the six Chinese directions. Its geometric lines and moving center form a Zen koan: more transparent than the ancient pyramids yet just as secretive. A hawk soars overhead. A billow of small birds floats onto the mown field to ferret seeds: another perfect day at Storm King.

During the following weeks, in August's steamy, pre-hurricane weather, di Suvero completed the 10-year cycle of building *Pyramidian* (1987–98). "Storm King is the most visible sculpture park in the U.S. There's nothing like it: the scale, the history," di Suvero said. He's been to Denmark's Louisiana and praises the Netherlands' Kröller-Müller, which owns a di Suvero from the mid-'70s, but the art there is "not built on this scale." Monumental art, picture-perfect vistas, and sculpted, engineered landscapes distinguish Storm King. In this giant playland, ideas and nature exchange energies.

Storm King's unique character can be attributed to two features, assets belonging to it alone: 500 acres of land and H. Peter Stern, president and chairman of the board. His powerful board includes former National Gallery of Art director J. Carter Brown, and his distinguished advisors include former Cornell University H.F. Johnson Museum director Thomas W. Leavitt. Founded in 1960 by Stern and Ralph E. ("Ted") Ogden, business partners at the Star Expansion Company, Storm King's original mission was to feature New York's Hudson Valley painters. However, as Stern explains, "We happened to appear on the scene as these large-scale sculptures emerged…Museums did not have room for them. We had the space and the open-mindedness. Neither Ted Ogden nor I had any preconceived notions about collecting. My personal collecting specialty is Turkish and Indian art." The catalyst was Ogden's visit to David Smith's farmland in the Adirondack Mountains. He was so moved by the experience of seeing Smith's work installed against this outdoor backdrop that he made it his mission to acquire the works from Smith's estate and create an appropriate outdoor environment for them at Storm King.

At the same time that he was thinking about art, Stern was conscious of how large sculpture could fit into the landscape: "We want sculpture that needs this kind of environment, an environment that offers something quite different from an urban

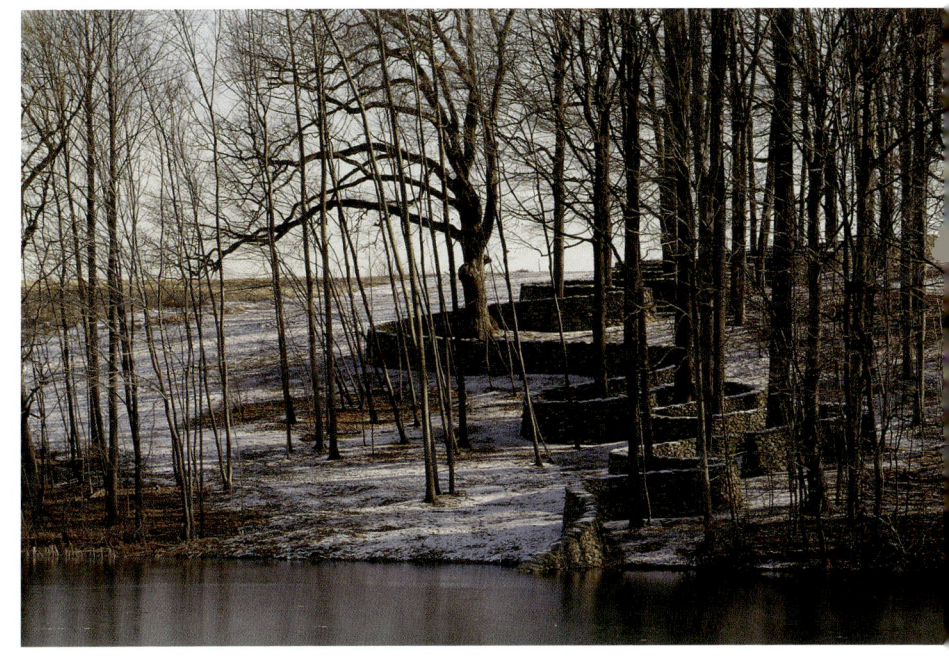

Andy Goldsworthy, *Storm King Wall*, 1997–98. Fieldstone, approximately 5 x 2278.5 ft.

one." At the time of the purchase, the original 200-acre park was in bad shape. Two million cubic yards of gravel had been removed for the New York State thruway. Stern and Ogden called in landscape architect Bill Rutherford to orchestrate Storm King's transformation. "He does not want his artistic signature to be recognized," Stern observes. "He wants the landscape to look as if God, not he, had created it."

Efforts to engineer grand, yet natural, vistas and walking paths and to match each sculpture to a chosen site are ongoing. Roads, parking lots, underground drainage, and a tram service are designed to be as invisible as possible from most sight lines. The art has minimal labels, and there is no signage to obstruct the view or to remind the viewer of caged museum objects. Instead, a color-coded map leads visitors along a marked path to areas labeled alphabetically; each area is named for its major artist. Works by more than 154 artists, several of whom are represented by more than one sculpture, are clustered in several different landscape areas. The art park (open annually between April 1 and November 15) has an annual operating budget of $3 million. Director and curator David R. Collens heads its small staff.

Storm King is a living sculpture. In an eastern field, across from di Suvero's giant steel creations, a farmer mows circular rows of alfalfa and begins baling it into big rolls. On the same field, David von Schlegell's three square aluminum frames on raised

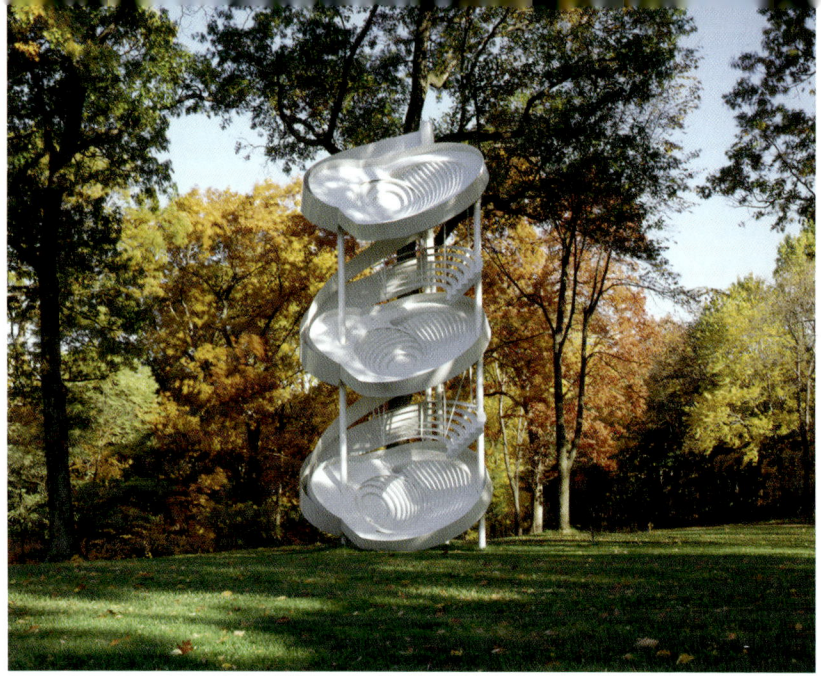

Alice Aycock, *Three-Fold Manifestation II*, 1987/2006. Aluminum and painted stainless steel, 351 x 168 x 144 in.

steel legs cast perfect square shadows that follow the sun. At the south end, Robert Grosvenor's low, black Cor-ten steel form hovers like a giant flattened top hat. Close to the entrance, a couple sensuously circles *Arch* (1975), one of Calder's last stabiles.

The south end of the grounds features works by Richard Serra and Andy Goldsworthy, which are reached by walking down a grand maple-lined avenue planted in the 1960s. Goldsworthy's *Storm King Wall*, built from freestanding local stones by the artist and his Scottish wallers, stretches for 2,278 feet. The wall curves around trees as it meanders toward a pond, then continues on the other side. Creating a dialogue with the hilly landscape and stolid trees, it invites comparison with the straight stone walls visible further up the hill, which were built by the earliest settlers in the region. The wall also symbolizes the entire Storm King enterprise of intertwining art and nature.

Richard Serra's *Schunnemunk Fork* also brings out the elements of its 10-acre site. Four weathering steel plates, each 2.5 inches thick, eight feet high, and 34 to 54 feet long, are half-submerged to form triangles in the earth that mark eight-foot declines in the elevation in the field. The steel plates mark their relations to each other, to their site, and to the facing Schunnemunk and Storm King mountains. As they contrast with the pale butterflies and dragonflies hovering around the surrounding Queen Anne's lace, the sun casts dramatic shadows, doubling the images of the plates in the high grass.

The sculptures in Storm King's collection are carefully sited. Kenneth Snelson's *Free Ride Home* seems to free-float above a central hillside, while Grace Knowlton's large concrete *Spheres* nest against the clefts and curves of the same slope. In the Normandy-style indoor exhibition space, Louise Bourgeois's *Number Seventy-two* forms a mysterious and intimate grouping of marble cylinders notable for its delicate hues and veins. The nearby hilltop features a cluster of David Smith's sculptures (his work was the subject of a three-year, three-part exhibition "The Fields of David Smith"). The humanism, humor, and human scale of these welded metal constructions provide physical contrasts with Ursula von Rydingsvard's giant-sized, rough-cut wooden vessel *For Paul*, which stands at the steep south side of the hill, and with di Suvero's seven steel constructions, many brightly painted and with moving parts, in a field below. On a hillock to the north, Noguchi's stone *Momo Taro* beckons with the presence and majesty of rounded stones made for sitting, climbing, and contemplation. Siah Armajani's *Gazebo for Two Anarchists* and Alice Aycock's *Three-Fold Manifestation II* are both architectural constructions that draw visitors to their sites.

Storm King's ambitious program of integrating nature and art includes long-range plans for re-structuring selected sites; one program in conjunction with the Lady Bird Johnson Wildflower Center based in Austin, Texas, called for replanting 80 acres with grasslands and wildflowers. "In addition to being a sculpture park, we are a nature conservancy," Stern says. "Star Expansion Company, owned by Ted Ogden and myself, acquired and donated over 2,300 acres of Schunnemunk Mountain."

"We've had every advantage here," Stern observes. "We began with no preconceived plans, and we have been listening to inner voices to discover what will work. Akin to marriage, there has been pleasure and suffering along the way." The rural location, 55 miles north of Manhattan near the U.S. Military Academy at West Point and the city of Newburgh, contributes to Storm King's legend and legacy. As Peter A. Bienstock describes it in *Earth, Sky and Sculpture: Storm King Art Center*, the park "presents two kinds of experience, one intellectual and spiritual and the other primitive and natural. Its carefully shaped landscape and superbly…sited art are in the great tradition of the sculpture garden: its margins, blending into the wild and finally merging into it, suggest the elements of nature that have captivated humans but that have also challenged them, and which they have for thousands of years sought to bring under their control and into their service. Few sculpture gardens in the world so dramatically unite these elements." For those who come to see and experience this cultivated wilderness, Storm King challenges and delights the eyes, the body, and the mind.

<www.stormking.org>

Middelheim Open Air Museum of Sculpture: A Conversation with Menno Meewis

by Robert Preece

Located on a lovely 62.5-acre site on the edge of Antwerp, the Middelheim Open Air Museum of Sculpture features some of the most important sculpture exhibitions in Belgium. It also acts as a reference collection for modern sculpture from Rodin to the present. Middelheim features a 240-square-meter pavilion for exhibitions and over 250 permanent outdoor sculptures. For temporary exhibitions, artworks are shown inside the pavilion and outdoors, with a fluid connection between the two sites, and permanent works are often purchased from these shows.

Middelheim's beginnings date back to a large international exhibition organized in 1950 by a committee representing the City of Antwerp. This show consisted of 167 sculptures by 104 sculptors, including Rodin, Ossip Zadkine, Jean Arp, and Henry Moore. The sculpture biennials continued until 1989, with up to roughly 60 artists participating in each show. The collection now offers a selective overview of modern sculpture, including works by Arp, Calder, Pablo Gargallo, Barbara Hepworth, Floris and Oscar Jespers, Giacomo Manzù, Moore, Louise Nevelson, and Zadkine.

While Middelheim's early emphasis was on filling historical gaps in its collection, since 1993 its mission has shifted to a focus on contemporary art, "with the condition that it's possible to show it in the open air." The contemporary collection includes works by Guillaume Bijl, Tony Cragg, Luciano Fabro, Per Kirkeby, Panamarenko, Franz West, Jessica Stockholder, Carl Andre, and Timm Ulrichs. Recent purchases have added pieces by Joep van Lieshout, Ann Veronica Janssens, Luc Delue, Pedro Cabrita Reis, and Dan Graham. In 2005, Middelheim presented "Idyll—as to answer that picture," its first group exhibition since the biennials ended. The show, which included sculptures by Miroslaw Balka, Lee Bul, Boy and Erik Stappaerts, Yukata Sone, and Corey McCorkle, focused on idyllic visions and the temporary adjournment of reality—a perfect theme in the idealized landscape of the sculpture park. Paul McCarthy's monumental inflatable sculptures, including five specially created works, added an element of edginess in the summer and fall of 2007. Menno Meewis has been the director of the museum since 1992.

Robert Preece: What are the main challenges in running the Middelheim Open Air Museum of Sculpture?
Menno Meewis: It's a combination of different things. It's very important to have an exhibition program, and we also have a museum for contemporary art. This means that we have to purchase contemporary work. What's very interesting for the museum is

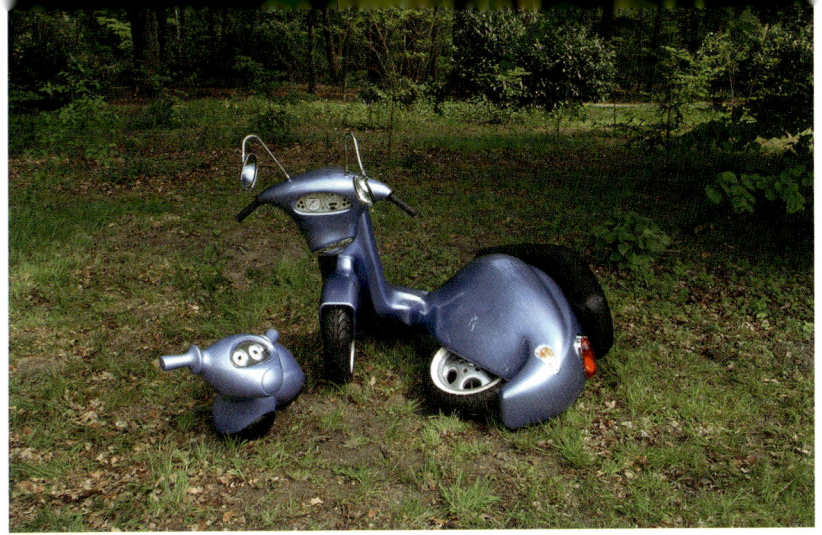

Patricia Piccinini, *Nest*, 2006. Fiberglass, vinyl, acrylic, and scooter parts, 87 x 146 x 127 cm.

that we collect both modern and contemporary art. Most contemporary art museums start with art after World War II. We have more than 100 years of sculpture. A second important thing is to have more space. That's what we did two years ago. But we don't have enough money to acquire more property, so we're working in different phases. Next year, we'll make a new entrance and add new roads.

RP: Are there particularly unique challenges in running a sculpture park in Belgium, or specifically in Antwerp?

MM: I think it is the same as anywhere else in Belgium. Museums here are not very rich. We don't have a lot of facilities — or possibilities.

RP: Why not? Belgians pay enough taxes.

MM: Yes, that's so. But for contemporary art, it's sometimes very difficult. Even in Brussels.

RP: What is Middelheim's procedure for selecting artists?

MM: We have a committee of advisors — with people from other museums, from universities, art critics — and we meet twice a year.

RP: Is there a general vision for the contemporary programming?

MM: It's always a choice. Because our exhibitions are mostly connected with a purchase, we're starting from our collection — what we'd like to purchase, what story we'd like to tell. That's why we bought a Lawrence Weiner — we didn't have a conceptual work in the collection. We didn't have Minimalist art, so we bought a Carl Andre.

RP: So when you select an exhibition, one of the criteria is how well the work will fit into a 100-year history?

MM: If it's an exhibition with an acquisition, yes. We buy carefully, because we always buy large work — and this has an immediate influence on the whole museum. It's not

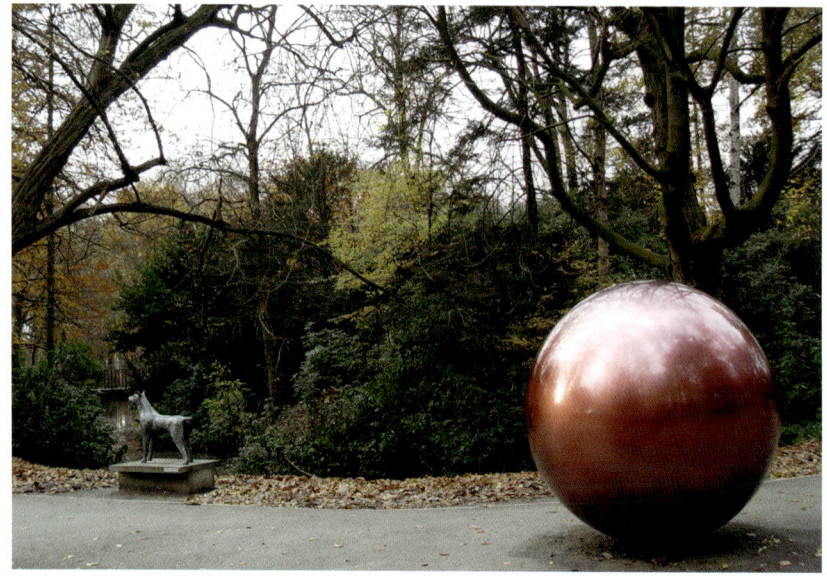

Corey McCorkle, *Yayoi*, 2005. Fiberglass and car paint, 200 cm. diameter.

so easy to take it away and put it in storage.

RP: Are there particular issues involved in designing, producing, and installing a public artwork at Middelheim?

MM: It's completely different working with open air. For instance, it's very difficult to work with other open-air museums to have traveling exhibitions. Other museums have white rooms, but for open air, the setting is always completely different — the landscape, the scale. We are in a very old park that dates back to the 14th century. It's very difficult for us to bring in Land Art, for example.

RP: What kinds of restoration issues do you face?

MM: We have a lot of bronze works that need maintenance and restoration. The stone sculptures are not always very easy to work with. It's a problem. When we purchased works from the biennials, some were meant to stay only two or three months. Now they've been in the collection for 20 or 30 years.

RP: What are your future plans for the museum?

MM: We didn't organize any exhibitions in 2004, because we wanted to invest in the infrastructure of a new outdoor exhibition space. We are also creating a new entrance with a small building, installing new roads, and siting three or four monumental works. The roads and entrance will be designed by artists.

<www.middelheimmuseum.be>

Hakone Open-Air Museum: Sculpture in the Mountains of Japan

by Ken Scarlett

Hakone Open-Air Museum, established in 1969, was the first sculpture park in Japan and the third outdoor collection of modern sculpture in the world (following Middelheim and Storm King). Diverse and eclectic, Hakone offers a wide range of major works by prominent Western and Japanese artists of the 20th century. The collection features well-known and expected sculptures such as Rodin's *Balzac* (1891–98), the surprising such as Manzù's somber *The Door of Death* (1962–64), and a separate gallery with 300 works by Picasso.

From the moment one arrives, there is an element of the unexpected. Beyond the foyer, the entrance route progresses rapidly downhill by way of a long escalator set between concrete walls. After a somewhat claustrophobic tunnel, visitors emerge into a vast and welcoming open space (probably unaware that they have passed beneath the railway line) to find sculpture dramatically placed against a mountain range and under a vast open sky. It is a well-staged, theatrical introduction to the museum.

Directly ahead, on top of a towering white pillar of concrete, the silhouette of Carl Miles's *Man and Pegasus* (1949) commands attention; the style may be out of fashion, but the work remains impressive. The winged horse is seen from beneath, while the male figure appears to fly effortlessly through the air. From this point on, the collection appears to proceed chronologically, from Rodin's *Balzac* to Maillol's *Action Unchained* (1906), to four symbolic female figures, *Strength, Victory, Liberty,* and *Eloquence* (1918–22) by Bourdelle, displayed against the sky in a nearby open courtyard. Originally planned as supporting figures around the base of a colossal monument to the Argentinean general Alvear, they have the strength and dignity to survive independently.

The installation abandons its just-begun historical introduction as a massive bronze, *Reclining Figure: Arch Leg* (1969–70) by Henry Moore, comes into view. For a number of reasons, this is a very significant work in the Hakone collection. Nobutaka Shikanai, former president of the Fujisanki Group, Japan's largest communications conglomerate, once visited Moore at his home at Much Hadham. Deeply impressed by the artist's display of outdoor sculpture, Shikanai determined to establish a sculpture park in Japan and commissioned a work, which became *Reclining Figure: Arch Leg,* thus beginning the collection.

As a young man in his 30s, Shikanai "conceived a passion for modern sculpture and sold off a family collection of traditional Japanese art to buy works by Giacomo Manzù and Emilio Greco."[1] His interest in Western sculpture was at odds with the traditional attitude of some Japanese, who saw the influx of Western art as a threat "to the Japanese spirit" and an attack on the "national identity."[2] Not only did Shikanai believe that sculpture was the most exciting development within 20th-century visual art, he was also convinced that it could attract a mass audience. He set out to create a sculpture park that would draw as large an attendance as possible.

He chose Hakone—two hours south of Tokyo and already a much-visited tourist resort on the edge of a national park with mountains, forests, and lakes—as the site for this imaginative venture. He engaged Bukichi Inoue, a Japanese sculptor and architect, to design the buildings, as well as the winding paths that link, or separate, the various groupings of sculpture. As executed, the plan skillfully accommodates the rapidly sloping land, deliberately using the proximity of the mountains while also incorporating views of the distant horizon. The park was not intended as a formal Japanese garden; instead, it was to serve as a relaxed place of enjoyment, with contemporary sculpture as the main attraction. Today, the grounds include various eateries, shops, play spaces for children, and a hot spring where tired tourists can sit and bathe their feet.

Certainly the influx of visitors during my visit was impressive. Shouts and delighted screams emanated from the area specifically set aside for young people. More than a place for leaving children while their parents view the sculpture, this children's park includes a variety of specially designed spatial experiences. In Bukichi Inoue's *My Sky Hole*, one person at a time enters a small door in a black acrylic cube to find a spiral staircase winding underground to a dim narrow space covered in soft gray fabric. Here, one can sit and contemplate a circle of sky before following another set of spiral steps up and out through a transparent cube of clear plastic. Shigeo Matsubara's *Cosmical Color Space* (1968), on the other hand, is meant to be experienced by a great number of children at once. Twelve large, hollow, steel squares, painted in brilliant colors, each balance on a corner so that small people can walk through them, physically experiencing the space and the changing visual combinations of color and form. Nearby, children may climb in and out of Isamu Noguchi's radiant red *Octetra* (1973), and further downhill, they can scramble inside a vast expanse of rope netting hanging from a very high ceiling in a large hall. Together, these works offer a series of imaginative three-dimensional experiences.

Hakone deliberately sets out to please a wide range of spectators, including children, interested members of the general public, and informed 20th-century sculpture enthusiasts. Just beyond Moore's *Reclining Figure: Arch Leg*, one finds Calder's huge *Les Arêtes de Poisson* (1966), followed by Jean Dubuffet's *Aborescence* (1971–80). A view across an expanse of lawn reveals Ossip Zadkine's *The Dwelling* (1960), Naum Gabo's *Spheric Theme* (1976), the golden bronze of Arnaldo Pomodoro's *Sphere Within Sphere* (1978–80), and a range of contemporary Japanese works. *Never Ending*

Dialogue (1978), by Susumu Shingu, intrigues many people, as the sail-like forms atop its bright orange steel structure gently undulate and rotate in the breeze. Another kinetic work, *Sixteen Turning Sticks* (1969), by Takamichi Ito, consists of 16 rods in highly polished stainless steel that soundlessly rotate while forming endlessly complicated and intriguing patterns. Elsewhere in the park, George Rickey's *Two Lines Vertical, Hakone* (1965–76) silently and elegantly moves through the sky.

If the juxtaposition of works is sometimes a little confusing—Emilio Greco, Jean Arp, and Jean Dubuffet all in close proximity, for instance—the collection of large-scale bronzes by Henry Moore is undoubtedly displayed with skill and sensitivity. Shikanai had a great admiration for Moore's work and wanted his bronzes to be the centerpiece of the Hakone Open-Air Museum. In 1986, he acquired 16 works from George and Virginia Ablah of Wichita, Kansas, and with subsequent purchases, Hakone's Moore collection has now risen to an impressive 26 sculptures.

These works span four decades, from 1948 through 1985, giving a unique opportunity to compare similar themes such as family groups, reclining figures, and mother-and-child pairings. The earliest, *Family Group* (1948–49), displays a unified degree of simplification and abstraction and is justifiably one of Moore's best known and most loved. *Two-Piece Reclining Figure 1* (1959) reads as two weathered rocks, barely recognizable as human form, whereas two later bronzes skillfully combine imaginative abstraction with the basic structure of the human body. The only non-figurative work by Moore on display is *Atom Piece (Working Model for Nuclear Energy)* (1964–65), which lacks the impact of the nearby *Atmos* (1991) by Tony Cragg.

A collection of 300 works by Picasso gives Hakone yet another claim to fame. Housed in a separate building, the group consists of prints, paintings, sculpture, ceramics, tapestries, silverware, and objects in gold and glass. Hakone also features a highly imaginative reconstruction of Picasso's Cannes studio, La Californie, based on photographs taken by David Douglas Duncan over a 17-year period, from 1956 until Picasso's death. Unlike the reconstruction of Brancusi's studio adjoining the Pompidou in Paris, where everything is

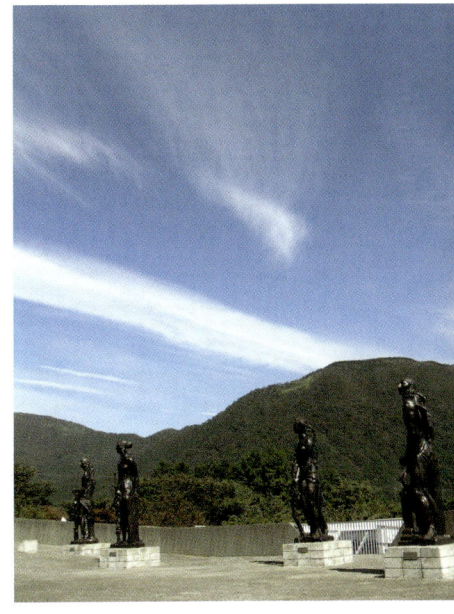

Emile-Antoine Bourdelle, *Grande Statue de la Force, Victoire, Liberté, l'Eloquence*, 1918–22. Bronze, view of work installed at Hakone.

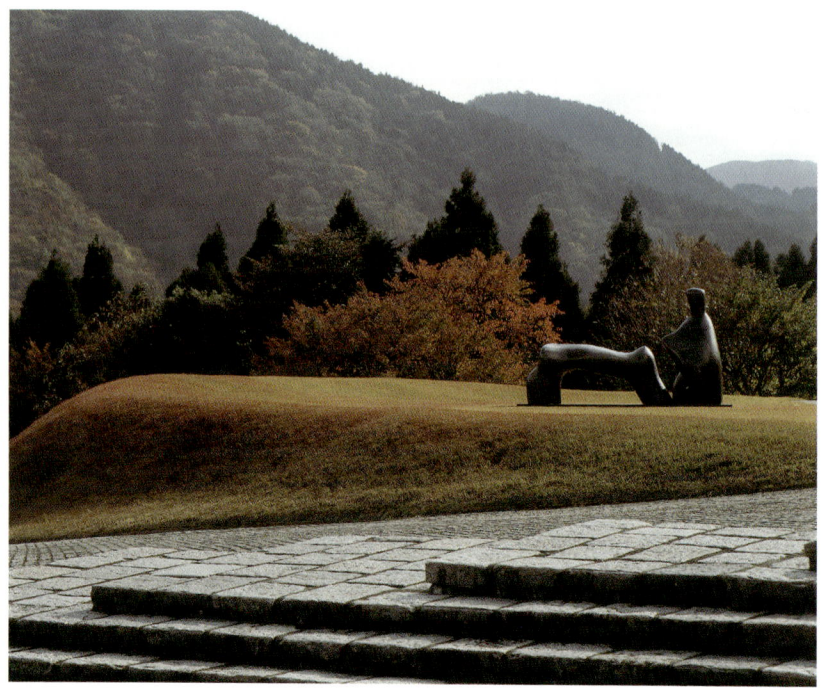

Henry Moore, *Reclining Figure: Arch Leg*, 1969–70. Bronze, 259 x 296 cm.

meticulously and immaculately in its place, the Picasso studio functions like an utterly convincing stage set. Easel, work-bench, chairs, and tables have been accurately remade, but painted matte white to make clear their status as reproductions.

One could continue to enumerate the surprises and delights of Hakone — Marta Pan's *Floating Sculpture 3*, painted the same golden orange-red as the carp swimming lazily in the still water, Joan Miró's irreverent *Personage* (1972), Niki de Saint Phalle's outrageous *Miss Black Power* (1968), and Magdalena Abakanowicz's stark and lonely *One of a Crowd* (1992). This eclectic collection of work by some of the major sculptors of the 20th century, with its wonderful high points (and occasional lapses), grew from "The First International Exhibition of Modern Sculpture," held at Hakone in 1969. A number of works were purchased from the show, including sculptures by Hepworth, Noguchi, Adam, Bill, Pan, Penalba, as well as by a range of Japanese artists, such as Imoto, Mizui, Matsubara, and Takamichi Ito. The collection begun by Nobutaka Shikanai developed so rapidly that by 1981 — 12 years after the park's inception — a branch was opened in Nagano prefecture, a mountainous area above the tree-line, 2,000 meters above sea level. In contrast to the lush lawns and deciduous trees of Hakone, this sparse landscape, which is frequently shrouded in mist or covered with snow, offers dramatic views of the Japanese Alps. With sensitive planning at both sculpture parks, "a symbiotic relationship between the works of art in [the] collection and the beautiful natural environment" has been achieved.[3] Amazingly, neither nature nor art has been overwhelmed or spoilt by the high attendance. Shikanai, who died in 1990, not only led the way in the establishment of public sculpture parks and corporate support for the arts, he indirectly influenced the development of contemporary Japanese sculpture and has given great pleasure to a vast number of Japanese and overseas visitors. The tangible results of the Open-Air Museum undoubtedly surpass his original vision.

Notes

1   Sam Hunter, *In the Mountains of Japan* (New York: Abbeville Press, 1988), p. 25.
2   Ibid., p. 20.
3   Takatoshi Suzuki, *The Hakone Open-Air Museum. The Utsukushi-Ga-Hara Open-Air Museum, 1969–1999*. Introduction.

<www.hakone-oam.or.jp>

Yorkshire Sculpture Park at 30

by Oliver Lowenstein

In 2007, Yorkshire Sculpture Park marked its 30th birthday. As a central part of its celebrations, the park hosted the largest Andy Goldsworthy exhibition to date in Britain. The artist's previous YSP exhibition and residency, "Parkland," occurred 20 years before, in 1987, and his first show there was in 1983, only six years after the park's inception. Goldsworthy's return brought this history full circle, underlining how his path and YSP's, to a considerable extent, have mirrored each other.

Less remarked, but a significant part of these parallel paths, is that both man and organization are part of the fabric of Northern England's cultural life. Each has maintained a degree of geographical separation from London, the center of Britain's art establishment. Goldsworthy is well known for having made his way outside of and despite the conventions of the metropolitan art world. Originally born in Lancashire, he passed much of his childhood in Alwoodney, a town a few miles from Leeds, the nearest city to YSP. In early adulthood, Goldsworthy began to experiment with ephemeral time-based and nature-derived pieces in Northern places: Morecombe Bay's Lancashire coastline; the riverbeds of its tributary, the Lune estuary; and England's highest mountain peak, Scafell Pike, and other mountains of the nearby Cumbrian Lake District. This would have been only months before YSP first opened its gates, and recalling that time in recent British social history suggests a further layer of entwinement between Goldsworthy and YSP.

The late '70s in Britain was a time of social division and polarization, and what continues to be called the North/South divide was only too apparent during the Thatcher years. Through Goldsworthy's early career and his gradual recognition through the '80s, the split between North and South was teetering on rupture. While significant parts of the South saw economic boom, later followed by bust and recession, much of the North—the heartland of the Industrial Revolution—was hit hard by the consequences of recession. It was only when Tony Blair swept to power in 1997, at the helm of New Labour, that serious work began to bring these cities back to something of their former glory.

Recognizing that cultural industries could play a central role in supporting regeneration, New Labour brought an updated, strategic approach to the arts and arts funding, with artists as key workers. Although the primary focus was the "Urban Renaissance" of the big Northern cities, rural organizations attractive to urban audiences also played a significant role. Artists with name recognition among non-traditional audiences were courted and used to build the market in cultural tourism. YSP benefited from this strategy and has undergone significant development since 1999.

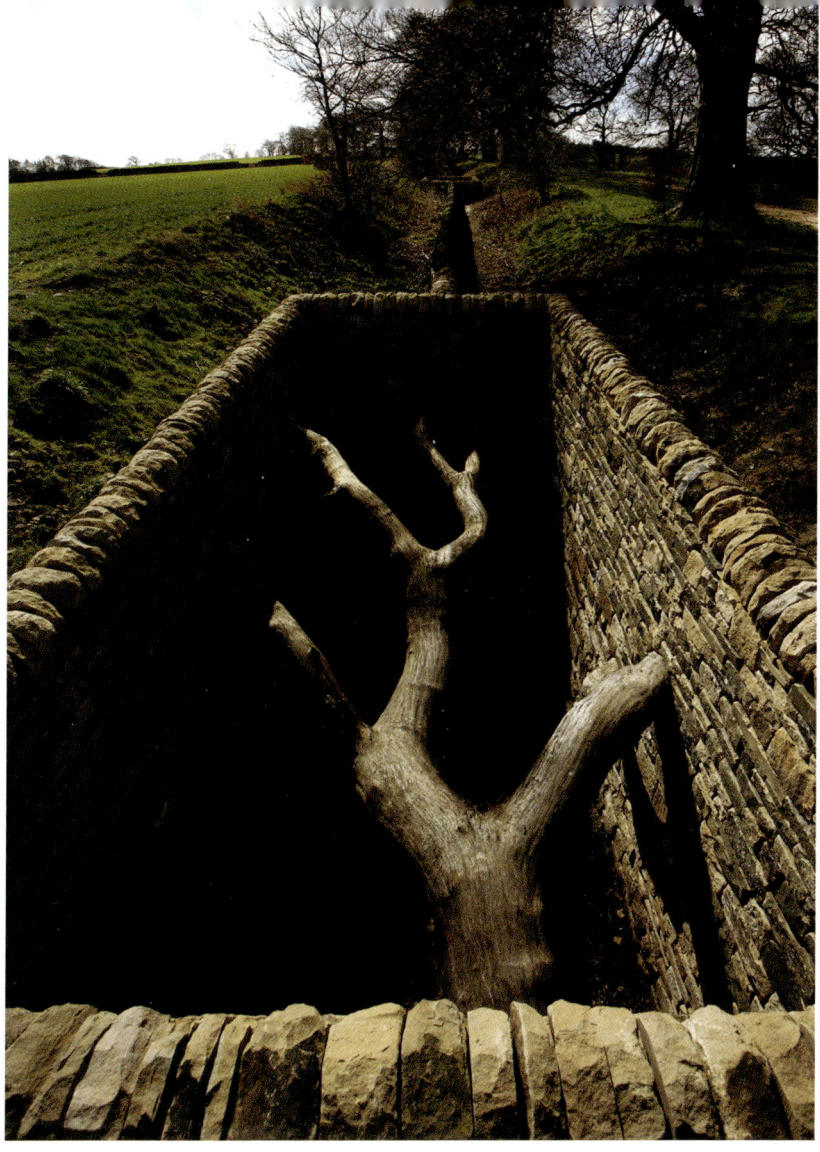

Andy Goldsworthy, *Hanging Trees. Oxley Bank. Yorkshire Sculpture Park*, 2006.

Yet it remains primarily rural, and agricultural. It is not surprising that YSP's influence continues to loom large in current regional regeneration planning, what is boldly called the Yorkshire Forward Renaissance Towns Initiative. This regional regeneration body recently announced that in Wakefield, the town nearest to YSP, a "historic conservation area…will be transformed" to include a new "landmark building of architectural quality (which) will house work by two of the 20th-century giants of British modern art, Henry Moore and Barbara Hepworth."

This future project builds on YSP's step-by-step development since 1999. That year, supported by Lottery and EU regional development funding, YSP bought an additional 237 acres of arable land on its southern boundary and took over the 100-acre Bretton Country Park, integrating the expanded estate under a single landscape management plan. YSP then initiated a master plan, involving a marked re-appraisal of direction. Central to the re-think was the park's relationship to the land and working on the land. A major capital development program of £13 million, between 2002 and 2005, funded the building of a new visitor center and, more recently, an underground gallery. Recognizing the strength of the expanded grounds, YSP noted that the diversity of its landscape offered an advantage in a climate of increasing interest in land-based sculpture and art centers.

YSP has developed a visual identity around a rural, or pastorally inclined, environmental pathway. Arriving at the entrance, the eye is first drawn to the closest of the 10 Henry Moore pieces in the immediate foreground of the rolling valley in which YSP is nested. The valley continues to be farmed, and YSP's expressed desire for its work to be not only on the land, but also in the landscape, is understandable. Many visitors are soon inside one of YSP's recent additions, the visitor center. Opened in 2002, the center was designed by Feilden Clegg Bradley, one of Britain's first sustainable architectural practices. Featuring a central walk-through corridor, the center is finished in a regional sandstone and carefully sited on the sloping hillside. Two years ago, FCB

James Turrell, *Deer Shelter*, 2006.

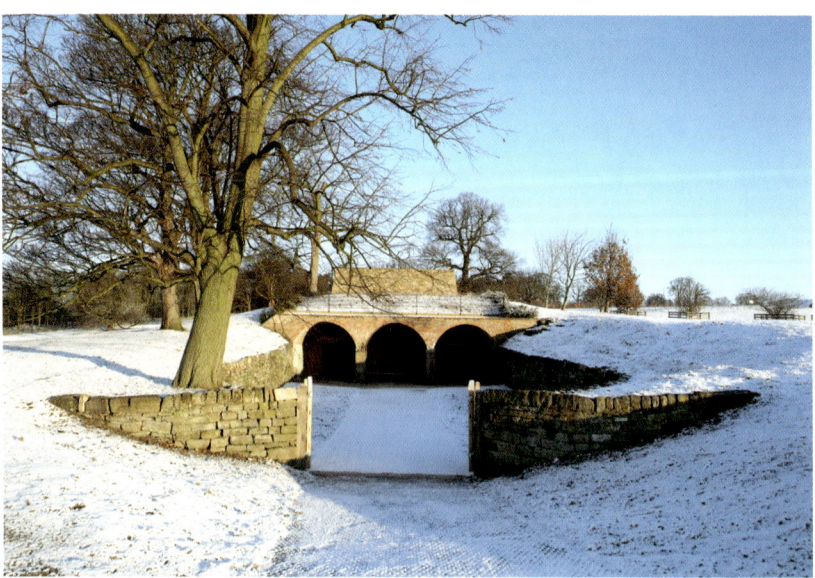

completed a second building, the underground gallery, located a stone's throw from the park side of the visitor center. This is an even more unambiguously environmental statement, a grass-topped earth building dug into the side of an embankment. From above, the grass-covered roof disappears into the hillside, affording uninterrupted views across the valley. Inside, the curatorial team installed what they call "Goldsworthy's greatest hits." For the identically dimensioned white cubes of the underground gallery, he prepared pieces immediately and iconically identifiable as his—a tangle of logs and branches cut from felling on the YSP Estate; 11 circular sandstone mounds, their individual stones stacked in order of decreasing size; a nest-hearth that recalls and aestheticizes tribal and pre-modern dwellings; and vertical expanses of cracked mud flats mixed with horse hair applied to all four walls of one room. Three arched brick vaults, another recurring form, stand outside.

Since the opening of the underground gallery, YSP's other major project has been a James Turrell sky chamber. Here, once again, the emphasis is on a connection to the elemental. Supported by the new Art Fund, Turrell appropriated an existing deer shelter and created within it one of his singular meditative spaces linking earth and sky. YSP's collection also includes major works by Barbara Hepworth, Anthony Caro, Lynn Chadwick, David Nash, Peter Randall-Page, Sol LeWitt, Jonathan Borofsky, Magdalena Abakanowicz, and Elisabeth Frink. A new generation of artists, many associated with post-performance and installation, is becoming increasingly relevant to YSP. Indeed, its strategy of matching a residency with a major summer show has nurtured many emerging artists who have been working outside the mainstream. Simon Whitehead, who was the 2005–06 artist-in-residence, states that YSP has been actively looking for new avenues, with different ways and different forms of presenting art practice. Whitehead's work originates in dance and movement, and he has developed a practice around the act of walking. At YSP, he spent over two years on his work, supported by YSP staffers. The result, *Walks to Illuminate*, was a series of night walks, with participants wearing lighted shoe-sculptures to show the way. The walks began in autumn 2005 and continued over the next year. YSP staff wore solar hats during the day to build up energy, and at night this stored energy powered the illuminated shoes. Night walkers, after a ritualized donning of shoes, became, in effect, the animators of the performance.

Commissioned by Arts Council England, Yorkshire, and curated by YSP, Wolfgang Winter and Berthold Hörbelt's *Cratehouse for Castleford* almost extends into community outreach. Castleford, a neighboring mid-size town still recovering from the disappearance of coal mining, offered just the kind of site preferred by the German artists, who use recycled everyday objects to reclaim lost public spaces and increase awareness of art's contribution to the quality of life. Their Castleford work consists of two metal shipping containers combined with bottle crates to create a semi-public space for local use. The bright orange crates are a variation on nearly 25 earlier structures completed around the world, in places as far afield as New York, Stockholm, Hanoi, and Obihiro, Japan. Recycling artifacts for "superuse" seems to be a growing trend. Even if Winter and Hörbelt's constructions don't quite scale the heights of Shigeru Ban's ongoing Nomadic Museum project, their work here contributes to the goal of regeneration.

It is perhaps inevitable that contemporary artistic practice be subsumed by regional regeneration efforts, yoked to the pressing needs of areas with continuing unemployment, poverty, and their consequences. Art today is also a part of the world tourism trail, and YSP, like other art establishments, plays to this as best it can. The fact that YSP is so caught up in land management and therefore promotes artists concerned with living and working on the land is a commendable strength. YSP has to push its rural, agricultural credentials, just as an urban venue has to put the best gloss on an urban agenda. Goldsworthy may aestheticize agricultural work and life into art, a consequence, perhaps, of a culture removed from the land. But it will be up to the likes of YSP to build—or grow—a 21st-century art culture truly responsive to our times and to connect the ecological needs of the land with urban audiences.

<www.ysp.co.uk>

The Kröller-Müller Sculpture Park

by Ken Scarlett

Both the Storm King Art Center, close to New York, and the Kröller-Müller Sculpture Park, near Amsterdam, were established around 1960, which places them among the earliest of the major sculpture parks. But whereas Storm King was conceived solely for the display of sculpture, the Kröller-Müller grew out of the personal collection of paintings (with some prints, drawings, and sculpture) assembled by Helene Kröller-Müller over a 30-year period. The gallery, which began as a temporary building housing the collection, has expanded, grown, and changed direction. As early as 1955, plans were drawn up for the display of outdoor sculpture, so it is accurate to state, as the museum's literature does, that "it was the first permanent sculpture garden designed especially for a museum's collection." Over the years, the outdoor sculpture collection has continued to grow, and now the Kröller-Müller is synonymous with the sculpture park.

Kröller-Müller had always assumed that her collection would be opened to the public and made several attempts to build a gallery. (On two occasions, full-scale models of proposed galleries were built in the countryside — one was on rails so that it could be moved to different locations, which gives some idea of the family's wealth.)

Marta Pan, *Floating Sculpture, Otterlo*, 1960–61. Fiberglass-reinforced polyester resin and pond, 216 x 226 x 185 cm.

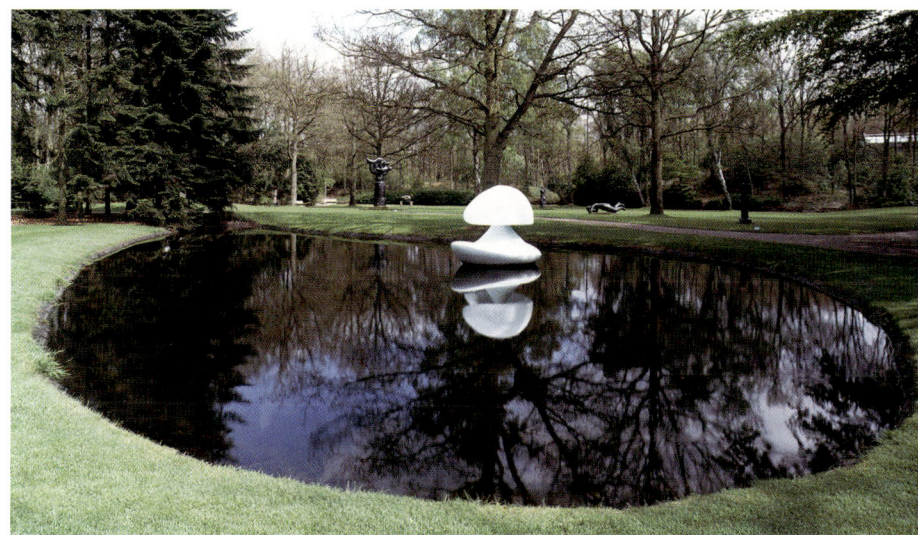

In 1935, she decided to transfer ownership of the collection to the Netherlands, and, in 1938, the Statemuseum Kröller-Müller opened in Otterlo, in what is now the National Park of Hoge Veluw. Free bicycles enable visitors to cycle through the undulating hills and leafy forests.

Helene Kröller-Müller made it clear that she wanted her collection to be kept together, which posed a problem for the institution's directors. The impasse was solved by taking a new direction—by establishing a sculpture collection in the parkland adjoining the gallery. In 1960, French sculptor Marta Pan was commissioned to design a floating sculpture and artificial pond. In the 1970s, and again in 2002, the outdoor area for sculpture was greatly enlarged. It now covers 25 hectares, but Pan's white abstract form, gently floating on the pond, is still the first work one sees on stepping out of the gallery. A highly reflective, golden-yellow bronze by Arp also attracts attention at the far side of the small lake.

The areas of immaculate lawn nearest the gallery are surrounded by high trees that create discrete viewing spaces. Within each exhibition area, compatible works are sensitively displayed so that, for instance, sculptures by Rodin, Bourdelle, and Maillol are all in close proximity. Figurative sculptures are grouped near the gallery, as if to lull conservative visitors into a sense of security—but the farther they walk, the more radical the works become. Sculptures have been skillfully placed to entice viewers, luring them from one area of display to the next.

Catching a glimpse of a work by Barbara Hepworth, one steps into a large space only to realize that it contains a number of her bronzes, as well as Henry Moore's superb bronze *Two-Piece Reclining Figure*. It seems that Hepworth and Moore, who were closely connected with the innovative open-air sculpture exhibitions in Battersea and Holland Parks in London in the early 1950s, influenced the early development of the Kröller-Müller Sculpture Park.

The Kröller-Müller doesn't pander to visitors: it assumes a certain perceptive intelligence and an ability to locate works within the extensive parkland. Richard Serra's huge installation *Spin Out*, which consists of three monumental sheets of steel, is set within a secluded area encircled by wooded hills and entered by a narrow earth track. But what a revelation when one steps into that vortex, where the steel sheets appear to rotate around the central space. Likewise, Ian Hamilton Finlay's *Five Columns for the Kröller-Müller* is secreted behind high hedges of rhododendrons. Entering by a narrow pathway, one comes into a private, tantalizing world of ambiguous meaning. Five classical pedestals carved in Portland stone, each one different in design and height, surround the straight tree trunks, which appear to become five columns. As befits classical pedestals, Finlay's works are inscribed on the bases— "Rousseau," for instance. Do these columns serve as a memorial to a grand tradition or are they ruins?

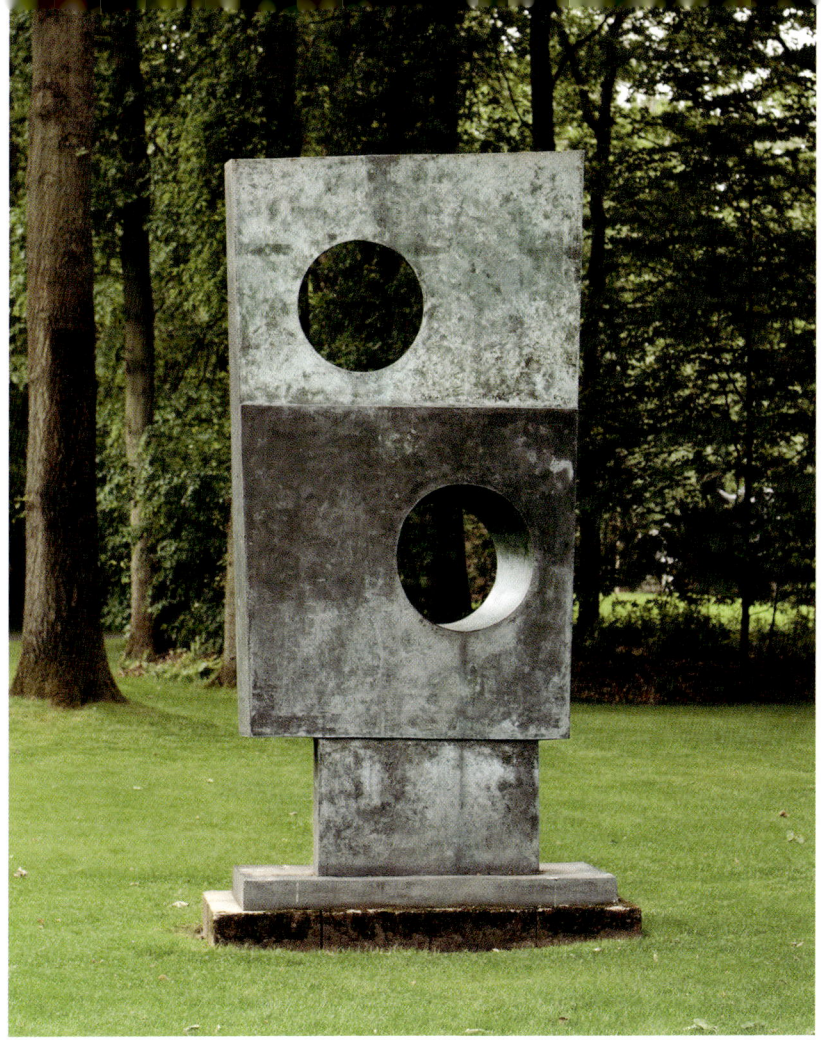

Barbara Hepworth, *Squares with Two Circles*, 1963–64. Bronze, 17 x 157 x 76 cm.

After such intellectual gymnastics, Jean Dubuffet's *Jardin d'Email* engenders spontaneous physical enjoyment. Built well above the ground, this huge work can be seen and heard from a distance, for it is often filled with adventurous adults and excited children. Entering through a small side doorway, which leads to a somewhat dark and narrow staircase, one steps out onto an undulating concrete landscape painted a brilliant white, with the edges of the contours picked out in black.

Kenneth Snelson's *Needle Tower* always attracts visitors, who crane their necks upward at this extraordinarily elegant structure. Constructed of steel and aluminum tubes held in tension by stainless steel wires, it is a miraculous balancing act that seemingly defies conventional engineering. Movement always attracts, and inevitably there are also groups of people watching George Rickey's kinetic work, *Two vertical, three horizontal lines*. The slightest breeze sets the steel blades effortlessly and silently shifting through space. One watches, fascinated, mentally trying to calculate the movement, which never appears to repeat.

To visit the Kröller-Müller is to be surrounded by sculpture placed in a supremely beautiful setting. When one departs, heading for the bicycle rack or the car park, yet more sculpture awaits. On either side of the broad path, which is the exit/entrance to the museum, there are a number of commanding works, including Mark di Suvero's *K-Piece*. Constructed of massive steel girders and painted a brilliant orange-red, this extroverted sculpture emphatically announces its presence. And just when one thinks that the exhilarating display is over, Claes Oldenburg's gigantic garden *Trowel* marks an intersection. Light-hearted, amusing, even ludicrous, it must bring smiles to many faces — a nice memory of the wonderful diversity of sculpture at the Kröller-Müller.

<www.kmm.nl>

Laumeier Sculpture Park

by Jan Garden Castro

Since its founding in 1975, Laumeier Sculpture Park has expanded into a 105-acre facility with meadow, forest, marsh, and formal garden settings. Its original 72 acres of rolling woodland and meadows, located across the street from suburban mall sprawl and 20 minutes from downtown St. Louis, were bequeathed in 1968 to the St. Louis County Department of Parks by Mrs. Henry H. Laumeier in memory of her husband. Several years later, parks department director Wayne C. Kennedy and banker Adam Aronson initiated the idea of a sculpture park when Aronson introduced Kennedy to artist Ernest Trova, who later donated 40 works to the park. Today, growing numbers of visitors, ranging from joggers, dog walkers, and bikers to distinguished members of the art world, come to Laumeier for the landscape, concerts, and annual Art Fair, as well as for the collection of permanent, site-specific, and temporary sculpture. Much of Laumeier's growth can be credited to its former director, Beej Nierengarten-Smith, who had an ambitious agenda for the park, including contemporary site programs with an emphasis on "new and innovative ideas using non-traditional sculptural materials."

In addition to Trova's famous *Falling Man*, there are many figural works in the collection. Manuel Neri's *Aurelia Roma* (1994) is a faceless form that self-consciously displays variegated pearly hues and both rough-hewn and highly polished surfaces. Judith Shea's *Public Goddess* (1992), a gold, headless torso imprisoned in a spear-tipped gate, is surrounded by a heart-shaped garden.

The park's first signature piece was *The Way* (1972–80) by Alexander Liberman. Weighing in at 55 tons, 60 feet tall and 100 feet long, *The Way* is constructed from 18 salvaged steel oil tanks and welded into a "configuration of post-and-lintel elements." For its 15th birthday, *The Way* was sandblasted and repainted Chinese red. Perched on a high meadow, it attracts visitors, wedding parties, and curious children. Other early acquisitions and loans by international artists include a playful Jerald Jacquard; a steel Anthony Caro resembling an easel and canvas; an embedded circular Richard Serra; Mark di Suvero's monumental steel *XV* (1971), a literal construction of the Roman numeral XV, and other works by the artist; and George Rickey's *Peristyle II* (1966), whose steel spikes deflect wind and light.

Starting in the 1980s, site and ecology became paramount concerns at Laumeier. Meg Webster's *Pass* (1991–92), a landscaped 1.5-acre garden, attempts to create a sampling of Missouri woodlands and habitats, and Ian Hamilton Finlay's *Four Shades* (1994), a circle of shade trees, is based on a verse in Virgil. Frances Whitehead's *Hortus Obscurus* (1996), a garden based on a changing assortment of

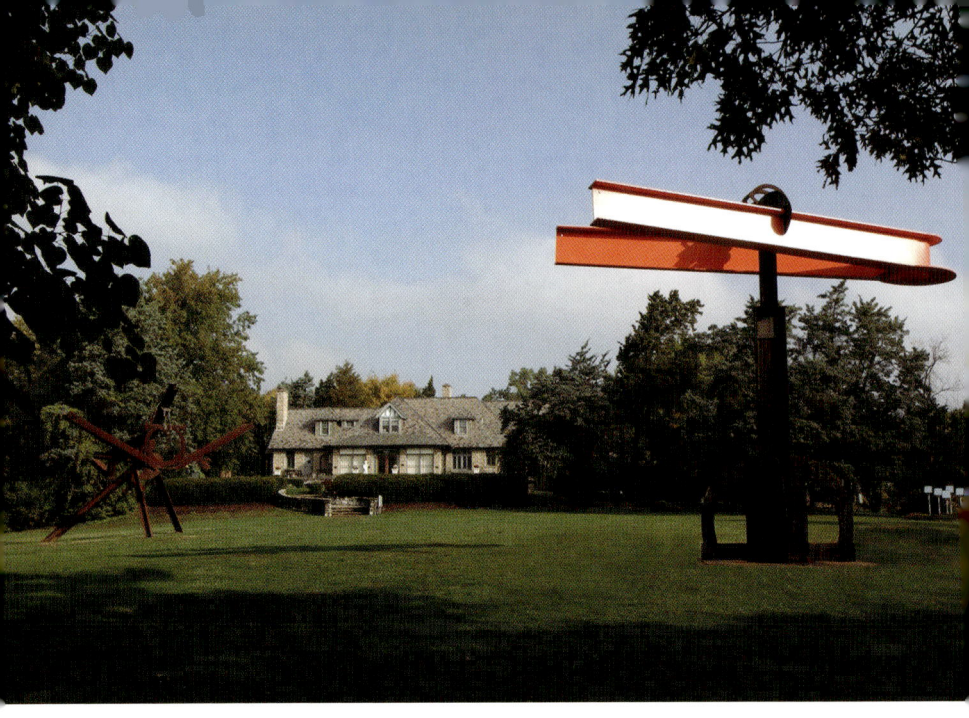

View of Laumeier Sculpture Park with (left) Mark di Suvero's *Bornibus*, 1985–87, and (right) *Destino*, 2003.

dark-hued blooms including black daylilies and tulips, black roses, vegetables, and herbs, is left untended so it can grow naturally.

Commissioned projects, in particular those by Jackie Ferrara, Mary Miss, Robert Lobe, Robert Stackhouse, Beverly Pepper, Ursula von Rydingsvard, Vito Acconci, Richard Fleischner, and Dan Graham, constitute Laumeier's primary triumph. Ferrara's towering cedar structure allows visitors to enter an intimate space and then look out at the surrounding forest and sky. von Rydingsvard's rows of hollowed-out cedar forms (1988–89) were inspired by her childhood memories of World War II refugee barracks.

Located at a forest creek, Dan Graham's *Triangular Bridge Over Water* (1990) consists of three grids that combine industrial materials—reflective glass, aluminum, and steel—with dramatic results. The glass reflects pinkish daylight and mirrors a gurgling stream and trees alive with birds. On the other side of this visually and acoustically vibrant bridge, a path leads to a pavilion and walkway circling Mary Miss's kidney-shaped *Pool Complex: Orchard Valley* (1983–85). Miss salvaged the old, ruined pool and unearthed hidden pathways in the site. "The way I was able to integrate new and old structures was a good experience for me," she explained. "It provided me with a strong working example of how this same attitude might be applied on a larger scale.

For instance, in urban renewal projects, instead of wiping the slate clean, the possibility of building on the existing context seems to me a very interesting one."

Robert Lobe's *The Palm at the End of the Parking Lot* (1995) is a dead walnut tree with severed limbs sheathed in a shimmering jacket of hammered aluminum. He worked the aluminum with an air hammer and other industrial tools. "The aluminum handles like clay under the hammering technique," he said. "This is a highly tactile experience—essentially I'm making love to this tree. I see the potential for a kind of form that can go beyond nature."

Although Lobe's piece has weathered well, other site works have presented tough conservation issues. In 1994, Andy Goldsworthy designed a pear-bottomed cairn of Celtic inspiration by layering stones from a nearby creek bed; his earlier pilgrimages to the site to add mud or autumn leaf layers to a nearby stone underscore the transitory and transformative nature of his outdoor sculpture. The cairn was damaged by visitors in spring 1996. When invited to rebuild it, Goldsworthy declined, asserting (as David Nash has done) that his pieces are intended to be temporary, and that the fallen cairn was simply the current state of the project. Laumeier staff decided to remove the stones altogether. A recently installed porcelain fountain by Brazilian artist Valeska Soares emitted perfumed water, which attracted and killed small insects, filling the fountain with tiny floating carcasses.

Vito Acconci, *Face of the Earth #3*, 1988. Natural concrete, gravel, reinforced rods, sod, and earth, 394 x 342 x 58 in.

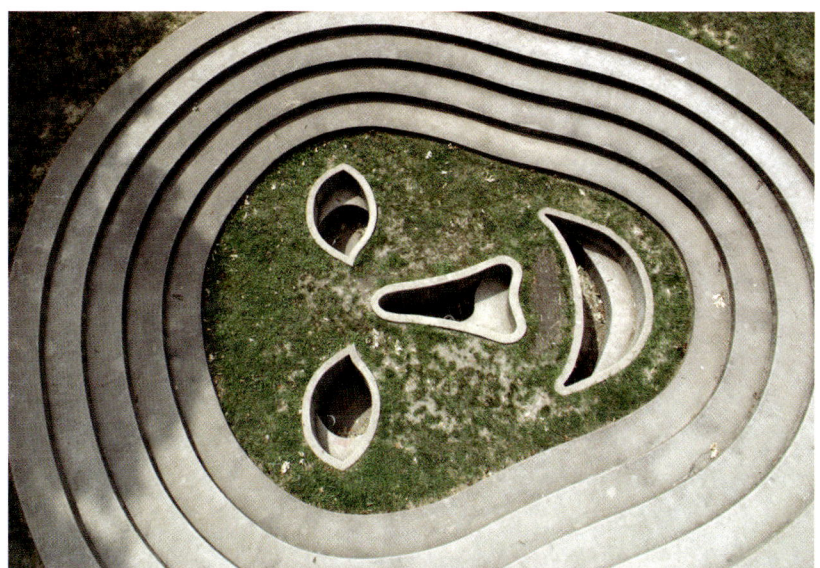

Beverly Pepper's *Cromlech Glen* (1985–90) is an enigmatic, womb-like mini-performance space nestled between two precipitous grassy mounds. The incline of the slopes, designed to be steeper than the "angle of repose," made the piece initially difficult to seed and plant, but ongoing conservation has restored the grass-carpeted surfaces. The mound ends were rebuilt twice. Stone steps were added to permit movement up one mound, along its crest, and down the other mound. This visually exciting piece is one of the most physically engaging earthworks in the park.

In addition to over 70 outdoor works, the gallery hosts three exhibitions every year. Hikers may tour at their own pace using a map with iconic markers. Laurily Epstein, co-author of *A Guide to Sculpture Parks and Gardens in America*, points out that "Laumeier's maquettes for the blind [eight presently in place] also give the sighted viewer an immediate lesson in how scale changes everything and adds an intellectually exciting dimension."

To celebrate its 30th anniversary, Laumeier commissioned a new Fine Arts and Education Center in 2007. The winning design, by Pugh + Scarpa architects, was selected from a field of 35 American firms and represents what Laumeier director Glen Gentele identifies as "an innovative, thoughtful approach to architecture." Gentele's vision for Laumeier is "to create a cultural legacy for art and nature that future generations will experience in one of America's great open-air museums." He sees current and future projects focusing on "an integrated framework for the flexible growth and development of the institution as a unique, sustainable community asset and attraction." Envisioned as an environmentally savvy structure bridging art, architecture, and landscape, the park's new education building takes the first step toward developing Laumeier's picture-perfect landscape in a responsible and innovative way.

<www.laumeiersculpturepark.org>

Emerging Art at The Fields

by Jan Garden Castro

"To some degree, we have a 'do it well and they will come' theory," Francis Greenburger, the founder of Omi International Arts Center (Art Omi), said recently. "We're less concerned about large numbers than about being an important venue for the type of art that we're exhibiting. We are art-centric rather than box-office-centric. We don't have to justify our numbers to anybody. What differentiates us from Storm King—which, of course, has a fantastic modern collection and contemporary exhibitions but is more tied to the modern period—is that we're trying to be on the cutting edge of where sculpture is today."

Driving is currently the best way to reach The Fields, Art Omi's sculpture park in Ghent, New York. Taking Amtrak to Hudson, New York, and then directing a taxi to Omi, 10 miles away, is also an option. The spacious 90-acre sculpture site in Columbia County is about two hours north of New York City and less than an hour south of Albany, on the east side of the state between the Hudson River and Massachusetts. Upon arriving, visitors find a recently completed visitors' center and a varied terrain of field, forest, and pond, with over 100 sculptures in many media by established and emerging artists.

Emerging artists with works recently on view include Kahn/Selesnick, a team of sculptors whose *Apollo Lunar Rover Crash Site*, a silvery fish-like form with a pointed nose cone, wheels, and a tail, lies in a glen. The mythic history of this strange object is detailed on the team's Web site <www.kahnselesnick.com>. *Lunar Rover* formed

Kahn/Selesnick, *Apollo Lunar Rover Crash Site*, 2007. Aluminum, wood, and mixed media, installation view.

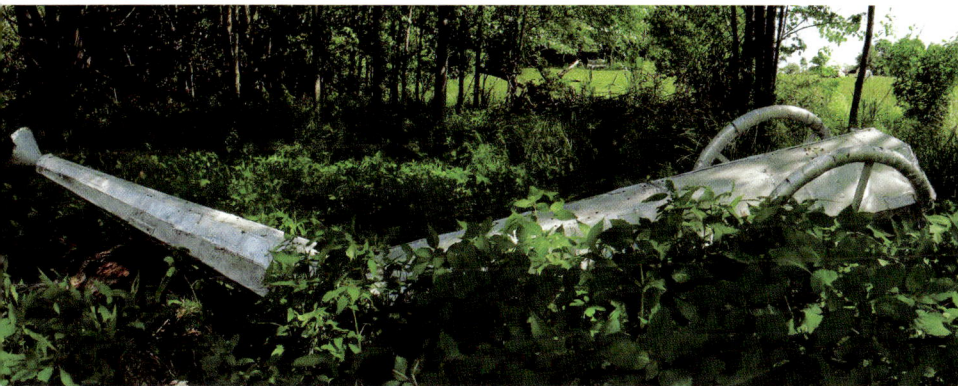

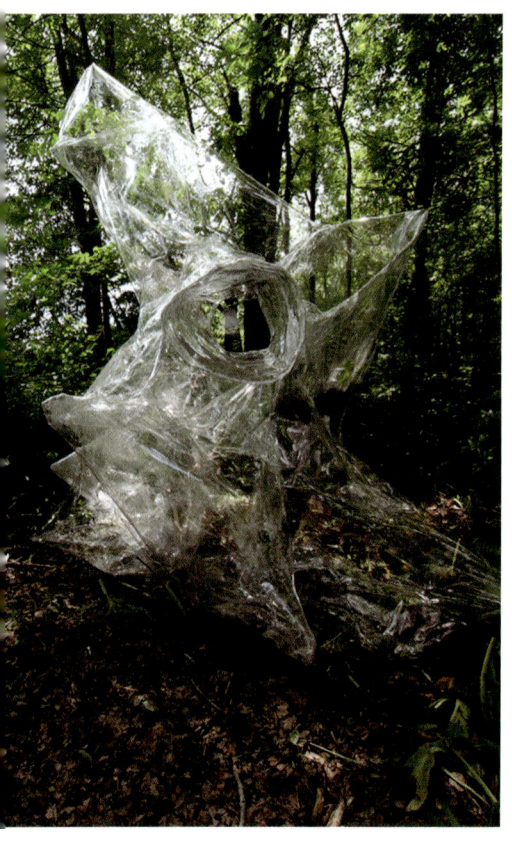

Mikala Dwyer, *Empty Sculpture*, 2006. Plastic, installation view.

part of "bivouac," an exhibition of "expeditionary" artists curated by Max Goldfarb. The show also featured work by Allison Wiese, Elinor Whidden, Garrett Ricciardi, John Osorio-Buck, Matthew Lusk, Mary Mattingly, Marie Lorenz, Jose Krapp, Charles Goldman, Ross Cisneros, and Michael Cataldi. In a nearby deep woods, Mary Ellen Carroll's '83 Buick Regal marked the remains of *In Reverse*, her performance at the summer 2007 opening: a cherry picker plucked up the car, moved it out of the woods, and dumped it in a nearby field, depositing it in a grave, where it was entombed with only its antenna showing.

The new visitors' center includes a reception area with skylights, a café, and an indoor gallery space. Designed by ft Architecture + Interiors principals Peter Franck and Kathleen Triem—who also serve as curators for The Fields—the one-story building hugs its site, and the post-and-beam construction relates to the vernacular of the area's farm buildings. Its cast concrete floor, stone veneer walls insulated with four inches of recycled blue jeans, glass viewing areas, solar panels, and low-maintenance, sedum-planted roof are designed to keep the building cool and energy efficient.

The Fields' nine outdoor exhibition sites are named after their landscape features. The new entrance features Beverly Pepper's slender, triangular Cor-ten construction *Paraclete* on a wooden base. The old entrance includes DeWitt Godfrey's *Picker Sculpture/July*, Cor-ten loops between two trees; two works by Alain Kirili; *Haunt*, a sound piece by Lewis deSoto; wooden *Vases on the Field* by Foon Sham; and an untitled, recently restored work by Robert Grosvenor. The Little Field includes work by Antoni Milkowski, and the Back Woods features Grace Knowlton's *Beached Whale* and Alena Ort's *Triad*—three stones with forged steel bands. The Lower Wheat Field includes Bernar Venet's *4 Arcs Disorder* and Vincent Mazeau's *January Sun*. In The Woods, we find Jene Highstein's *Inverted Cone* and Mary Ann Unger's *Untitled*

(*Misericordia*). Shimon Okshteyn's *Shoe Last*, a giant fiberglass model of a shoemaker's form, can be found in the Wheat Field. DeWitt Godfrey's *Socrates Sculpture*, which has the feel of a roller coaster, is cleverly constructed from hand-bolted ribbons of steel. In the Clover Meadow, Carl Andre's *Cascade* offers a stunning example of older work that maintains its "edge," as does Robert Lobe's *X-Ray*, which was recently moved from the Little Field.

The blue-tinged Catskill Mountains form a beautiful backdrop for the park and Art Omi's 125-acre main campus; the center encompasses a total of 300 acres of farmland and devotes about 90 to the display of sculpture. The facilities include Ledig House, three residency buildings named for the late German publisher Ledig Rowohlt that offer alternating programs for emerging artists, writers, composers, and dancers.

Founded in 1991 by Francis Greenburger, Omi International Arts Center grew out of his experience on the board of the Triangle Arts Trust, a nonprofit corporation in the formalist tradition founded by Anthony Caro and Robert Loederer, and Top Gallant, Andre Emmerich's 140-acre sculpture park in Pawling, New York. Greenburger, who heads both a real estate corporation and a literary agency, formed Art Omi with John Cross and Sandy Slone about a year after all three left the Triangle board. Greenburger had already purchased the land, and he asked Triem and Franck to develop the sculpture park. More than a dozen of the original sculptures came from Emmerich, who had decided to sell his estate; of these, one or two remain. The other arts programs evolved, and each now has its own board; Jed Cleary is currently serving as the director of collections. A separate executive committee, including Joseph Thompson, director of MASS MoCA, and Alan Fishman, chairman of the board of the Brooklyn Academy of Music, oversees Art Omi's organizational issues.

"Our mission for the sculpture park is to continue to present innovative outdoor sculpture," Greenburger emphasizes, "along with some established artists to give a context to the cutting-edge work. And we're thinking of an initiative to include some architectural forms within the park to rethink architecture...My dream for Art Omi generally is that it will continue to evolve as the first-class international art center that it is. And I use the word 'evolve' purposively. We want to respond to ideas and opportunities presented to us by people whom we feel are competent to execute them."

<www.artomi.org>

Grounds For Sculpture: Present and Past

by Patricia Summers

Founded by sculptor-philanthropist J. Seward Johnson to be about sculpture in every possible way, Grounds For Sculpture, in Hamilton, New Jersey, opened in 1992. But first its terrain had to be painstakingly created and landscaped and on-site buildings had to be relocated and/or renovated to serve as additional display areas, a process that took a few years. Today, 254 sculptures, including some commissioned for their sites, are on view on the grounds. The names of their creators read like a Who's Who in contemporary sculpture. The park boasts, besides two buildings for indoor exhibitions, Rat's Restaurant, a café, and a gazebo-café, open seasonally. One of the two gift shops, Toad Hall, also includes gallery space.

Visitors are also attracted by extensive programming. All of it is arts-related, if not specifically having to do with sculpture, and everything is open to the public. Besides seasonal exhibitions and gallery talks, park tours are conducted by a cadre of docents, and there are classes and workshops for everyone from tots to adults, with sculpture and photography being only two of the options. Concerts, dance performances, and poetry readings are also on the calendar. The Seward Johnson Center for the Arts, the starting point for school tours, houses a visitor center for orientations and special events. Its state-of-the-art educational facilities, with workshop space for children's art programs, opened in spring 2008.

In 2000, after years of operational support from J. Seward Johnson's private foundations, Grounds For Sculpture was incorporated as a public not-for-profit corporation. In 2002, it expanded to 35 acres, and by 2007, it was under new management and directed by a community board made up of New Jersey business representatives, philanthropists, and sculptors. "From the beginning," says Andrea Fabry, CEO, "Johnson always wanted to create a public place, ultimately dependent on public support." Accordingly, the organization's budget is met through individuals (including about 2,000 members) and foundations, the New Jersey State Council on the Arts and the National Endowment for the Arts, admission fees, and donations. Johnson's family philanthropy provides less than a quarter of the budget, a percentage intended to steadily drop.

Although he has stepped down from both management and the board, Johnson's earlier contributions remain, attesting to his puckish, whimsical, or self-indulgent bent. His landscape ideas include follies and surprises, and his three-dimensional renderings of Impressionist paintings, such as *Déjeuner Déjà Vu* (1994) derived from Manet's *Déjeuner sur l'Herbe*, are located around the grounds.

Fabry says that she prefers "sculpture garden," though she sometimes uses "sculpture park and museum" to suggest both outdoor and indoor exhibition space—

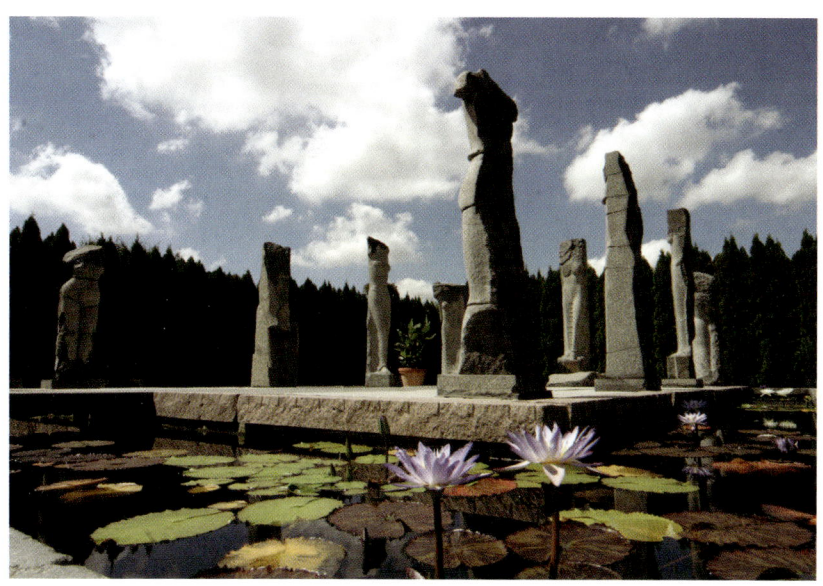

Carlos Dorrien, *The Nine Muses*, 1990–97. Granite, 132 x 240 x 360 in.

Grounds For Sculpture is definitely not just an outdoor attraction. Nor is it, in view of shows that change seasonally, a once-a-year place. In accordance with Johnson's original vision, "it should always change with the season, and the experience should always be different."

Each season brings changes on the grounds and in the buildings, with new group and solo shows, as well as additional outdoor works. Two artist residencies have provided insights and involvement for the many community members who took up the invitation to participate. For instance, during Patrick Dougherty's nine-week residency in 2004, area volunteers of all ages and specialties helped to gather and prepare the materials for the woven-wood structures they then helped to erect.

In spring 2008, Ellen J. Landis moved from the Albuquerque Museum of Art to become the second curator in the organization's history, following Brooke Barrie. She also handles educational events. Her tenure will coincide with development of a new strategic plan that may involve expanded programs and the continuation, or not, of artist residencies.

Since its opening, Grounds For Sculpture has been a steadily growing presence on the art scene. Now a fixture in the area, it's a popular site offering myriad ways to enjoy a visit. Starting with its signature entrance arbor, the more picturesque features include a water garden, a bamboo courtyard, a sculpture wall and colonnade, a peacock house, an amphitheater, pergola, lotus pond, and lake.

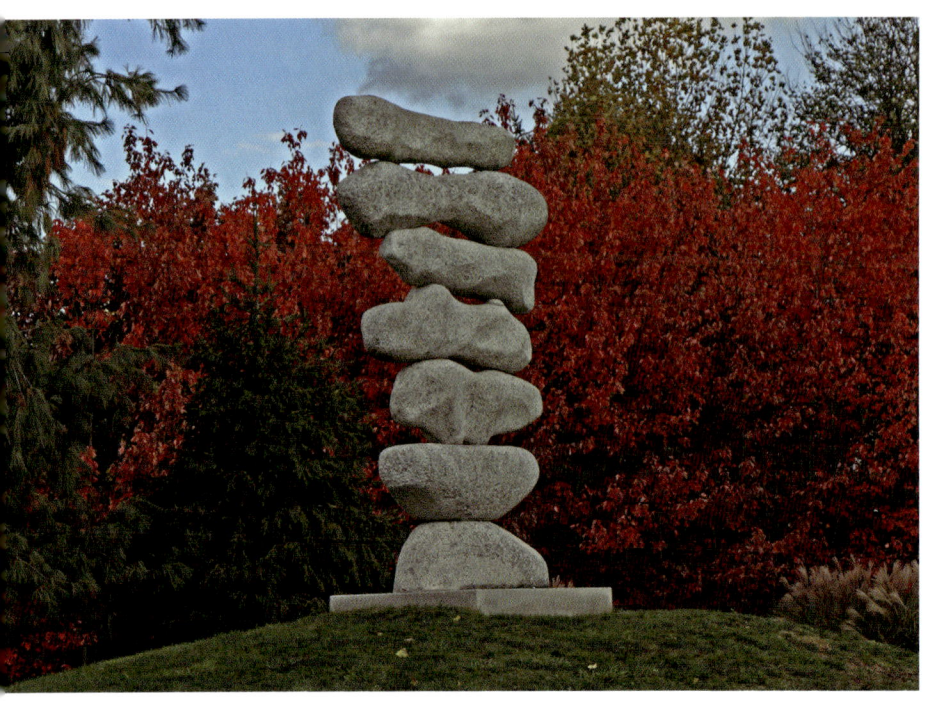

Isaac Witkin, *Eolith*, 1994. Blue Mountain granite, 168 x 96 x 48 in.

Long before the park and museum, with its rolling hills and lush landscaping, the site hosted fairs of all sorts. This function began in 1745, when King George II granted a royal charter allowing fairs for the buying and selling of livestock and other goods. In 1888, the area was established as a permanent annual fair site, complete with grandstand, half-mile track, and two exhibition buildings. Its wide range of attractions over the years reflected whatever was current, from agriculture to Annie Oakley, from horses to automobiles to dog shows.

In decline by the 1970s, the State Fairgrounds property was up for grabs after the last New Jersey State Fair in 1980. Four years later, the Atlantic Foundation purchased the tract that would become Grounds For Sculpture. Architect Brian Carey designed a lush mix of European garden styles to complement contemporary sculpture and, with glass walls and high ceilings, blurred the transition from outdoor landscape to indoor viewing areas. The 1992 opening of Grounds For Sculpture marked the beginning of a new, and continuing, aesthetic era in central New Jersey.

<www.groundsforsculpture.org>

Australia's McClelland Gallery and Sculpture Park

by Ken Scarlett

McClelland Gallery and Sculpture Park, less than an hour's drive from Melbourne, is fast becoming the preeminent destination for Australian sculpture, both historical and contemporary. Established in 1971, when Langwarrin was still a country area, the park has extensive grounds in which to display its rapidly growing collection. With the recent purchase of adjoining bushland, it covers 16 hectares of mown grassland and native eucalyptus bush. Driving through the gates, visitors become immediately aware of sculpture—on the sides of the gravel road, dotted across the sweeping grasslands in front of the gallery, in the car park, and on the pathway leading to the main entrance.

The first work to appear is Anthony Pryor's towering *Sea Legend* (1991–2001), which soars effortlessly aloft and establishes a sense of drama and expectation. Three wide-spread legs shift all of the action high above the spectator. Though this composition typifies Pryor's style, *Sea Legend* was fabricated after his death at the age of 40 in 1991. The original maquette was faithfully enlarged by John Fasham and his skilled assistants, a group that frequently works with sculptors on large-scale public projects.

Another major commission, Inge King's *Island Sculpture* (1991), can be seen across the undulating area of grass. Designed specifically for the small island at the center of McClelland's artificial lake, it is perfectly scaled for its site. It rests like a gigantic insect that has just alighted, brilliant red planes accentuating its predominately black welded steel construction. As one of Australia's major sculptors, King has carried out a great number of public commissions; the McClelland collection features eight of her works. Approaching 90 years of age, she continues to produce sculpture of great strength and originality, recently introducing a subtle figurative element into her work after years dedicated to abstraction.

In direct contrast to the flat steel plates of *Island Sculpture*, Sebastian Di Mauro's *Snuffle* (2002–03) consists of curving bright green forms installed on either side of the lake. Children are tempted to climb over these modern-day topiaries made of artificial grass, and the underlying steel structure is strong enough to support their weight. The plastic Astroturf sitting on the natural grass highlights Australia's acute shortage of water. Will plastic grass become the acceptable norm?

As one moves around the gallery building, the environment changes from wide expanses of mown lawn to natural bushland—a remnant of eucalyptus forest that has miraculously escaped the advance of Melbourne's ever-growing suburbs. The extensive grounds continually surprise and delight as viewers explore the various directions taken by Australian sculpture over the last 30 to 40 years. McClelland successfully

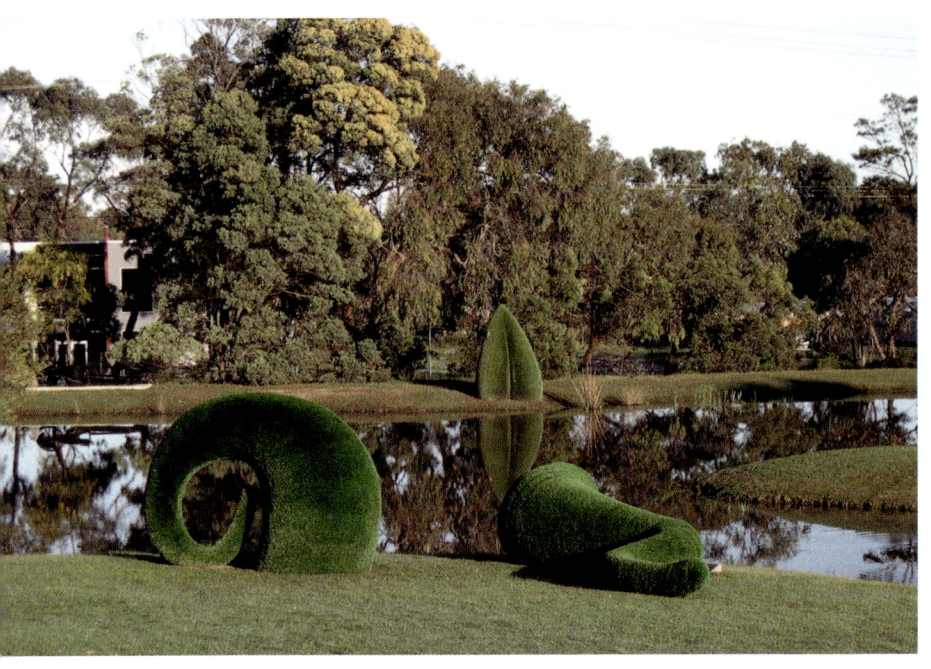

Sebastian Di Mauro, *Snuffle*, 2002–03. Astroturf and galvanized steel, two elements, 240 x 240 x 650 and 253 x 180 x 105 cm.

showcases the great sense of experimental vitality characteristic of this stimulating period of rapid development.

Ken Unsworth's audacious *Annulus* (2007), set in a clearing surrounded by gum trees, strains its apparently simple engineering to the limit. Three outward-leaning stainless steel poles support a myriad of hanging wires, each attached to rounded, water-washed stones suspended just above ground level. When the sun shines, each stone casts a rounded shadow, creating a wondrous pattern on the sandy soil. The work both defies gravity and accepts that gravitational pull holds everything in place: it is at once supremely logical and intensely poetic.

The biennial McClelland Survey and Award, which began in 2003 and carries a prize of AUS $100,000, has injected a dynamic quality to the sculpture park. Not only are the finalists' works on display for a period of six months, but the winning work is also purchased. To date, three new works have been added to the permanent collection. Ian Burn and John Clark's impressive *Plantation* (2003) consists of ambiguous ovoid forms arranged in serried ranks that suggest either threatening bomb-like objects or methodically arranged plant forms. Subsequent winners of this prestigious competition, Lisa Roet's *White Ape* (2005) and Rick Amor's enigmatic half-human,

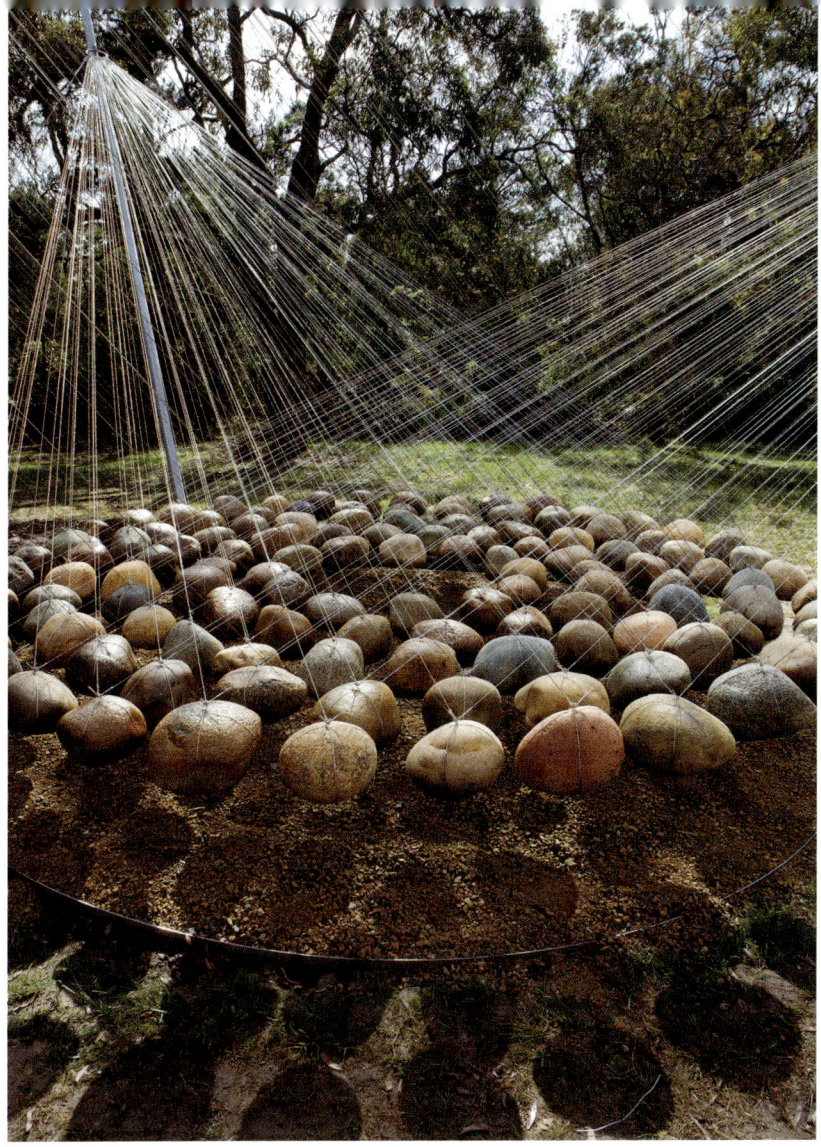

Ken Unsworth, *Annulus*, 2007. Stainless steel wire, steel, and river rocks, 600 x 1500 cm. diameter.

half-animal *Relic* (2007), demonstrate the wide diversity characteristic of current Australian practice.

Until quite recently, the collection focused solely on Australian sculpture, but the purchase of *Ratytus* (2005), a wonderfully elegant, wind-driven mobile by the New Zealand artist Phil Price, marks a significant widening of the purchasing policy. It would appear logical to broaden the collection to include work from neighboring New Zealand, whose artists produce identifiably different work.

While McClelland's outdoor space focuses on sculpture from the last 40 years, the gallery houses historical works, ranging from the early years of settlement to the present. Though this collection is still being assembled, ultimately it will enable visitors to understand the various influences that have helped to form Australian sculpture — influences that originated in England, Europe, the U.S., and, more recently, Asia. The collection includes early works by artists such as Thomas Woolner, who came from England to Victoria during the gold rush in the 1850s, follows the development of Australian sculpture through the 19th and 20th centuries, and comes emphatically up to date with an astonishing new acquisition — Ron Mueck's *Wild Man* (2008). Whereas Woolner set out to please with his elegant profile portrait of W.C. Wentworth, Mueck deliberately sets out to confront the spectator with the aggressive nudity of his over life-sized work.

A visit to McClelland always offers challenges and delights. Its tranquil setting creates an ideal backdrop for experiencing a diverse and stimulating collection. And to round off the expedition, one can retreat to the airy, light-filled café to sample excellent seasonal food and superb local wines.

<www.mcclellandgallery.com>

The Sculpture Park at Goodwood

by John K. Grande

The Cass Sculpture Foundation, founded by Wilfred and Jeanette Cass, recently expanded the grounds of its Sculpture Park at Goodwood by purchasing a new venue called the Chalk Pit, increasing the overall area of Goodwood to 26 acres. The park exhibits a wide range of contemporary British artworks, each with its own spatial context, and also makes them available for purchase — a policy that guarantees a gradual transition in the works on view over the years. Large-scale sculptures by leading British artists are commissioned each year for display on the grounds in West Sussex. Since its inception, Goodwood has displayed works by many renowned sculptors, including Eduardo Paolozzi, Antony Gormley, Richard Long, David Mach, Rachel Whiteread, Richard Deacon, Alison Wilding, Marc Quinn, Cathy de Monchaux, Gavin Turk, Richard Wentworth, Andy Goldsworthy, and Anthony Caro. Sales help fund new commissions, thereby encouraging the development of new and challenging sculpture.

Wandering through the grounds, visitors can see some remarkable expressions of the three-dimensional urge. Bill Woodrow's riveting *Regardless of History*, first exhibited on the empty fourth plinth at Trafalgar Square in London (spring 2000–summer 2001), questions the notion of permanence. A monumental head broken from a fallen

Bill Woodrow, *Regardless of History*, 2000. Bronze, 920 x 480 x 237 cm.

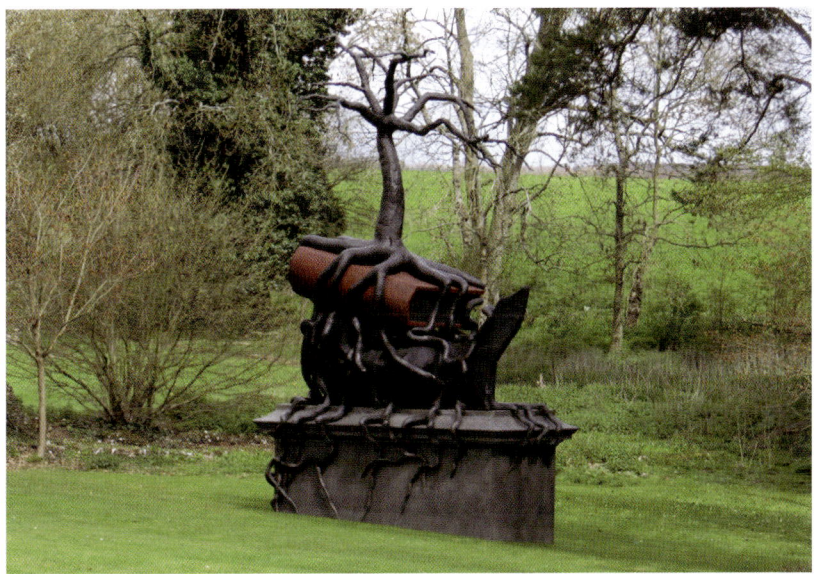

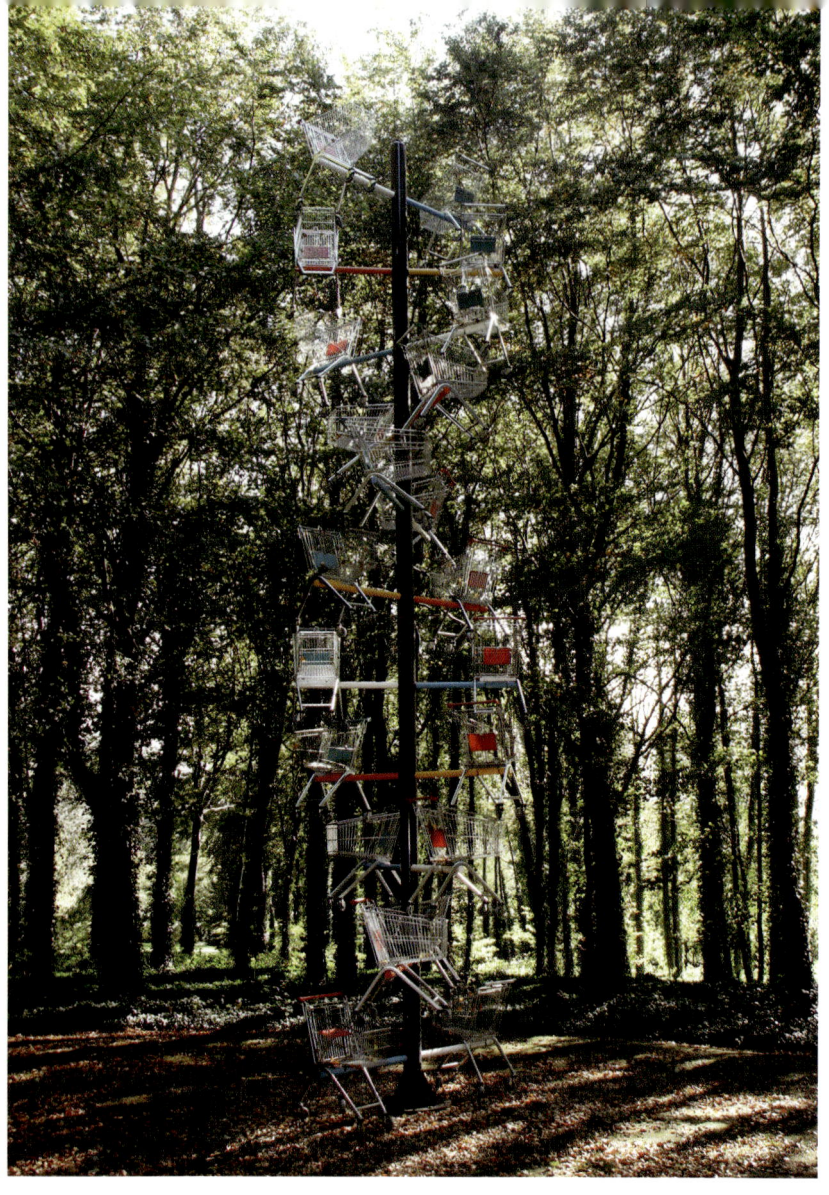

Abigail Fallis, *DNA DL90*, 2004. Shopping carts and steel, 1000 x 250 cm. diameter.

statue rests under a huge red book. A tree surmounts both symbols of human culture, its roots binding them in place. Woodrow's overriding message is that knowledge — our collective and accumulated history — is temporary, its remnants ultimately dominated by nature. Abigail Fallis's *DNA DL90* (2004) is a tantalizing large-scale tower of supermarket shopping carts. Here, the function of the carts turns ironic: their placement in the park seems unreal until you realize that nature provides the products usually carried in them. Steven Gregory's playful and whimsical *Fish on a Bike* (1998) recalls Victorian novellas and children's stories, a ludicrous fantasy sculpture that attracts large audiences. *Give and Take* (2003), an enigmatic work by Peter Randall-Page, is carved from a glacial granite boulder. Its repeating circular relief forms recall biological growth.

To celebrate its 10th anniversary, the Cass Sculpture Foundation brought together a colorful array of 13 large-scale sculptures by Tony Cragg. When Cragg first emerged on the sculpture scene, he explored a variety of media, playing with discarded and recycled plastic objects, toys, and containers. He represented Great Britain at the 43rd Venice Biennale in 1988, the same year that he won the prestigious Turner Prize.

Cragg's recent cast and molded forms have a beautiful, almost poetic hybridity. Seemingly practical or functional shapes shift ever so slightly to become contiguous riddles of three-dimensional form in space. These sculptures are like visual quips or puns, set in the worlds of manufacture and nature and inhabiting the borders between science and fiction. Sometimes they defy a set form only to arrive at a point where one form references other familiar forms. At times, they hinge on or echo the machine age. Two stone columns seem worn by time, as if wind or water had eroded their surfaces. There is a tinge of the archaic as well. Cragg makes us ask questions about the nature and origin of form itself.

Bulb (2001), whose sculpted stone surface appears natural and partially eroded, has the look of soft strata or clay. There is a tinge of the ancient to it, and it tips its hat to the organic. Here, formlessness takes on and represents form. The work seems to suggest that it is part of a greater whole or an implicit continuity at which we can only guess. It looks like a geology of the imagination—the human element is always there. *Tongue in Cheek* (2004) has a purely British, Brave New World look. This gold-colored bronze, with its perforated surface, resembles a lost artifact from the machine age. Its skin within a skin creates a double entendre of form within form. Cragg's works existed independently of the beautiful Chalk Pit and nearby forest, describing a fluid spatial relation to the environment yet remaining for and of themselves.

Recent commissions at Goodwood have included works by Wells Small, Tessa Campbell Fraser, Bryan Kneale, Lynn Chadwick, Phillip King, Peter Burke, and Helaine Blumenfeld. They join the more than 160 large-scale sculptures that the Cass Foundation has commissioned from over 120 British artists over the last 15 years. The rotating collection at Goodwood is the most visible tool the foundation has in its mission of "enabling the future of British sculpture today."

<www.sculpture.org.uk>

Frederik Meijer Gardens and Sculpture Park

by Gerry Craig

Was art ever meant to be seen at anything but walking speed? For centuries, art was a daily experience that could not be avoided—one encountered it on the way to the temple, cathedral, or mosque and in other public spaces. The automobile did not exist, and art was not a destination: it was an integration of culture into the larger environment. While art in public places has never completely disappeared, the ability to interact with it has become increasingly institutionalized.

In contrast, the Frederik Meijer Gardens and Sculpture Park creates a symbiotic relationship between walking-speed pleasures. Merging a substantial art collection with equally ambitious garden exhibits and extensive education programs, the mission of this nonprofit is to promote the enjoyment, understanding, and appreciation of gardens, sculpture, the natural environment, and the arts. That mission is accomplished through 125 acres of natural wetlands, woodlands, meadows, indoor sculpture galleries, the Midwest's largest indoor conservatory, an amphitheater, farm garden, and children's garden.

The first substantial support for the gardens and park came from the public-minded Lena and Frederik Meijer. The gardens opened in April 1995, after many years of planning and fundraising by the West Michigan Horticultural Society. The Meijers were asked for their support in 1990, and they welcomed the concept of a major botanical garden and home for their growing sculpture collection. They contributed $1.5 million, offered to donate their entire sculpture collection, valued at $2 million, and Meijer Inc. offered a 70-acre site to the Horticultural Society for the project. Unlike most collectors, the Meijers never intended their collection to be private, and they take pleasure in building a public collection that can be enjoyed outside the rarefied air of museums.

The Meijers became interested in sculpture when they were introduced to the work of Marshall Fredericks, known for his large-scale bronze animals. Fredericks's 1983 public commission for the Meijers' home town of Greenville, Michigan, launched their passion for collecting. Over the next five years, they purchased more than 30 of his works, a collection now featured in the children's garden. When the first curator and director of the sculpture program, Joseph Antenucci Becherer, was hired in 1999, the Meijers told him that they wanted to create a collection of international significance. Becherer says, "The Meijers are people of their word." Beginning with a 1999 purchase of Rodin's *Eve*, the collection grew rapidly to include other important modern and contemporary works, now the focus of the collection. The sculpture park opened in 2002 with 24 works by artists such as Magdalena Abakanowicz, Mark di

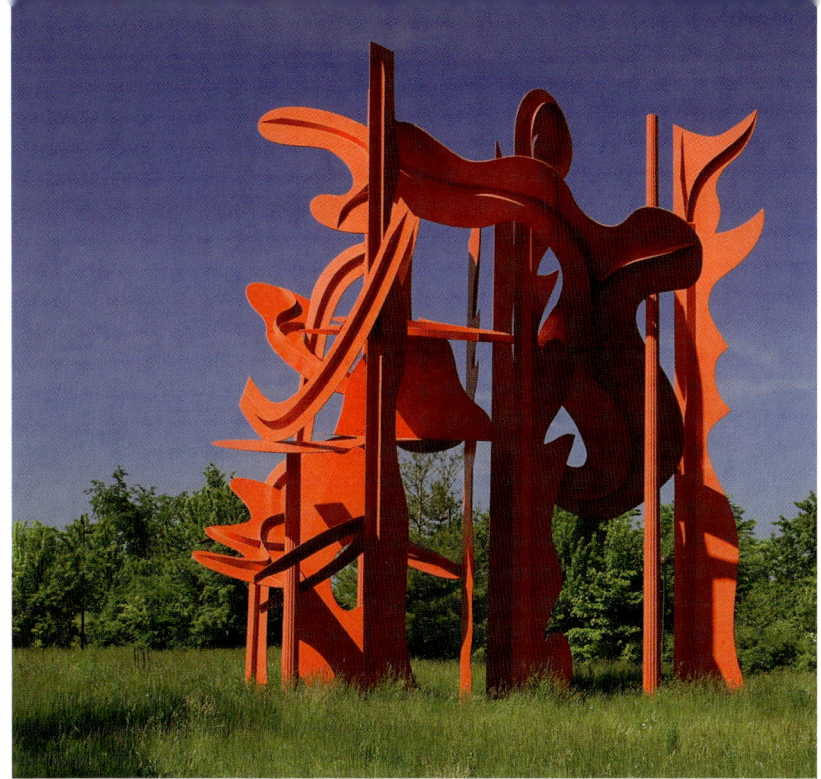

Alexander Liberman, *Aria*, 1979–83. Painted steel, 42 ft. high.

Suvero, Claes Oldenburg and Coosje van Bruggen, Antony Gormley, Bill Woodrow, Dietrich Klinge, Barbara Hepworth, Igor Mitoraj, and Aristide Maillol. The Meijer Foundation provides substantial funding each year for new acquisitions, backing the purchase of works deemed significant by Becherer, his staff, and an advisory committee of art collectors and professionals.

The park's collection is predominantly influenced by an early Modernist sensibility. Much of the work is based on the figure, even when abstracted. Exceptions are the exquisite *Scarlatti* by Mark di Suvero, seen on a rise in an open field of wild flowers, George Rickey's *Four Open Squares Horizontal Gyratory—Tapered*, set in a pool of water, and Carolyn Ottmers's *Full Circle*, perfectly located behind a running stream. The less formal siting of these works compared to the structured views and horticultural bases for the classic works provides a different context for viewers to understand the goals of contemporary sculpture.

Becherer says that an attempt to build an encyclopedic collection shapes the acquisitions, and purchasing dollars are spent to develop the early modern and contemporary holdings simultaneously. The sculpture staff of seven and the advisory committee also consider works that do not duplicate others in the region,

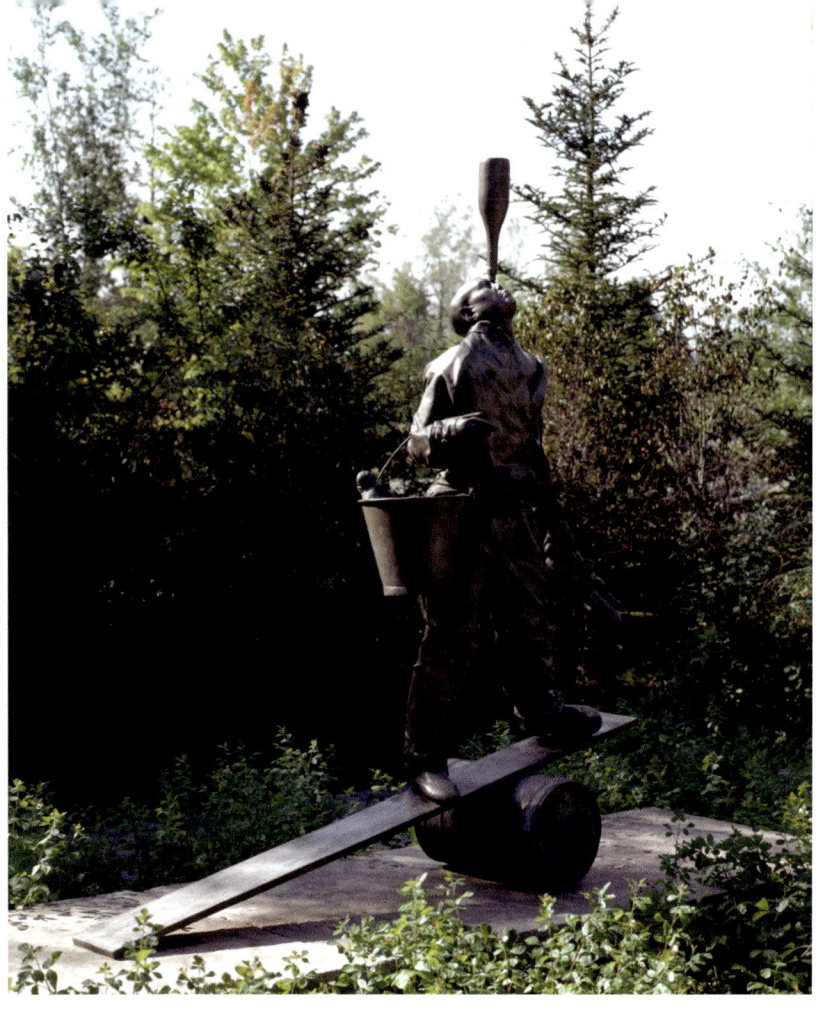

Juan Muñoz, *Broken Nose Carrying Bottle Number One*, 1999. Bronze, 63 in. high.

such as Maya Lin's *Ecliptic Park* in downtown Grand Rapids. Since they started collecting, they have secured a menacingly tender Louise Bourgeois *Spider* and several key Henry Moores. While the most recent contemporary work has been under-represented, that is changing, as new purchases of works by Jonathan Borofsky, Chakaia Booker, and Tony Cragg have been installed, joining Deborah Butterfield's *Cabin Creek* and Keith Haring's *Julia*. A Sculpture Competition for Emerging Artists also secures a new work for the permanent collection each year; Ottmers's work was the inaugural piece placed as a result of the juried competition.

The indoor galleries allow the staff to introduce other contemporary sculptors during inhospitable weather. Exhibitions are programmed in conjunction with the plant conservatory, such as last year's Japanese Autumn show—15 centuries of ceramics joined with bonsai trees loaned from around the country. Other shows have included the sculptures and drawings of George Segal, Dale Chihuly, Anthony Caro, Henry Moore, and Jaume Plensa. The galleries offer educational and interpretive opportunities for work like di Suvero's, in which the moving parts beg for interaction. The large swinging wood platform of *To Intuit* (1983) was a gathering spot for old and young. "It is highly unusual that touching the art is not only allowed but encouraged by the artist," said Becherer. And there were signs that told you so. Yet social conditioning is hard to break. As one little girl tried to climb on, her mother was overheard to say, "Oh no, honey, it looks like a swing but it's not a swing."

This desire to make art fun, interactive, and accessible is integral to the intelligent and community-minded decisions of the Meijer staff. They are making art a destination, even if sculpture isn't the sole attraction. Gardening is America's favorite hobby, and here visitors learn what gardens share with art: the ability to encourage contemplation and imagination.

<www.meijergardens.org>

Into the Woods: The Carell Woodland Sculpture Trail

by Susan W. Knowles

Less than five miles from the bustle of downtown, a walk in the woods on the outskirts of Nashville yields a surprisingly rich encounter with some of the best contemporary sculpture coming out of Europe and America. Inaugurated in June 1999, the Carell Woodland Sculpture Trail most recently installed Siah Armajani's *Glass Bridge* (2003). The trail was conceived by John Wetenhall, former director of the Cheekwood Museum of Art, as a way to transform a significant portion of the institution's 55 acres into a lively and welcoming exhibition area for contemporary art. Wetenhall's vision, to carve a path for wandering alone with the thoughts of 15 creative artists, makes use of a previously ignored space—the wooded perimeter of the Cheekwood grounds. Amidst the rustling leaves, fallen tree limbs, and overgrown ground cover of a sparse and long-neglected forest, a winding path was cut and covered with wood chip mulch. Along the way, sculptures hide in the woods. They are far enough apart to allow visitors to concentrate on one piece at a time, close enough to form visual relationships, and spaced at distances just attention-spanning enough to keep a dialogue going inside the viewer's mind. It is an artistic conversation that needs no words, as refreshing as the fresh air and rugged path that accompany it.

The trail, more than the extensive renovations to the museum or the construction of an innovative learning center, has forced Cheekwood, home to an extensive collection of decorative arts and 19th- and 20th-century American paintings, into the postmodern discourse. Inserting a layer of irony into the identity of a place that stands, in an inescapable way, for elitism, these contemporary works comment on their surroundings. The diverse and multiple voices that once drifted through only in temporary exhibitions now linger in the air. The permanence of the new narrative is a bold move, for context is king in a place like Cheekwood, where the aura of the 18th-century British leisure class is almost inescapable.

In a pleasant twist of irony, the new sculpture trail was almost completely funded by Monroe Carell, a Nashville businessman who has amassed millions from fees collected at Central Parking lots all over the country. The guiding vision that inspired Carell to open his checkbook was that of James Turrell, artist-physicist-philosopher. Carell, at Cheekwood's urging, went to see a Turrell installation in New York. He emerged convinced that Turrell had the ability to create works capable of expanding anyone's personal metaphysics. Corporate art patron Hugh McColl (Bank of America/NationsBank) once stated that the reason his bank supports public art projects is that an encounter with a work of art allows a momentary pause in one's normal thought pattern.

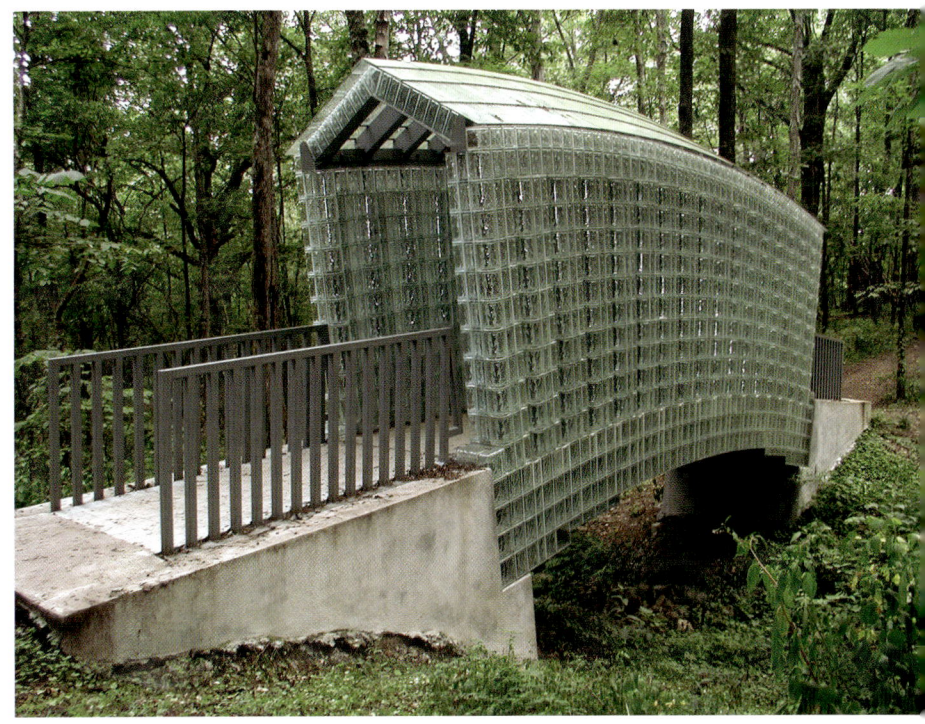

Siah Armajani, *Glass Bridge*, 2003. Glass, steel, and mixed media, 20 x 40 ft.

The trail starts with George Rickey's *One Line Horizontal Floating—Twenty Feet*, which hangs suspended above a grassy landscaped alcove behind the Cheek Mansion, framing a distant view of downtown Nashville and pointing now and then toward the diminutive tall buildings. It descends through the square arch of Eric Orr's *Cheekwood Prime Matter*, in which a potentially gimmicky sequence of flowing water, spouting fire, and steam seems to stop time every 15 minutes while a majestic 100-year-old tree nearby becomes wreathed in fog. The viewer continues to walk downhill and into increasingly dense wooded spaces. Ulrich Rückriem's *untitled boulder*, a large block of granite in the center of the path, poses an abrupt challenge. Out-of-scale for these woods and too polished to be a natural outcropping, it calls attention to itself by showing four differently textured faces on the same block of stone, pulling curious viewers around to see all sides and revealing its quarry marks in the process.

Many people walk right past Tom Czarnopys's bronze tree trunk *Girdled Figure*, whose trapped prepubescent human form conveys the anguished vulnerability of a tree already marked by a girdling (slow-killing) ax. In *A Memorial to the Aboriginal People of this Land Who Lived in and With These Forests*, Yone Sinor, descended from

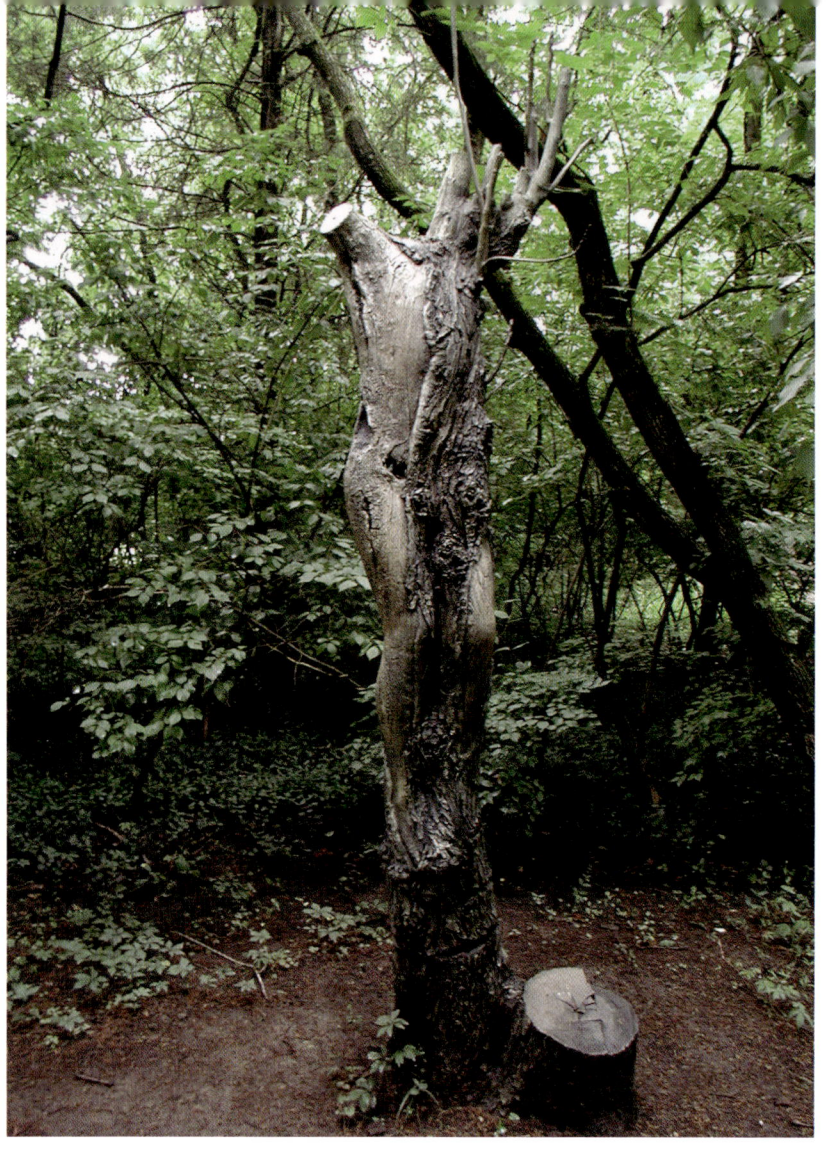

Tom Czarnopys, *Girdled Figure*, 1997. Bronze, 115 x 30 x 29 in.

local Cherokee, has created a ruined round house of standing poles of local cedar, well-camouflaged in a wooded grove—a reminder that the first settlers, who built their log houses in clearings, emulated the ways of the Indians and sometimes co-existed peacefully among them. Next, a huge ghostly gray rabbit, crouched on all fours, rises through the trees. Viewed from behind, where well-developed labia and small breasts are easily visible, Sophie Ryder's giant galvanized wire *Crawling Lady Hare* is both a child's fantasy and a slightly sinister feminist critique.

Finally, one emerges from the woods and encounters a view of the austere neo-Georgian Cheek Mansion high on a hill above; at one's feet are the huge scattered stones of an Ian Hamilton Finlay piece. For a moment, it looks as if the Cheek Mansion has come tumbling down, another ironic ploy. The quotation incised in Latin lettering on the broken blocks talks about today's order being tomorrow's disorder, based on a quotation from the French Revolution.

If the ancien régime stands above us, then the next frontier is, literally, before us. At trail's end is Turrell's *Blue Pesher*, a domed igloo-like structure entered through an angular concrete tunnel. Through its oculus, one can see the moon but no stars, Turrell says, for there is light inside the dome, and the sky appears deep blue long after it has gone to black outside. The inquisitive will discover that a dome carries sound horizontally and also directly down to a listener standing in its very center. Inside, a slanting-back bench provides a place to still the mind and contemplate the silent blank sky, observing one's own observations, meditating on the ever-increasing speed of information transmission, spotting the steady progress of a brighter-than-stars satellite, listening, perhaps, to the future.

<www.cheekwood.org>

The Ephemeral Sculpture Garden

by John K. Grande

Sculpture parks and gardens, which come in many forms and exhibit a diversity of art forms, reflect the broad spectrum of ways in which humanity can approach nature and art and their intersections. The urge to create and place art in the land can be traced back to prehistoric stelae, stone circles, and rock carvings. Ancient sites such as Stonehenge or Carnac in Brittany manifest our desire to civilize or humanize a site. The medieval garden was a way of keeping the wilderness out, and the Renaissance garden (containing sculpture) evolved into Fontainebleau. In the 19th century, there were remarkable and naturalistic innovations by North America's pioneer of landscape architecture, Frederick Law Olmsted. More recent antecedents of the contemporary sculpture park include Robert Smithson's *Spiral Jetty*. Smithson was acutely aware of ecology and of entropy (or de-differentiation, as Anton Ehrenzweig called it) and the way it works on humans and the physical environment. The maximal scale of Land Art engaged the environment wholeheartedly and challenged our reading of art as a fetish or object of wealth and patronage. Earth could be considered a material for sculpture. Since the 1960s and 1970s large-scale Land Art has merged with other, more earth-sensitive tendencies in tune with the cycles of nature.

Over the past 25 years, ephemeral sculpture has grown into an art form in itself and has moved toward a more site-sensitive and entropic relation to nature, both in conception and realization. Ephemeral sculpture has often been linked to performance, as was the case for Ana Mendieta, Robert Morris, Alan Sonfist, Allan Kaprow, and Dennis Oppenheim. While some of these works are temporary, others have a prolonged life, seeking to reunite the languages of art and ecology. The new ephemeral sculpture has transformed Land Art into eco-art, no longer necessarily large scale (it can be quite intimate), but sensitive to biology and geology, and even to more transparent and transient effects like climate.

In May 1982, Agnes Denes created *Wheatfield*, two acres of wheat planted in downtown Manhattan, one block from the World Trade Center and Wall Street and facing Bartholdi's Statue of Liberty in New York harbor. *Wheatfield* enabled city dwellers, some for the first time, to see the foodstuffs they ate growing where they lived. The wheat was harvested before the site was developed. By the time of Denes's project, Alan Sonfist had already conceived and created *Time Landscape*, which grew out of the same performance and conceptual roots as Smithson's work. Forty years after its inauguration, *Time Landscape* stands as a living urban monument to the ecological art movement, reconnecting life to the canvas that is nature.

In developing an interactive nature-specific dialogue, rooted in actual experience in a given place and time, with nature the essential material and ingredient of the process, contemporary artists are following these and other examples by developing a new language of expression. The emphasis is holistic and bio-regional. Above all, it displays a respect for our integral connectedness to the environment. The earth is a living, breathing organism whose elements—climate, geography, geology, and other life forms—are an inviolable part of the human creative process. The land is no longer just a subject that we represent through art.

In an ephemeral sculpture garden, links are established between human culture and the culture of nature. Elements from nature are the paint, and nature is the canvas. Artists are the catalysts. There is no subject or object. This earth-sensitive language of expression is tactile and physical, playing visually with various organic and inorganic elements in a given site. The creative growth experience is interactive. As we enhance our understanding of nature's place in our society, our civilization, and our personal lives, we better understand that our future inevitably involves understanding and respecting natural processes.

Sculpture always has a landscape within it, an experience drawn from nature. When a sculpture embodies a landscape while actually being in it, the challenge

Nils-Udo, *Clemson Clay Nest*, 2005. Red clay, pine, and green bamboo, 20 x 35 ft. diameter. View of work at the South Carolina Botanical Garden.

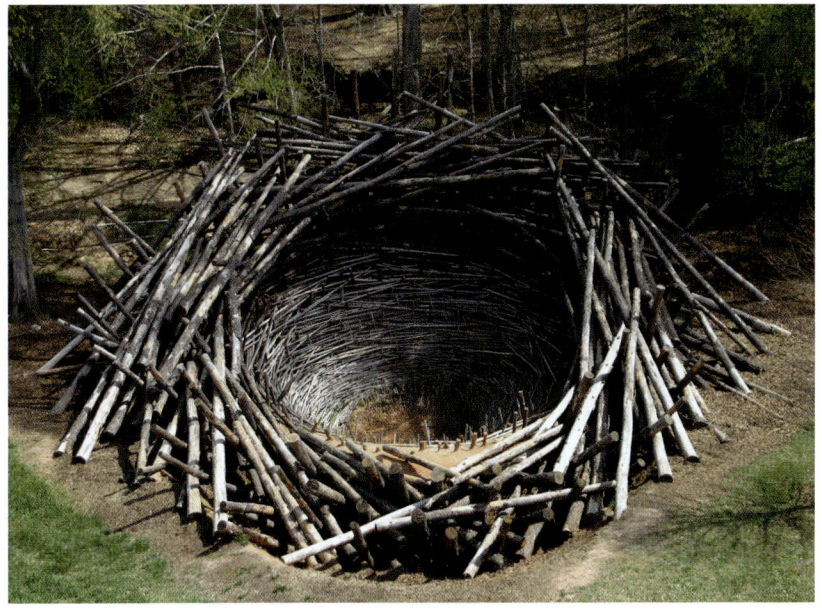

becomes broader, involving aspects of architecture, aesthetics, landscaping, and creative and individual expression. Earth-specific sculpture is the landscape. The South Carolina Botanical Garden (SCBG) is one of the largest permanent sites devoted to art in the land in eastern North America. It is a living laboratory of natural and human-built structures, supporting "extended ephemeral" projects. The structures evolve, integrate into, and gradually return to nature. The art is site specific but exists in a general garden framework. SCBG offers a prime example of the ephemeral sculpture garden, with works by Nils-Udo, Yolanda Gutiérrez, Chris Drury, and Yvette Dede and Hiroko Inuoe. Kathleen Gilrain's *Impressions of Lost Life* (2000), deep in the forest, evoked the cycle of life and death as it was allowed to decay. North Carolina native Patrick Dougherty, like Herb Parker and Brian Rust, has created two works in the park.

Danish environmental artist Alfio Bonanno, who created a work at SCBG in 1997, is also the founder of the ephemeral sculpture garden TICKON, on the island of Langeland in Denmark. Another pioneering institution, TICKON includes works by David Nash, Bonanno, Sonfist, and many others. Layers of perception intertwine with differing visions of what landscape, or cultivation, or wilderness might be, but they all share cultural commonalities whatever the origin of the artists or viewers. The same is true of the Forest of Dean Sculpture Trust, with its unique regeneration of an abandoned mining site as an art nature trail.

Preservation and conservation are terms reserved for purists in the art world, while perpetuation and consecration of nature's role in our lives are the values used by ephemeral sculpture gardens in their living sculpture laboratories. The selection of works, the acceptance of the continuum of life, and the gradual transformation process all involve patience and perseverance, and a little help from friends, students, and local residents. One of the newest ephemeral sculpture collections was recently launched by the Virginia B. Fairbanks Art & Nature Park at the Indianapolis Museum of Art. Ten artists and collectives—Haluk Akakçe, Kendall Buster, Sam Easterson, Peter Eisenman, Alfredo Jaar, Tea Mäkipää, Andrea Zittel, Atelier Van Lieshout, Los Carpinteros, and Type A—have been awarded the first commissions to create site-specific work designed for the park's 100 acres of untamed woodlands, wetlands, lake, and meadows. Mary Miss is undertaking the first permanent project, an elevated bridge and walkway that will descend through the tree canopy and serve as a pedestrian gateway between the museum's major buildings and the park. Other, smaller-scale ventures have been undertaken at the Centre of Art and Nature in Lillehammer, Norway; the Centre Art Terre in the Laurentians in Canada; the Grizedale Forest Trail in England; the Tree Museum near Bracebridge, Ontario; the Lough Boora Parklands in Tullamore, Co. Offaly, Ireland; Connells Bay Centre for Sculpture on Waiheke Island, New Zealand; and England's Gunpowder Park, where 90 hectares were recently set aside for land regeneration and innovative science and art. Gunpowder's site, near London, features out-

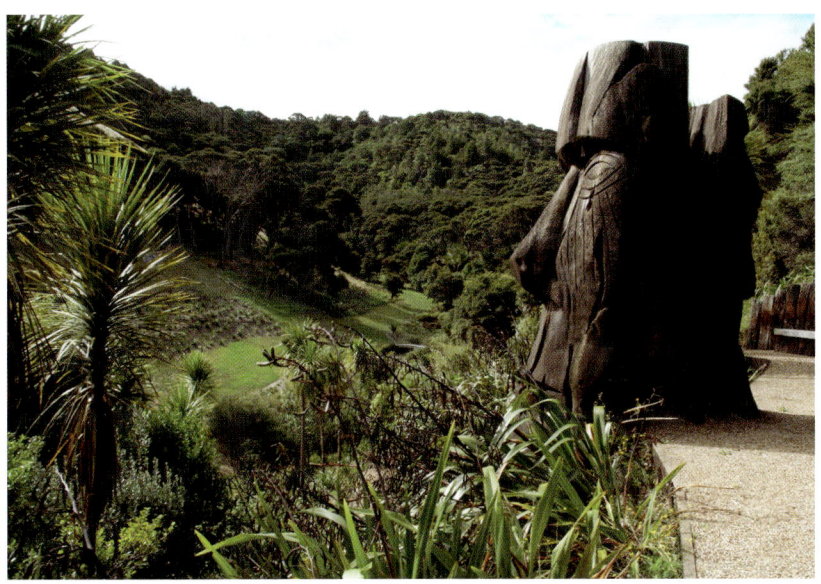

Fatu Feu'u, *Guardian of the Planting*, 1999. Macrocarpa stump, 600 x 190 x 210 cm. View of work at the Connells Bay Centre for Sculpture, New Zealand.

door ephemeral sculpture, performance, and educational biodiversity projects. Le Vent des Forêts in Lorraine, France, has sponsored an ephemeral sculpture and residency program since 1997; more than 140 works have been created and installed along a 45-kilometer stretch linking six rural villages, including Fresnes-au-Mont. And Quebec's Jardin de Métis, bordering the St. Lawrence river estuary, is a truly beautiful summer initiative involving artist/architect groups.

The Irwell Sculpture Trail and CITE, based in Greater Manchester, provide an alternative model to traditional sculpture park organization. A public art commissioning and advisory agency that advocates art in the public realm, especially in the context of urban and rural regeneration, CITE specializes in public art strategy, project management, and artistic direction for public art commissions. It also commissions ephemeral works for the 30-mile-long Irwell Sculpture Trail, which extends along the River Irwell and passes through a variety of locations—from rural Lancashire to former industrial sites leading to Salford, a former mill city next to Manchester. Participating artists range from recent graduates to internationally recognized sculptors.

Yatoo, a South Korean artist collective, has generated works with a culture-specific response to nature for more than two decades. In Gongju, an old city of the Baekche Kingdom where nature has played a role throughout history, it is understood that human culture and nature are intertwined, and this is how Yatoo's sculpture site

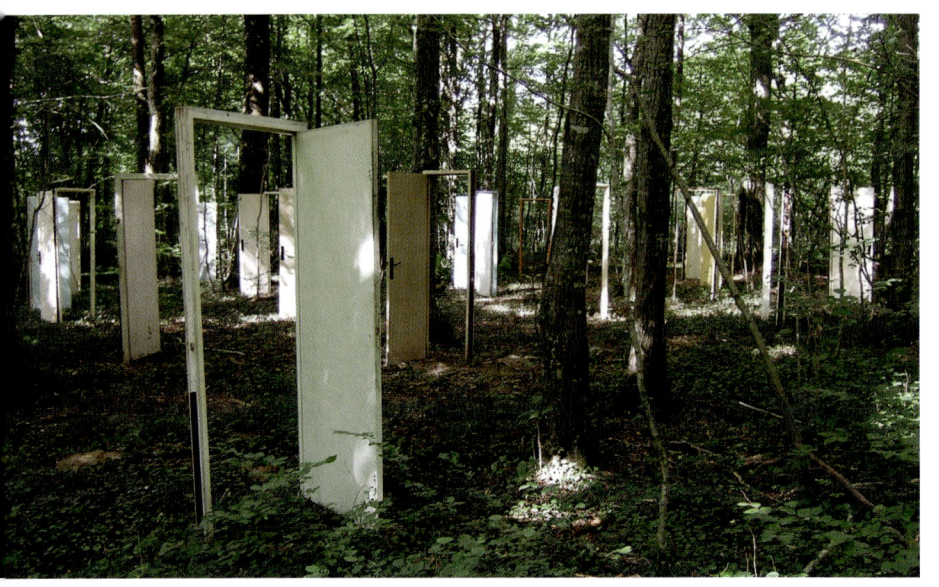

Igor Antic, *Paysage multiplié*, 2007. 40 doors and metal rods, installation view. View of work at Le Vent des Forêts, France.

has evolved. The history of nature parallels human history: each influences the other. Yatoo has embarked on a journey that involves exploring materials from nature within the context of nature. And this brings a new accent to the world of art, to the context of nature, for Yatoo explores a living history with precise and diverse expressions.

Each artist invited to Yatoo has a voice that works through nature as a medium. As Yatoo has evolved over the past 25 years, its realizations have challenged assumptions about what fine art is or can be in today's society. Nature participates in this ongoing performance, a theater of life with rhythms and principles of birth, growth, and dissolution. This cycle continues to evolve, as the art evolves. There is no final point to the process, something the Yatoo group understands. Ko Seung-hyun, Kang Hee-joon, Ri Eung-Woo, Ko Hyun-hee, Kim Hae-sim, Jeong Jang-jig, and Lee Jong-hyub, original members in 1985, have evolved their vision to embrace a broader scale, leaving traces around the world. They offer an exchange of aesthetic ideas, demonstrating that an understanding of ephemeral beauty is essential to a sustaining art.

The same might be said of Arte Sella, which is sited in the woods of Borgo Valsugana, Italy (near Trento). Founded in 1986, this art and nature park emphasises process and experimentation over the idea of finished works. Like many similar venues, Arte Sella sponsors artists to create new works in dialogue with the site and rarely shows works that use artificial materials. Its annual exhibitions have maintained a balance between Italian artists and international participants, and at the end, while some works are moved to the gallery space, many are left to decay. In the words of Laura Tomaselli, "Nature in the Val di Sella is powerful, austere, silent, and authoritative. The centuries-old trees, the rugged rocks, and the water, which flows and emerges unexpectedly, inspire in those who contemplate them and adventure toward them a certain awe and respect. The works of Arte Sella are given up to nature, which in time takes them over and changes them."*

The ephemeral sculpture garden brings together natural history and human aesthetics in an unusual collaboration, an aesthetic of the future. Bio-specific prototypes for creativity are more than just a principle. Ephemeral sculpture gardens go further than the traditional Japanese Garden aesthetic, for they enable nature to participate in the design and to be a growing part of the process. This is an ethic that many designers, landscape architects, and artists are now considering an essential part of future design. The ephemeral sculpture garden is a living laboratory that is truly environmental. Its earth-sensitive principles can be adapted to any area of endeavor. Beyond this, such artworks and sculpture parks demonstrate the practical role of aesthetics in providing us with imaginative and beautiful examples of environmental integration.

Notes

* Laura Tomaselli, Arte Sella brochure, 2000, pp. 11–12.

TICKON and Sculpture in Nature's Eyes: A Conversation with Alfio Bonanno

by John K. Grande

A pioneer of the site-specific nature installation, Alfio Bonanno uses nature's materials, cutting, lifting, carrying, bending, and placing them. Ephemeral and earthbound, his works establish links with nature and remind us that it is both a spiritual source and practical provider for humanity's needs. When he arrived in Denmark (he was born in Italy and grew up in Australia) in the 1970s, with roots in Arte Povera's nonconformist use of materials, Bonanno was one of the first to involve himself in art actions that created art with and within nature's sphere. The founder of TICKON (Tranekær International Center for Art and Nature) in Langeland, Denmark—a venue that has attracted many of the world's leading artists to work on site in natural settings—Bonanno has extended his message beyond his own outdoor installations, encouraging other artists to work with found natural materials and introducing viewers to new ways of experiencing art in the landscape. His concerns are as much social as environmental.

The environmental artworks at TICKON continue the traditional practice on the site: historically the Counts of Tranekær used the island of Langeland to create an interaction between the manmade and the organic by planting and shaping the existing landscape. In 1990, Count Preben Ahlefeldt-Laurvig passed the initiative on to Bonanno and his small group of like-minded supporters, donating 60 acres of land surrounding Tranekær Castle for the exhibition of artwork deeply engaged with nature. TICKON, the resulting nonprofit foundation, commissions site-specific environmental sculptures. It is not an institution in the usual sense, but a project that brings Danish and international artists to work in Tranekær's park.

TICKON is more like an untamed forest than a manicured garden; visitors encounter art by walking along a wandering path through wooded areas, pastures, and around a lake across from the castle. With a common passion for nature as animating force and starting point, selected artists have integrated their work into the surroundings. For some, the interposition is so cautious that only a photograph bears witness to it, while others build with natural materials that will grow or pass away, and still others use bones, stone, words, or the whispering of the wind.

To launch the park, Bonanno and the TICKON committee invited 16 European and American artists to create site-specific works on the grounds. The park was conceived from the beginning as an ongoing project, with new artists invited on a regular basis to make both permanent and ephemeral works. The first group of artists in 1993 reads like a Who's Who of art in nature, including Andy Goldsworthy, Chris Drury, David

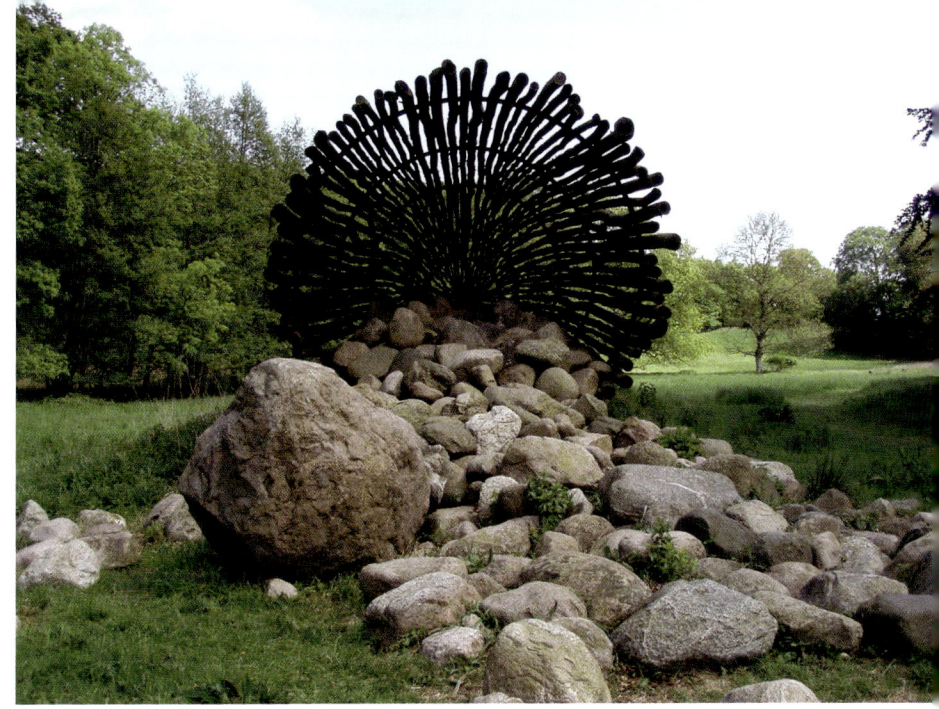

Alfio Bonanno, *Between copper beech and oak*, 2001. Charred larch, steel rings, and granite boulders, 12 meters long.

Nash, Alan Sonfist, Jussi Heikkilä, Nils-Udo, and Herman de Vries. Patrick Dougherty, Steven Siegel, and Marc Barbarit have also worked at the park. Bonanno is currently working to expand the park's scope to include a center for art, nature, and science.

John Grande: After World War II, at the age of 19, you returned from Australia to Contrada d'Urne in Sicily. In the spring of 1966, after a landslide, you discovered a beautiful amphora uncovered by the natural disaster. But when you tried to remove it, the terra cotta crumbled back into the earth, just a stain in the mud. This trace of ancient history—seen, then returned to nature—must have left a lasting impression. Such ephemerality is the foundation of your sculpture, and of your efforts at TICKON.

Alfio Bonanno: I have always been fascinated by traces in the landscape, something that tells a story you can build on. It gives meaning to our existence. That particular instance must have left something with me; it was so full of symbolism. When I helped my father build stone walls to prevent erosion, we often found pieces of ancient pottery. Water was collected there way back in time.

JG: Your project at the Miró Museum in 1985 was a breakthrough, bringing much-needed attention at a time when environmental art was less recognized than it is today.

AB: The Miró Museum gave me the opportunity to create a three-week installation at its Espace 10. This was my international debut, and since I was struggling with nature work, it was very important. I invited my friend, Danish composer Gunner Moller Petersen to create a composition called *A Sound Year*. This six-hour composition tells the story of the changing seasons with electronic sound. It's very beautiful, very realistic but also artificially created. It was an ongoing installation that moved from the summer through to the autumn, winter, and spring. We used animals, birds, fruit, plants — everything related to nature. I did line drawings with branches. These natural objects are signs and symbols that inspire me to imagine that they were a basis for our language.

JG: The language of your sculpture, your use of all manner of natural materials, carries traces of human involvement, of individual expression. You do not segregate nature from human activity.

AB: I am saying, "Look at this stone, look at this tree." I like to touch things, to smell things. I like to be in the middle of things. That is why I am working out there and not in galleries. For me, the strongest form of expression is out there where the work is born, where it belongs, in real life. That is where it collects its strength, even more so because it is vulnerable. Site-specific work outdoors has a life and participates.

JG: Having worked 30 years with environmental art, what can you say about its evolution?

AB: I began working in the natural environment because I couldn't do without it. I needed it, my body needed it, my mind needed it. I was curious. I didn't do it because of the art, and that's crucial. A lot of art today is being done for the exhibition. Though I am not free of that, going out and working in an open environment is a powerful and demanding experience, and not only in "natural" landscape.

I have a lot of respect for my surroundings and everything that's in them, ourselves included. That doesn't mean I hold back. I intervene, but it has to fit in. Even if it stands out, it's got to have a feeling of belonging in some way. Far too much sculpture and installation work imposes itself on a site or is just placed there. Siting is very important: a site is my collaborating partner. When a work is successful, it accentuates the feeling of a place. The work needs the site to breathe and function.

JG: What do you mean when you talk of art in nature being a silent revolution?

AB: I gave a lecture in Copenhagen to some students and younger artists a few years back. They asked, "Do you really mean that you create sculpture because you respect nature and your environment. Is that it?" And I said "Well, isn't that enough?" So much of the art being done seeks to be sensational: it has to be big, imposing, and monumental. Working with and within a natural environment, you learn to look and listen, to respect and appreciate simple moments of truth and participation. I am against signage, the artist's name or the title. The works are almost anonymous, just there like everything else. It is a form of expression that reaches out to a very broad and growing public audience, many of whom have never set foot in a gallery or museum. Here, we have a basis for a true and much-needed natural dialogue. It is a silent but determined revolution.

JG: Public participation is a part of many of your projects.

AB: The public is part of the process, whether it be in the planning phase, during, or after completion. It can involve politicians, organizers, helpers, assistants, the art world, and the local population. Involvement of a broad range of people is an important aspect of site-specific environmental art.

JG: At the Botanical Gardens in Copenhagen, you built a series of islands out of fresh willow and sycamore branches for the animals and birds, a strategy that David Nash also followed in his *Sheep Fold* at TICKON. Less concerned with aesthetics than functionality, this language is more vernacular, like a dialect spoken in materials. Are you something of a primitive in your approach?

AB: I do feel a little bit like a primitive. Sometimes I get accused of being naive. The art world seems to want another type of expression, and it totally ignored the floating island project. The most important thing was that the terrapin turtles climbed up and sunbathed on the islands and birds built their nests on them. The islands were con-

Alan Sonfist, *Maze of great oak of Denmark within stone ship—1001 young trees*, 1993. Granite boulders and trees, 25 x 55 meters.

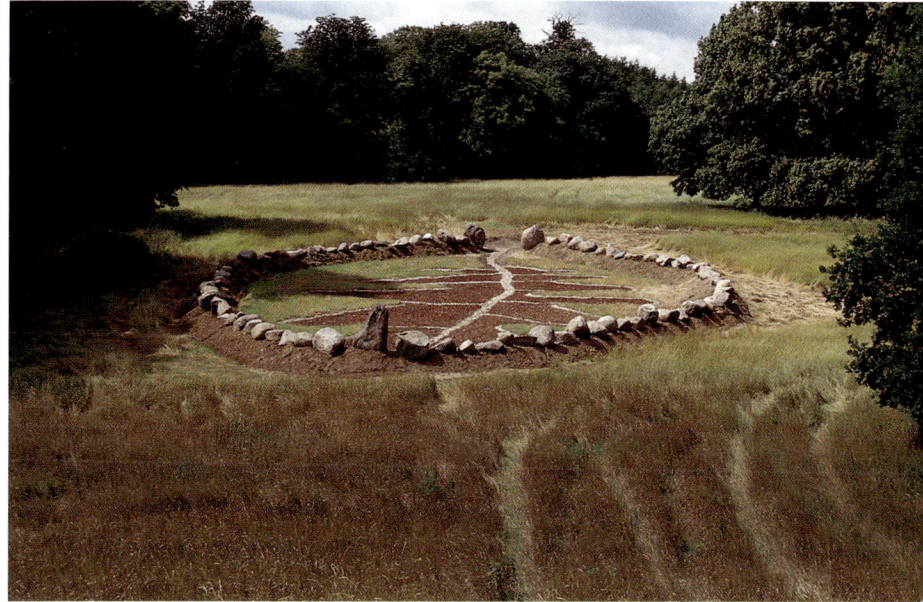

structed in a simple and practical way for use and growth — that was the point — not to create an aesthetic and artificial form so that we (not the turtles) had an excuse to call it art.

Over the years, I have found that waiting to see a site before deciding is important. Each site has its own story to tell. If I am patient, something happens. After a day or two, or an hour or two, I connect with the site, and it tells me what to do. The key to what I have to do is there, I just have to find it.

JG: How do people perceive nature and nature art differently now, compared to your experience in the 1970s, the '80s, the '90s?

AB: Nature art has now become an explosion. Everyone is playing around with natural elements. People are doing nature sculpture as they would go into a studio and paint. But one has to understand the processes involved — feel the necessity — most of all because it's a living space. Nature demands more attention and respect. Some younger artists are doing interesting work that reflects the technological world — but nature as they conceive it is more like a virtual reality. I feel this work has a nostalgic touch — almost the feeling of something lost — that is cold and clinical, reflecting a distance from the nature they represent. A growing global awareness about our environment brings a focus on ecological balance. Bells are ringing, warning us about our existence and survival. It is fascinating that we can simultaneously discuss the serious problem of the ozone hole and its consequences while preparing to send tourists for a week in space in orbiting hotels, at a cost of $50,000–$100,000 per person. We humans are, and always will be, the most complex, destructive, and unpredictable species.

JG: At Odense in 1995, with the Centre for Landscape, Environment and Culture in the 21st Century, you proposed a pilot project involving a huge abandoned garbage dump that serves 200,000 citizens. The goal of this ongoing project is to emphasize recycling, redevelopment, and interdisciplinary co-operation, with art as the catalyst. From the air, the dump and the sculpted landscape are intended to have distinct visual components created out of garbage. Local citizens are to be involved throughout. Fragments of industrial waste are to become freeform sculptural elements. Barges will be used to transport people to the site. Garbage becomes the spectacle, the focus for public participation, involvement, and tourism. How is the project progressing?

AB: The Odense project is huge. I have been involved with it for the last six years. Instead of hiding garbage, we would make it precious, something to discuss and to dialogue on. This is why we are hoping to make a huge cut in the dump, like an entrance to an amphitheater. We want to bring in huge elements, pieces of machinery, pieces of airplanes, and cranes, to enhance the visual aspect of the landscape so it tells a story. People have to be reminded that we are a wasteful society, that we consume a lot and have serious problems getting rid of our garbage. There is always the danger that the dump might become a superficial cultural landscape where people will jog or have art and sculpture exhibitions.

JG: The vernacular language of your art, and the kind of art you support at TICKON, is closer to native Amerindian arts. It's inclusive, an expression of the contemporaneity of nature in today's world.

AB: I am proud that you say that. It's a privilege and an honor. A lot of art critics do not understand that. It has to do with the respect for things. One of the most important things I have learned over the years is to rely on my instincts. They will pull me through, and that is human and universal.

<http://turist.langeland.dk/?vm=6361>

The Tree Museum, Canada

by Gil McElroy

In her 1968 hit song "Big Yellow Taxi," Joni Mitchell mourns the "paving of paradise," noting that "they took all the trees / put 'em in a tree museum / and charged the people / a dollar and half just to see 'em." About 100 miles north of Toronto lies the real Tree Museum, in a region of lakes and forest known as the Muskokas. For over 100 years, it's been a popular vacation retreat for urban Torontonians seeking to escape the summer heat. It's an area of golf courses, upscale cottages and resorts, camping sites, motels, and cabins. This is Cottage Country, and up here, the trees are free for the seeing, as is the Tree Museum itself.

The museum is located not far from the small town of Gravenhurst, best known as the birthplace of Dr. Norman Bethune, inventor of the mobile blood bank during the Spanish Civil War and later a hero of the Chinese Revolution. A sign at the edge of a secondary highway just south of town marks the Tree Museum's entrance, but it's a long walk into the woods along a winding dirt road, past a beaver dam that prevents a large pond from inundating a low-lying section of the only way in and out. A small house and some outbuildings are located at the end of the road, set on the shore of Ryde Lake. At various sites on the property, site-specific installations by a select group of contemporary Canadian artists are installed.

The museum is the brainchild of a handful of Ontario-based artists who banded together as the Tree Museum Collective in 1997, when they were offered use of this northern Ontario property owned by Mentor College, a private school located just outside of Toronto. The collective's first exhibition, mounted a year later, consisted of works by three artists spread across the Ryde Lake property. Not surprisingly, site-specificity was critical to the exhibition's success; the site's geological and topographical features—such as its many granite outcroppings, scoured clean and striated by retreating glaciers at the end of the last Ice Age—come heavily into sculptural play. For instance, in *Danse* (1998–99), Tim Whiten sandblasted four separate life-size figures—dancing skeletons, actually—into the exposed surface of a large, gently rounded granite hillock. Situated to denote the four cardinal points of the magnetic compass, his figures, though inspired by Hans Holbein's *Dance of Death*, have a more compelling relationship with the petroglyphs etched by ancient aboriginal peoples into rock surfaces at numerous sites not too far distant from here.

Badanna Zack's *A Mound of Cars* (1998) is, in many ways, Western culture's contemporary equivalent to petroglyphs. Using a number of abandoned cars found on site, which she stacked into a heap one atop the other, Zack created an enormous dirt- and sod-covered pyramid that she then sliced in half lengthwise, revealing the interior

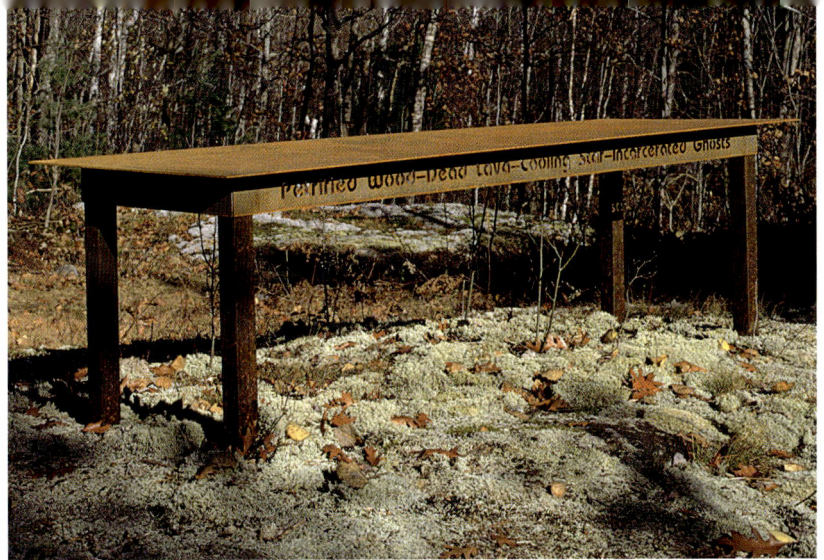

Anne O'Callaghan, *Relic of Memory,* 1998. Welded steel table with laser-cut table, 2.5 x 8 x 2.8 ft.

layers of rusted and wrecked automobile bodies like exposed geological strata. Zack's piece echoes the geological processes that, over the course of eons, have given particular shape to this part of Canada. At the same time, it critiques a mentality that views natural sites, wherever they might be found, as little more than dumping grounds for all things toxic, obsolete, or merely unwanted. Archaeological overtones abound in *A Mound of Cars*, pointed reminders of our species' need to comprehend the deeds and events of the past—our natural and cultural histories—in order to come to terms with the possible future.

Anne O'Callaghan's *Relic of Memory* (1998) thematically extends the evocation of the historical processes at play along the shores of Ryde Lake. A long, low rectangular steel table—rusted from its exposure to the elements—sits on the high side of a sloped clearing in the bush atop moss-encrusted rock. A text is etched into the side of the table, words identifying some of the previous inhabitants of this place ("Huron—Hatherly—Ruttan") and words denoting more poetic elements of its natural history ("Petrified Wood—Dead Lava—Cooling Star"). Farther down the grade from the table, O'Callaghan has installed a skeletal framework of two rusted steel arches held together by a connecting ridge pole, minimally forging architectural allusions, perhaps, to early aboriginal structures, as well as to the homes long abandoned by settlers unable to make a go of it in this difficult land, buildings left to stand vacant as nature, abhorring the vacuum, slowly reclaims that which it had temporarily been denied.

Since that first exhibition of three site-specific works, the Tree Museum has grown to include works by 35 artists, including Robert Wiens's *Log II* (1999), a sculpture formed of tree branches and twigs bundled and woven together to resemble a

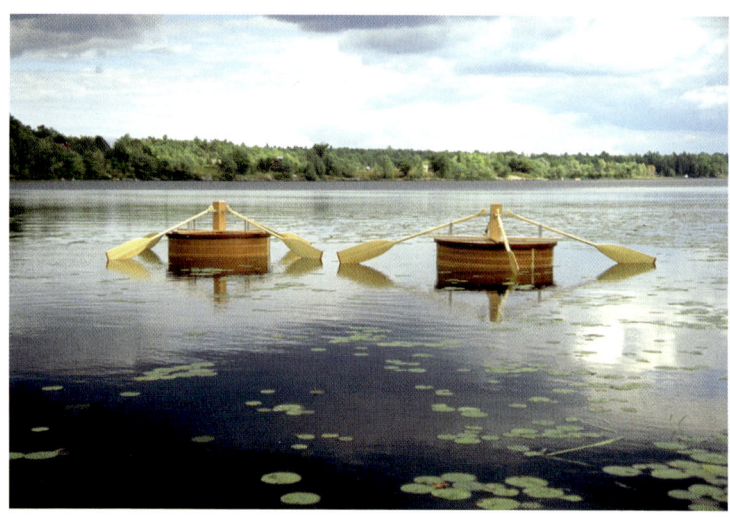

Lois Andison and Simone Jones, *Tidal Pool: Ode to Tom Thomson*, 2001. Wooden basins, paddles, custom hardware, motors, and custom electronics, installation view.

section of fallen tree in the midst of a small clearing near the lake shore. The 2002 exhibition, "Finding the Intimate in Nature," added works by Ellen Dijkstra, who is accustomed to an always-inhabited Dutch pastoral landscape, and Lyla Rye, who grew up in Canada's vast expanses of wilderness. More recent shows have featured Catherine Widgery, Ryszard Litwiniuk, Nancy Paterson, Barry Prophet, John Dickson, and Diane Borsato, among others. In 2007, Michael Belmore, Noel Harding, Jaffa Laam, Wen-Chih Wang, EJ Lightman, and Persona Volare contributed works to "What is Place."

In 2001, Reinhard Reitzenstein came to the Tree Museum to build *Shed*. Working on an open section of the property some distance off the main road, he constructed a small shed using materials found on site, covering its front with a façade of wooden disks cut from poplar logs to evoke the idea of the quintessential "log cabin." He then skewered the whole thing, puncturing the building with an entire poplar tree—branches and all—inserted through one side and out the roof. Out of true and out of place, the poplar "world tree" grows up through that which it might otherwise shelter, wreaking structural and cultural havoc like some mythologically demented 21st-century version of Tzuk-Te, the Mayan world tree, or Yggdrasil, the Norse equivalent. No matter our efforts to push or hold back the wild—to "pave paradise"—in the end, it seems, the trees will always have the final say.

<www.thetreemuseum.ca>

The Forest of Dean Sculpture Trail

by John K. Grande

Nestled in the Gloucester region bordering Wales and Hereford in the lower Wye Valley, a longtime mining area now returned to forest, the Forest of Dean Sculpture Trail features works by some of England's most recognized sculptors. Jeremy Rees, the founder of Bristol's Arnolfini Gallery, whose background was in forestry, brought enthusiastic support to the sculpture trail concept as it emerged in 1982. Martin Orrom, also with a forestry background, Rees, and Rupert Martin, the Arnolfini's curator, collaboratively guided and organized the early stages of the trail, introducing a group of exceptional works. While some have since disappeared into nature, others remain, and the trail occupies an important position among Britain's diverse sculpture parks.

The flame-like sheaves of metal in Cornelia Parker's *Hanging Fire* (1986) hang majestically to form a crown around a tree trunk. *Melissa's Swing* by Peter Appleton consists of a suspended sound sculpture named for the sculptor's daughter. The intimate and personal character of this sculpture park, where big names co-exist with new and emerging artists, makes it one of Britain's most significant contemporary venues for sculpture and performance events. Nature interacts with the art in ingenious and fascinating ways, and the siting of works reinforces the diverse range of styles and techniques.

One of the major features in the park is a group of part-process, part-entropic David Nash pieces, most notably *Black Dome* (1986), which emphasizes identification with the land, site, and a nature-specific aesthetic. Consisting of 900 pieces of charred larch, Nash's work was inspired by old charcoal hearths. As a sculpture that will return to nature, decaying gradually over time, it carries a cadence of natural majesty within its creation and eventual disappearance. Nash states, "The Forest of Dean [has] a long history of charcoal manufacture. I conceived making a mound out of charcoal, a brittle material. The whole idea was that it would rot down to a mound of humus and that only certain plants could grow on it." A debate still continues as to whether *Black Dome* should be preserved or simply left to dissolve, and it has been partially covered with ash to make it safer should passersby attempt to walk on it. Nash's *Fire and Water Boats* (1986), sited near a stream, has already been restored, the original elements replaced by the sculptor after they disintegrated.

A sculpture by Keir Smith also recalls the region's industrial past. In *Iron Road*, 20 jarrah wood railway sleepers appropriated from a disused regional rail line have been carved into a poetic expression that relates the past of the forest to its present. Here, the artist becomes a filter and sounding board, directing our attention to unseen

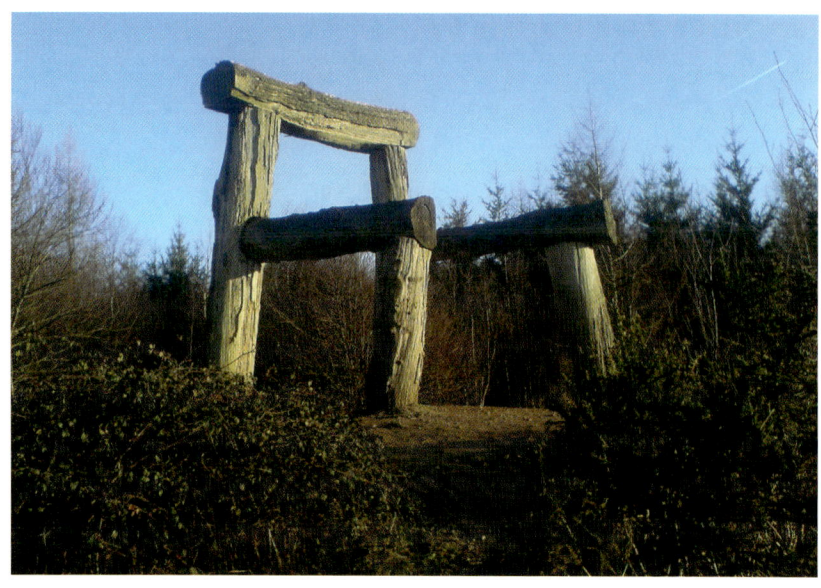

Magdalena Jetelová, *Place*, 1986. Oak, approximately 14 x 14 ft.

histories. Bruce Allan's *Observatory* (1986) contributes a surreal-looking set of stairs to the setting. One steps up only to catch a glimpse of a pond that itself is not a natural feature, but a water-filled scow or sink hole: nature returns to what was once a mine site, transforming it yet again. An early Sophie Ryder deer stands nearby.

Ian Hamilton Finlay applied incised stone plaques in different languages to the trees that form *Grove of Silence* (1986). Peter Randall-Page's large-scale *Cone and Vessel*, created from a Scots pine and an oak, draws attention to the tiny fragile shapes that exist in nature. His intricate interpretation of a pine cone and acorn cup reside under their respective trees. Set in the forest along a pathway, Kevin Atherton's stained-glass work reinforces the cathedral-like aura of the forest canopy.

In her conceptual intervention, Erika Tan has introduced non-indigenous, cast bronze bamboo forms into the forest; they have the look of artifacts from a lost civilization. Sited imposingly on a hill from which one can see the other side of the valley and sense the scale of the land, Magdalena Jetelová's *Place* (1986) resembles a giant's chair, evoking folktales and rusticity. The bird houses in Ingemar Thalin's *Life Cycle* (2002, now destroyed by vandalism) sheltered photographs offered by local residents, going beyond the simple object and integration with nature to introduce a social component into the sculpture park. In another symbolic sculptural action, Carole Drake buried five steel plates in the forest floor. The effect suggested the way that nature can capture, conceal, and subsume human history.

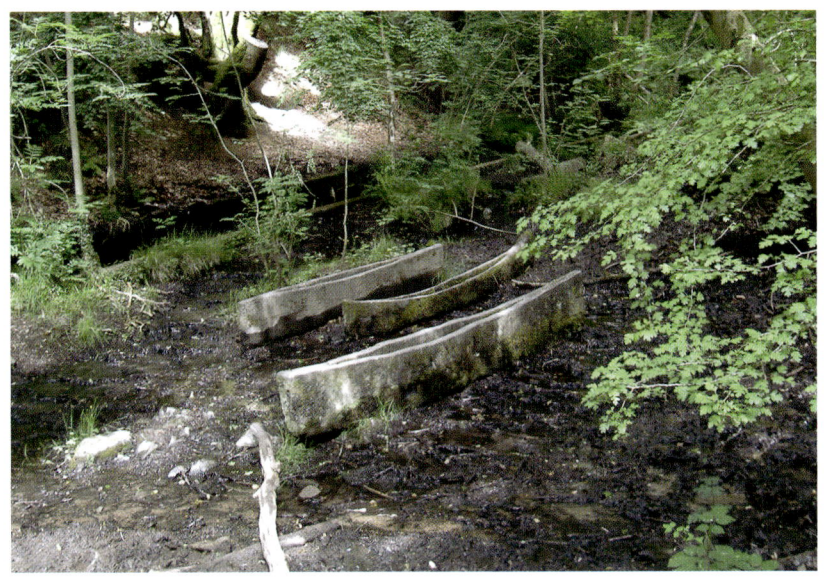

David Nash, *Fire and Water Boats*, 1986. Charred oak, installation view.

Set high up in the forest, Miles Davies's *House* (1988) almost resembles a mineshaft heading in the wrong direction—upwards. Usually a domestic image, this house alludes to the industrial, and the occasional clanging of steel can disorient visitors. Neville Gabie's *Raw* (2001) is cut into a Navy oak that once formed part of a stand of trees planted in the Napoleonic era. An oak was selected and felled, and its absence opened a space in the canopy above. Gabie dug up the ground where the oak had stood to create a space that evokes the vast volume of water consumed by such a tree. He then decided to build a perfect cube of oak, a solid block of matter, by cutting sections of the tree by hand and fitting them together like a Post-Minimalist jigsaw puzzle.

While maintaining existing works has been a primary concern, the Forest of Dean Sculpture Trail has now entered a new phase. Sculptors and performance artists participated in a recent "Reveal" event on the grounds, and Erika Tan and Jane Spray recently contributed ephemeral sculpture interventions along the trail. New proposals are being solicited from artists for the forest's nature/culture experiment; Annie Cattrell was commissioned in 2007 to create a permanent work in the park, commemorating Rees. The Forest of Dean is a place where nature and culture intertwine in an intricate, historically real way.

<www.forestofdean-sculpture.org.uk>

Sculpture in Woodland

by Robert Preece

The entrance to Sculpture in Woodland is so discreet that we almost missed it entirely. Traveling with a Dublin-based college friend, I rode through the rolling, green Irish countryside, which looked like something straight out of a tourist brochure. Suddenly, our taxi screeched to a halt: we saw the artwork through the trees. Situated about 20 miles south of Dublin in County Wicklow, "The Project"—as it is affectionately called—is a special treat hidden away in a forest. In fact, it has maintained such a quiet profile that a local paper called it the area's "secret gallery."

Established in 1994, Sculpture in Woodland features site-specific work selected to "create a greater awareness of wood as an artistic and functional medium" and "to establish a wood culture through the medium of sculpture." It is located in a 600-acre public forest called Devil's Glen, which is owned and managed by Coillte—a semi-state body responsible for Ireland's woodlands. According to former administrator Ciara King, "The idea was the brainchild of former Coillte forestry consultants Martin Sheridan and Donal Magner. They thought it would be a very exciting idea because it centers around wood and incorporates artistic, social, and forestry concerns."

At present, the project includes 18 commissioned works by sculptors from Ireland, England, France, Portugal, Latvia, Canada, Mexico, Japan, and the Republic of Korea. Two curving, pillar-like forms flank the entrance to Devil's Glen. *Antaeus*

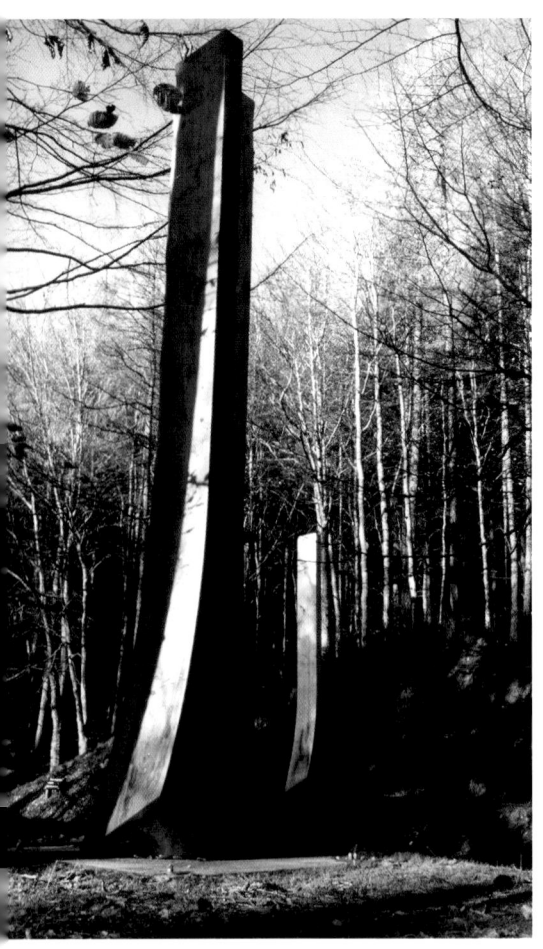

Michael Warren, *Antaeus*, 1998. European larch and poplar, 18 ft. high.

(1998), by Irish sculptor Michael Warren, refers to the mythical Greek giant who remained invincible—as long as some part of his body was in contact with the earth. The poplar and larch work emphasizes the verticality of the surrounding trees, its carved expression playing off the more natural forms, and may suggest the bond between trees and the earth.

For new visitors, finding the works becomes a treasure hunt. There are no markings, and the brochure doesn't have a map. On our one-mile journey to the parking lot, we discovered two works flanking the road. On the left, an untitled work (1996) by Mexico's Jorge du Bon sticks out off a bluff, resembling an extended telescope, raised and pointed like a cannon. For du Bon, "The structure is realized by means of cuts in an intellectual process. The dead tree comes back into a new life when nature cannot keep it anymore." We imagined the work as protecting the forest, looking out at the encroaching development beyond. It also draws an implied line across the road to Maurice MacDonagh's *Round* (1996), which is concerned with the mass, density, and gravity of trees. For MacDonagh, "*Round* takes the form of a large charred minimal cylinder constructed from concentric circles of Sitka spruce. This follows the process by which the tree itself forms wood and underlines the theme of the work—exploring the nature and substance of trees and how we experience them."

Further along at the car park and adjacent picnic area, two works stand assertively. Jacques Bosser's *Chago* (1997) is a 415-centimeter-high, thin, rectangular sculpture made from European larch. It refers to an African god of fire, who "appears, leaving in

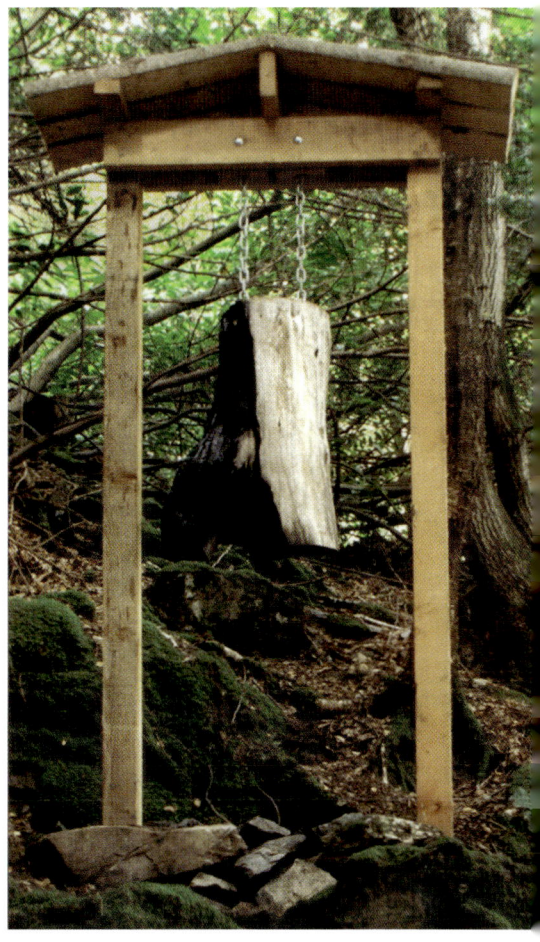

Kat O'Brien, *Seven Shrines—Na Seachta Scrinta*, 1996. Maple, silver fir, Douglas fir, sycamore, and Sitka spruce, seven elements, 10 x 4 x 1 ft. each.

his wake large blackened and burned-out tree trunks. To appease the gods, the locals insert pieces of metal in their wooden objects of worship and make a wish." Nearby, Derek Witticase—English-born and Irish-resident—installed *Pound* (1998), composed of 16 carved, organically shaped columns. Playful and magical, they appear almost out of a fairy tale. For Witticase, "The word 'pound' has connotations of weight, monetary value, a secure enclosure and force." The work is "about space being valuable and about valuing our environment."

Along a hidden path, we found Naomi Seki's untitled piece (1996), which recalls a machine with its rigid, implied rectangles and long boards extending outward suggesting motion. The Japanese artist says, "This work is concerned with visualizing the combination and balance of things—wood and wood—with different weights in different things." Kat O'Brien's *Seven Shrines* (1996) extends along the trail in seven accumulating "details," addressing "the seven generations born since the beginning of the Irish famine." Encountered in near darkness, the shrines looked haunted, with their flowing biomorphic forms suggesting a connection between tree and human trunks, and recalled the mystery of the forest at night.

Sculpture in Woodland has recently been granted charitable status by Ireland's revenue commissioners. At present, it is funded primarily by Ireland's Forest Service at the Department of Marine and Natural Resources, the Irish Art Council, Wicklow County Council, Coillte, and the Wicklow County Enterprise Board. Since 1999, as funding permits, three artists have been commissioned each year: an invited Irish artist, an invited international artist, and one artist selected by open competition.

According to King, "For the commissions, we've left it open. We don't want to restrict the artists. We are asking that it mainly be in wood, and that it is durable to survive for a minimum of 10 years. We aren't looking for temporary work at the moment because we are only getting the collection off the ground. Our other concern is safety, because it's a public park—for example we couldn't have sharp edges where people could get at them."

So, how long will Sculpture in Woodland remain a "secret gallery"? With recent efforts to raise the site's profile, probably not for long. As King says, "It's free, anyone can visit, and it's a beautiful setting." Indeed it is, and well worth the trip from Dublin—before the secret gets out.

<www.sculptureinwoodland.ie>

Wave Hill: Sculpture in the Garden

by Jonathan Goodman

One of New York City's most beautiful estates, Wave Hill has a long and distinguished history. Wave Hill House was originally built in 1843 by the jurist William Lewis Morris. Theodore Roosevelt's family rented Wave Hill during the summers of 1870 and 1871, when the future president was 12 and 13. (Roosevelt's stay is said to have increased his feeling for nature.) Mark Twain rented Wave Hill from 1901 through 1903, and Arturo Toscanini lived there from 1942 through 1945. Today the visual impact of the landscape remains remarkable: visitors walk along the Great Lawn and view the Hudson River and the Palisades beyond.

In 1960, Wave Hill was given to the City of New York; five years later, it became a nonprofit organization. Wave Hill is currently an institution dedicated to examining and creatively enabling an exchange between nature and people. Its 28 acres include gardens and greenhouses, and it sponsors diverse programs in horticulture, environmental education, land management, and the visual and performing arts. Early in Wave Hill's public history, it was used as a sculpture garden, with works from the collection of Joseph Hirshhorn installed on the grounds. Later, contemporary art programs were set up; until recently, these were fairly short lived. The current visual arts program, curated by Jennifer McGregor, is composed of three venues: the Glyndor Gallery, where thematic exhibitions of contemporary artists are shown; generated@wavehill, for which an on-site artist produces a landscape project every summer; and Wave Hill House Gallery, where four shows of emerging artists occur each year.

Willie Cole's *Everything and Anything* was the third generated@wavehill project (earlier installations were by Laura Anderson Barbata and Sylvia Benitez). Cole's installation was sited on the lawn next to the aquatic garden. Anything but natural, the work consisted of five rows of 10 white PVC turnstiles. Two of the center turnstiles were missing, enabling participants navigating the rows to pause and consider their position in a poetic, chance-filled maze.

The turnstiles functioned both as a reminder of city life—as McGregor pointed out, city dwellers use turnstiles to take the subway and to enter certain buildings—and as a maze with metaphorical meanings. As participants made their way through the turnstiles, they could read their inscriptions—almost 200 phrases beginning with "everything" or "anything": "everything you considered," "everything you think of," "anything believable," "anything fought for," and so on. A kind of poetry ensued, in which one made a series of choices to pass through a life maze. An urban piece sited in a green environment, the piece did not reference the grounds at all. Asked why it was so much at variance with its bucolic surroundings, McGregor replied, "Since we've had really wonderful pieces done with natural materials, we were looking more for an artist who would work with industrial or manmade materials. The earlier projects enabled visitors to experience the grounds, whereas Cole's work is an entirely different type of project."

Cole explained further: "I surprised people by requesting permission to dig holes in the ground. I wanted to do a whole field of the turnstiles; I also wanted a space in the middle so visitors could reach a clear spot and contemplate — even lie down so as to get a different view. But an entire field of turnstiles wasn't allowed." In fact, all of the outdoor pieces at Wave Hill must be approved by the horticulture department, which in this case limited the piece to 50 turnstiles. McGregor said: "When people come here and the grounds are beautiful, they think it's the perfect environment for sculpture. But it's really very challenging; the horticulture department sees the landscape in a certain way — for example, they see the way the curves of the foliage lead to the seating area of the grounds where Cole's piece has been placed. Part of their conception is based on the space surrounding the installation. Anything we put in the middle of the field is going to change the grounds, so what we're doing has to be temporal, has to come in and come out without a trace."

Members of the different departments are also involved with the artist-selection process. McGregor does some initial research and selects three artists to be inter-

Roberley Bell, *Arcadia Bell*, 2000. Steel, Astroturf, artificial flowers, and real flowers, dimensions variable.

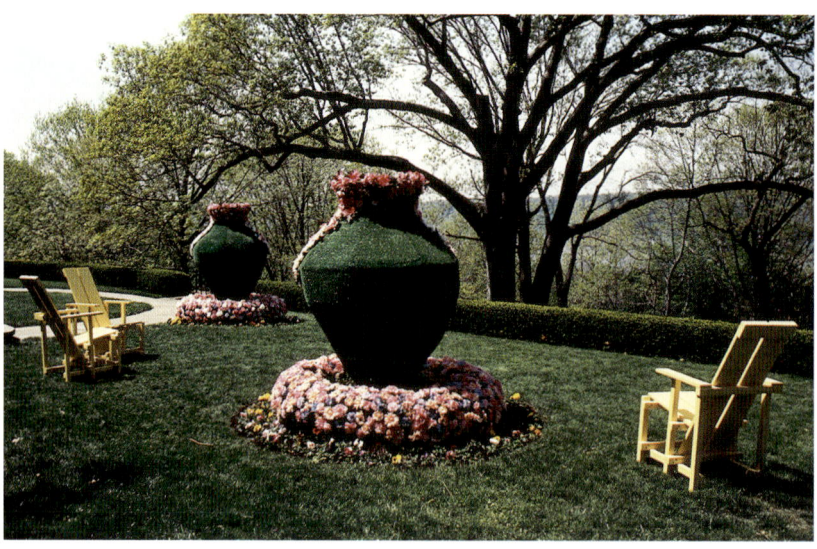

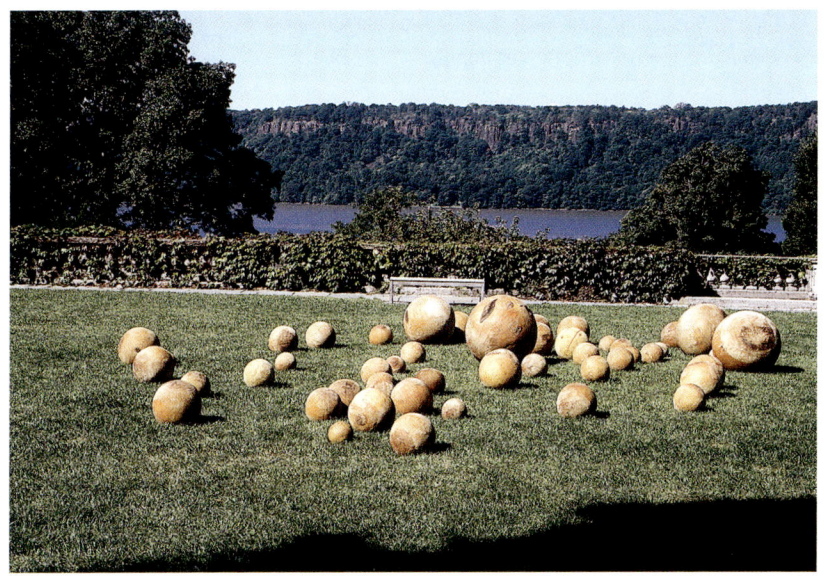

Luis Castro, *Ese Botero es mio (recordando Felipe Pirela)*, 2001. Maple, dimensions variable.

viewed by representatives of different departments, including, in the case of Cole, a member of the Forest Project Summer Collaborative work-study program for high school students from the Bronx (10 worked with Cole on his project), and, often, someone brought in from the outside. The artist talks about his or her idea for an outdoor piece, and then the group chooses an artist based on initial impressions. McGregor strongly emphasizes the cooperative nature of the Wave Hill projects: "I was really looking for a way that the visual arts program could interface with other departments; obviously, we're working with the education department really closely on this, as well as with the horticultural department."

Indeed, education is a major part of Wave Hill's mandate. The education program includes outdoor-based workshops for school children from the Bronx and other boroughs. There is also a learning center, used for school groups on weekdays and family projects on weekends, which acts an indoor interactive museum; other programs include craft projects, nature walks, and literary workshops. One of the most important and challenging interactions for artists working at Wave Hill is the Summer Collaborative project. Cole acknowledged the complexity of the experience: "It was a bit challenging to work with students. They are teenagers, so they weren't always driven by the same sense of urgency as I was. But, even so, several became very excited." As it turns out, the students' contributions were not only physical—they thought up many of the phrases used on the turnstiles.

McGregor said of her audience: "Many people come because they are interested in gardens. However…I [also] want Wave Hill to be a place for people to think about artists doing experimental work. We have a living environment that is always changing with the plants, and so there is no reason to have the sculpture hold us back. That's what I love about the way we're showing artists—we're responding to the way artists are working now." McGregor feels that maintaining permanent works on site fixes the collection to a particular moment in time, something she doesn't wish to do. As she said, "I [could] walk to Cole's installation and see how people respond. For me as a curator, that's really important, especially because it's a non-art audience. We're introducing people to really interesting concepts and artists, and I've been knocked over by how much people embrace them." Recent exhibitions and projects on the grounds of Wave Hill have included "Thoreau Reconsidered," featuring work by Ellen Driscoll, Spencer Finch, Alan Michelson, and Richard Torchia, and Nina Katchadourian's *Please, Please, Pleased to Meet'cha*.

<www.wavehill.org>

The Garden-Book: Environmental Art at La Marrana

by Andrea Bellini

While contemporary art installations in urban contexts are still a somewhat rare phenomenon in Italy, frequently due to the indifference of local governments, environmental art has become an undisputed favorite. Thanks to the commitment of private art lovers, who are more sensitive to the new forms of contemporary expression and less subject to the complex bureaucratic norms that regulate Italian historical city centers, an intriguing network is being created that features no fewer than 36 sculpture parks and environmental art parks. They include, in northeastern Italy, the Garden of Villa Verzegnis; in central Italy, the Centro d'Arte Ambientale di Casacalenda in Molise; and in Sardinia, the Museo su Logu de s'Iscultura at Tortolì.

These sites are now joined by another interesting place, located in an extraordinary natural setting on the border between Liguria and Tuscany—the Parco d'Arte Ambientale La Marrana at Montemarcello, Ameglia (La Spezia), a promontory jutting into the edge of the Mediterranean Sea, on the eastern side of the entrance to the Gulf of La Spezia. Owned by the Bolongaro family of Milan, La Marrana has made a name for itself as one of the most important centers of environmental art in central

Claudia Losi, *Sentiero Sfera (Path Sphere)*, 2007. Silk, birch and larch wood, glass, and aluminum, dimensions variable.

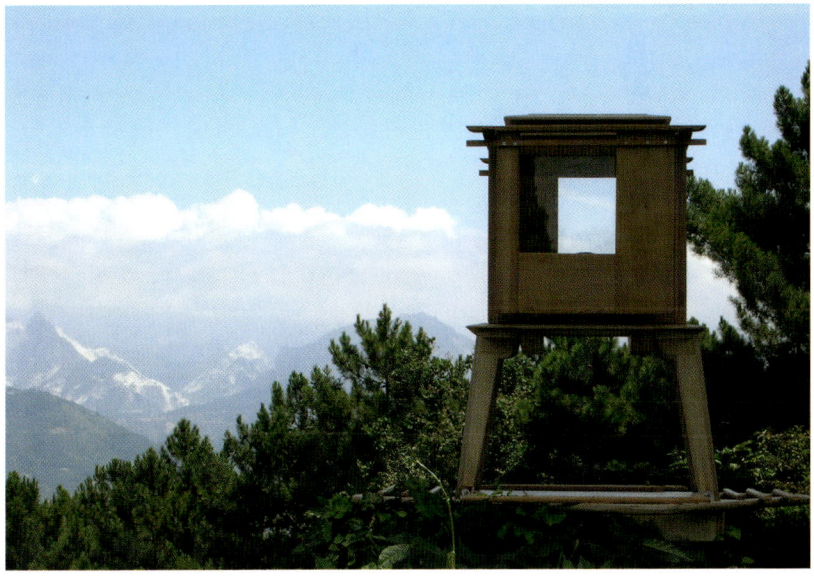

Italy. Aiming to create something new and specific in the context of Italian environmental art parks, Grazia and Gianni Bolongaro decided to favor multimedia works, creations that often include the use of light and sound.

The suggestive shouting of children introduced the first work installed at the park in 1997, by the Iranian artist Hossein Golba. The children's voices, fading into the surrounding trees and bushes, were accompanied by a long path (*Passi* [*Footsteps*]) whose fresh clay was marked by the footsteps of a little girl. *Passi* is part of the permanent collection at La Marrana. Golba refers to a notion of travel, a journey of initiation, that is very poetic in its allusion to the beginning of life, the start of the existential adventure represented by the footprints and voices of children. His other work, *Innesto (Graft)*, also alludes to a poetic, sacral-anthropological dimension: it consists of a series of books tied with white fabric to the branches of various olive trees, a fragile juxtaposition between nature and culture, joined together to share the same destiny.

The following year, Kengiro Azuma executed a sort of path with seven works on the theme of art and nature, which concluded with a long iron wall featuring an irregular profile that blocks the view of the valley and starts from a long series of roads, factories, and various examples of territorial defacement. *Il Sogno (The Dream)* is also part of the permanent collection. In this case, the Japanese artist seems to have had the poet Giacomo Leopardi in mind: for both, the limited view makes it possible to dream of the infinite, of what is impenetrable to our gaze, of the invisible world that marks the culmination of what is visible.

In 1999, the Italian artist Luigi Mainolfi executed a diverse group of sculptures with iron scaffolding, works that represent animals, vehicles, objects, and cages set out in a three-dimensional space. This is the last in a series that combines a rational geometrical structure with a free, dreamy, and at times playful imaginative process. What has been left behind in the park are Mainolfi's columnar self-portrait, hair blowing in the wind, and a cubic structure partially enveloped by brambles—the memory of a house, with the profile of an ascetic's chair, a space for unfettered dreaming.

After the Bolongaros met Philip Rantzer at the Venice Biennale, they invited the Romanian artist to create a work for the sixth annual exhibition at La Marrana. Rantzer's contribution refers to private memory, to a childhood lost on account of emigration and continuous travel. His imaginary world is in fact wholly bound up with the idea of the past, with a continuous attempt to preserve it, to create a bond with it. Rantzer constructed five evocative wooden rooms (which remain at the park), a sort of journey by stages back through memory, in which he placed old objects—teddy bears, childhood souvenirs, bicycles, and kinetic games. The overall atmosphere is evocative and poetic, an intimacy enhanced by the placement of the rooms in the woods bordering the garden. In this isolated area, Rantzer's sweet melancholy finds its ideal dimension.

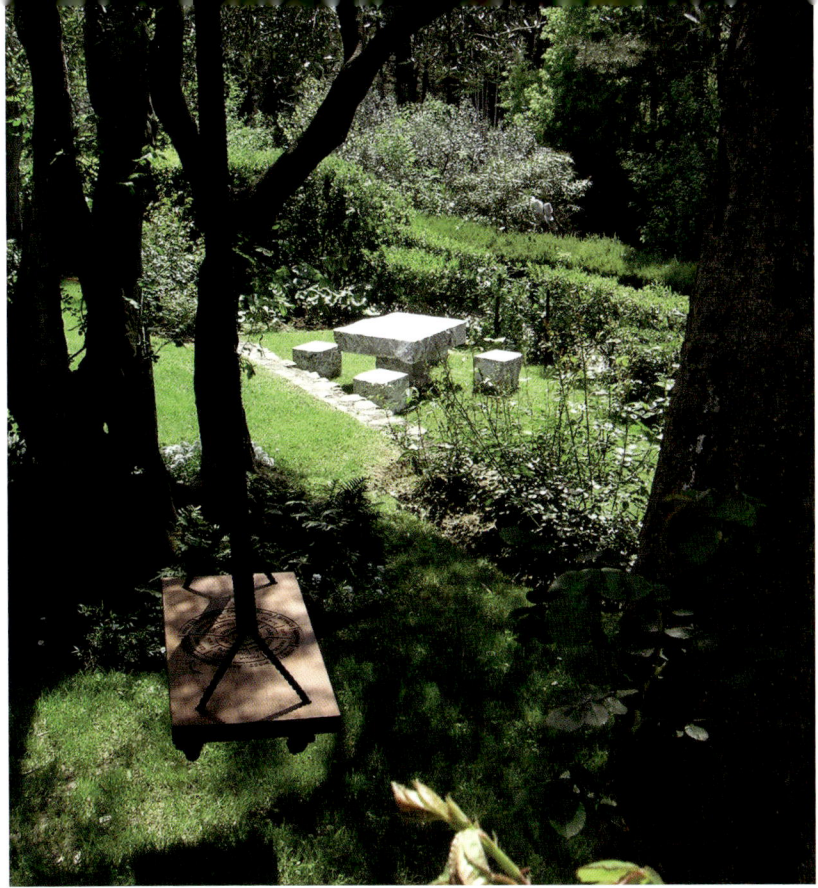

Ottonella Mocellin and Nicola Pellegrini, *Things aren't what they appear to be*, 2005. Mixed media, installation view.

In 2001, the Bolongaros asked curator Giacinto di Pietrantonio to select that year's artists. For the exhibition "Processo alla natura" (Trial against Nature), he chose Mario Airò and vedovamazzei (the artist team Simeone Crispino and Stella Scala). Airò installed a sound work in which a voice uttered propitiatory phrases and good wishes and a glass-topped table (which remains in the collection) with a pen inserted in the center of the glass to highlight the contiguity of art and nature and the potential of their poetic co-existence.

    vedovamazzei presented another suggestive sound work — a bench that activated a series of loudspeakers whenever a visitor sat down. The loudspeakers (hidden in the woods) emitted the sounds and cries of a memorable battle fought by the Romans against the Ligurians in 155 BCE right in the area of the Park of Montemarcello. The whizzing of arrows, the galloping of horses, and the din of battle immersed the visitor in a mythical temporal zone that was both heart-stirring and agonizing.

In 2003, Maria Magdalena Campos Pons installed *Interiorità o Luna sulla collina* (*Interiority or Hillsided Moon*). Several translucent polymer hemispheres were illuminated from inside and decorated with fragments of a poem by César Vallejo on the relationship between interiority and the moon. Videos and loudspeakers reproduced moving images as well as the poem, presenting a poetic dialogue between heaven and earth, with a sliver of the moon planted on earth and amplified by the poetry and music composed for the occasion by Neil Leonard.

In 2004, environmental works by Joseph Kosuth and Jannis Kounellis further enhanced the collection. Kosuth engraved the names of 55 cities on 55 stones in a pre-existing path, each one oriented according to its geographic position in relation to the park (*Located world La Marrana*). This is the third work in his "Located world" series, following installations at Singen, Germany (1999), and Sapporo, Japan (2001). Starting from these places, Kosuth has executed a "map of the world" according to an idea of measurement that tends to abolish the cultural and geographical dialectic between center and periphery. Kosuth's path abolishes boundaries and hierarchies. Representing a physical and mental journey, it invites viewers to imagine a single right of citizenship, a right that people freely make and decide for themselves, independently of the various microcosms of origin, geography, religion, and society.

At La Marrana, Kosuth opts for the least intrusive visual solution, using an already existing path. While the names in Singen were made in white neon spanning the city's walls and those in Sapporo were etched into the large glass panes of the Astrodome, those at La Marrana are engraved in stone. This solution is more in keeping with the nature of the garden itself and its time-evoking interventions. The work is almost hidden within the park's interior. Avoiding all immediacy and representational frontality, it invites research, physical displacement, and reflection. *Located world La Marrana* respects the spirit of the garden as a path of gradual discovery, as a place of "aesthetic education," to use Schiller's expression, intended for intellectual and emotional growth. Kosuth's simple inscription on stone revives the traditional conception of the garden as an articulated symbolic and eschatological system in which an entire era's culture is realized and expressed. The garden has always been conceived not just in terms of arboreal architecture, but as a place for creation and meditation, a home to allegorical systems punctuated by memorials, boundary stones, inscriptions, and maxims. In their structural semantics, the garden and the park historically reflect transformations in the poetic and philosophical vision of the world.

For his piece, Kounellis dug a broad pit in a clearing created by a lightning strike, in which he placed 23 bronze bells (*Senza titolo La Marrana*, 2004), each one inserted into the other in a suggestive helix moving from the bottom to the top. Kounellis defined the work as "an esoteric vertical that represents a physical anchor in the ground." This subterranean work emblematically evokes a geological umbilical cord, stretching to the natural and anthropomorphic center of time itself.

La Marrana (whose collection now includes more than 28 works; recent shows have featured Jan Fabre [2005], Ottonella Mocellin and Nicola Pellegrini [2005], and Hamish Fulton and Claudia Losi [2007]) is not an immense or out-of-scale property. It is a small and precious contemporary garden that, thanks to the complexity of its artworks, aspires to incarnate the role historically played by gardens in Italy and Europe since the Middle Ages, when they were considered a sort of big book—open-air "halls" and places for learning where topics and issues of relevance to humanity could be discussed.

<www.lamarrana.it>

The Wanås Foundation: Patronage and Partnership

by Gregory Volk

You wouldn't normally expect the buildings and grounds surrounding a 15th-century castle in southern Sweden to be the site of an impressive, risk-taking international sculpture project, but that's precisely the case with the Wanås Foundation. Since 1987, Marika and Charles Wachtmeister have invited international artists to respond to this unorthodox location, usually in group shows that eschew curatorial categories and rhetoric in favor of bringing together a temporary constellation of artists for a period of vivid experimentation. There is something familial and collegial about how this has developed, with artists suggesting other artists and a network of relationships and sensibilities developing through the years. For the installation period leading up to the opening, most of the artists are present, resulting in a real mix of creative processes and robust daily life. Marika Wachtmeister, the driving force behind the project, while well-versed in art, is actually a lawyer and not a trained arts professional at all. Still, as she has grown into her self-made position—she got the idea for a sculpture project after moving from Stockholm with her husband to his comparatively remote and rural family home—she has become a vibrant force, not only in Sweden, but internationally. Moreover, the enterprise

Antony Gormley, *Together and Apart*, 1998/2001. Cast iron, 189 x 48 x 24 cm.

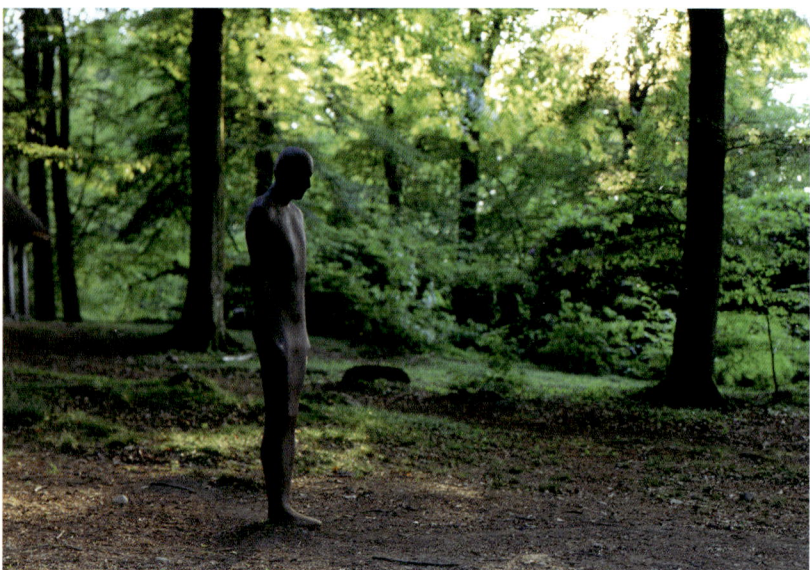

that she stewards doesn't really feel like an institution: an adventure-in-process, Wanås has its own idiosyncratic way of doing things.

The exhibition in 2000 featured 10 artists, most of whom had already received considerable acclaim. What resulted were intriguing and at times radical variations on the tradition of outdoor sculpture or sculpture park works. Miroslaw Balka, among the most acclaimed of a younger generation of Polish artists, presented a grave-like sculpture in Wanås's renowned sculpture garden, which stretches way back into the forest. Installed near a pond, his pseudo-grave, made of polished black granite and open at the top, was filled with blue and yellow plastic balls—playful things that encouraged passing children to climb down into the enclosure (*Play-pit*, 2000). Understatedly fusing carefree youth and a sharp sense of mortality, Balka's oddly gorgeous work seemed simultaneously brooding and humorous. His piece was conceptually coupled with an interior work in the barn: looped paper chains, suspended between the walls, resembled party decorations for a child's birthday, until you realized that they were made from newspaper obituaries. Near *Play-pit*, at the edge of the pond itself, New York-based Swedish artist Ann-Sofi Sidén, otherwise known for her video and film projects, installed a crouching, anatomically precise statue of herself peeing into the grass (*Fidiecommissum*, 2000). Sidén's work freezes and immortalizes a surreptitious bodily act that would otherwise seem pure anathema in the stately, aristocratic grounds of Wanås, in the process upending a longstanding tradition in which similar figures are almost always male.

In downstairs rooms in the barn, a spare marble form suggestive of Post-Minimalist abstraction, by Monika Larsen Dennis from Stockholm, served as a pedestal on which one could kneel, almost reverentially, while resting one's chin in a small concave hole. There was a kind of quiescence and peacefulness to the work, suggestive of rich inner calm, and also an interesting mix between hard, cool marble and soft, yielding skin (namely your own). This was one part of a two-part work, *Reconsidering choice* (2000), which continued outside in the sculpture park with a series of trees repeatedly shot by a pellet gun, so that the embedded pellets interrupted the natural bark with rough mini-fields: here the feeling was frantic, obsessive, and disturbed.

The whole project of the Wanås Foundation at once fits in with and seriously disturbs these aristocratic grounds, replete with exquisite palace, manicured lawns, farm buildings and former servants' quarters, a pleasant pond, and an aura of stately decorum that must be maintained. You're always aware of just how unusual this project is: a vibrant and in some ways unruly "now" bursting from a place that seems distinctly beholden to "then," namely the rhythms and mores of a provincial aristocracy that stretches way, way back into Sweden's past. But, at the same time, Wanås continues a tradition of patronage in which local aristocrats commissioned artists for portraits and sculptures and updates it entirely, with an eye toward risk and experiment. This is patronage for a new era, and Wanås is distinguished not for ordering desired works, but for its partnership with participating artists, which involves an almost total devotion to realizing their projects as they wish.

Through its past shows, Wanås has acquired quite a collection of works, all situated in the sculpture park. One finds a long line of paired boulders by Richard Nonas; a slightly sloping concrete form by Jene Highstein, like a kind of low-to-the-ground plateau; a pair of seemingly totemic iron antlers by Marina Abramović attached to a freestanding construction in a field, precisely where you would expect deer to be wandering and grazing; a remarkable thatched architectural construction by Martin Puryear; and a pyramidal form, sliced open at its center to form an entranceway, by Gunilla Bandolin. Quite a number of Swedish artists are included, but one of the strengths of Wanås, right from the beginning, has been its international focus. It is not a local sculpture park, but an ambitiously international one that just happens to be pretty much in the middle of nowhere, in art world terms. As younger generation experimenters have been invited, the collection has expanded beyond its roots in Post-Minimalism to encompass all sorts of fresh approaches. It is an active, ever-changing place without allegiance to any particular look or style. Among the more compelling of these past innovations is a series of artificial trees by Roxy Paine, tucked among the other trees, and one of Janet Cardiff's coolly dazzling Walkman-accompanied "walks," in which you go for a stroll in the forest, all the while listening to Cardiff's hypnotic voice telling stories, calling attention to things, speaking to you personally and intimately, as if she's some inner companion lodged in the depths of your mind.

Adding to the liberties being taken is a backwards waterfall by Olafur Eliasson (*Yet Untitled*, 1998/2000). On one section of a stream running through the park, Eliasson rigged a small system of pumps and plateaus that reversed the water and sent it jetting and spilling upstream and higher. Mixing artificiality and nature, technology and a lingering beauty, Eliasson's can-do gadgetry functioned as a kind of practical miracle (think of Biblical stories in which the seas parted or the rivers ran backward) while still serving as a peaceful and meditative moment in nature—albeit one wholly engineered by the artist. New York-based Honduran Paul Ramirez Jonas accomplished something similar, but in an entirely different way. He devised a system of discreetly installed bells heading out into the forest, which were electronically wired to the castle's front door (*Echo*, 2000). When a visitor rang the bell there, other bells trailed off in a line deep into the forest. The effect was at once startling, whimsical, and sublime. This was just one of an ambitious suite of works involving sound by Ramirez Jonas, who's known for his tinkering quasi-inventions that nevertheless have a real sculptural elegance. Elsewhere, an ensemble of

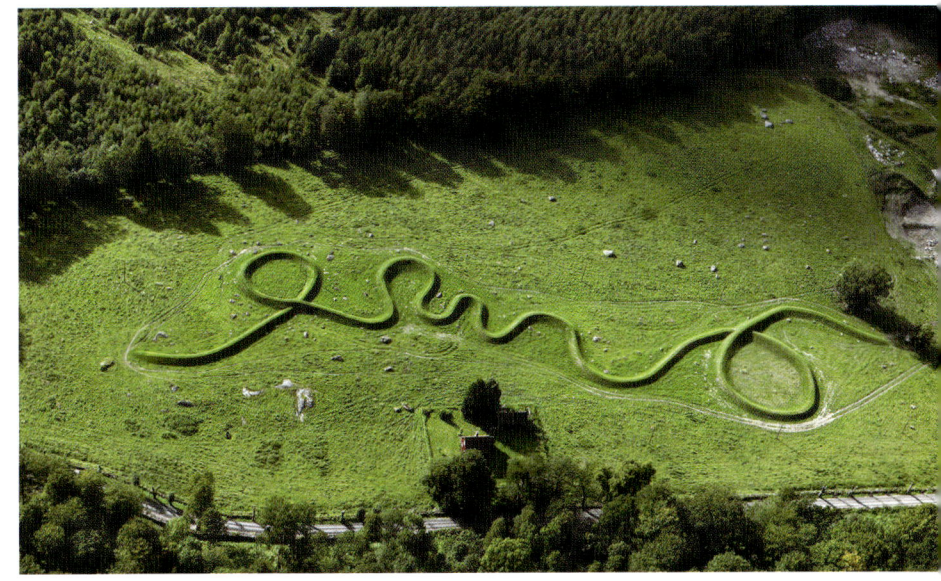

Maya Lin, *11 Minute Line*. Grass, earth, and stone, 500 meters long.

homemade instruments (a drum, a whistle, a flag, a tambourine, a bicycle pump), electronically wired and set to a timer, intermittently burst into a kind of tragicomic fanfare replete with all sorts of slight but fetching kinetic activity; it was at once vigorous (even ecstatic) and whoppingly forlorn. Out among the cows, bells aligned on a fence were fitted with salt chunks for licking. If played correctly by the cows (obviously an impossible feat), they'd yield a crisp version of "When the Saints Come Marching In."

Close to 200 artists have exhibited at Wanås over the years, and the sculpture park's permanent collection features more than 30 works, mainly by Nordic and American artists, including Antony Gormley, Jenny Holzer, Cris Gianakos, Jene Highstein, Richard Nonas, Roxy Paine, Martin Puryear, Jason Rhoades, Kathleen Schimert, Sarah Schwartz, and Gloria Friedmann. In 2004, Maya Lin created her first major installation in Europe, set among the grazing cows in one of Wanås's fields. *11 Minute Line*, which was the first large-scale installation at Wanås outside the sculpture park itself, measures approximately seven feet in height and 1,500 feet in length, creating a winding line in the landscape.

Wanås, which started out as a personal vision, has become a truly valuable place and is justifiably receiving increased international attention — which is remarkable when you think of just how remote it is. Not only is it a highly unusual forum for contemporary sculpture, it's also a laboratory for artists and ideas, a fanciful place that allows for idiosyncratic projects to be realized that wouldn't find much chance or support elsewhere, a place where artists are encouraged to push their ideas to an extreme, and ultimately, a one-of-a-kind forum that is radically re-imagining what a sculpture park can be. Factor in the life that occurs there, with artists arriving, oftentimes long in advance of the show, to set about realizing their projects, the communion that develops, and the sense of shared adventure, and you get an idea of what is happening at this distant venue an hour or so outside the southern city of Malmö.

<www.wanas.se>

Site-Specific Sculpture at Fattoria di Celle

by Paula Bortolotti

Fattoria di Celle, located between Florence and Pistoia, hosts the outstanding collection of site-specific art that Giuliano Gori and his family began in the early 1980s. International artists are invited to create installations in the outdoor spaces of the park and farmland, as well as inside the various farm buildings of the historic villa, which was built in the late 17th century. Fattoria di Celle is one of a large number of sites rich with sculptures and installations of Land Art, spread throughout the region.

Gori moved to Celle Farm in order to realize a project that had been forming in his mind for some time: he wanted to see how contemporary artists would respond to a new kind of commission, one in which "natural space would become an integral part of the artwork and not just a container for art." This idea derived from Land Art, which was prominently represented in important exhibitions in Italy and throughout Europe during the 1970s. While visiting these exhibitions, Gori noticed that artists presented works specifically created for the spaces, using mostly temporary materials. He intended to propose the creation of permanent installations, following a Renaissance model, "when princes and city councils entrusted the best artists with building monuments and city embellishments."

Sol LeWitt, *1-2-3-2-1*, 2004. Aluminum, five parts, 11.5 x 2.9 x 2.9 meters.

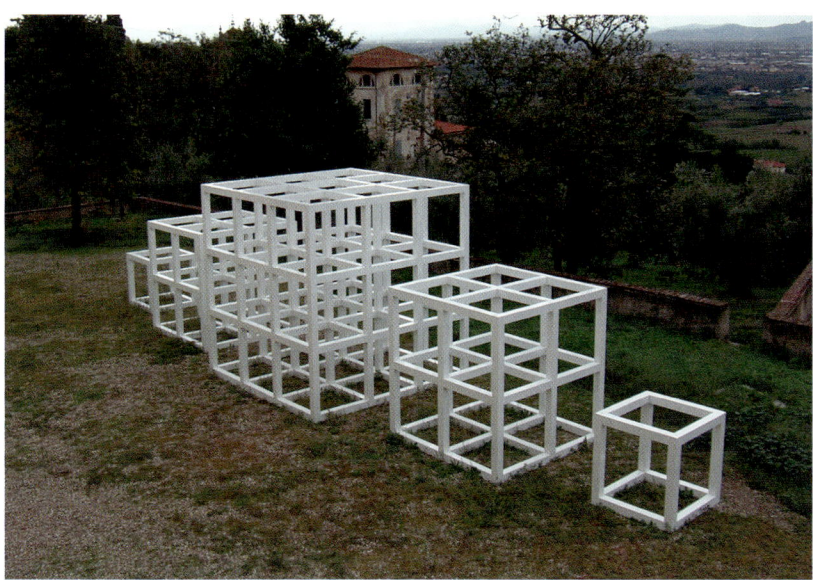

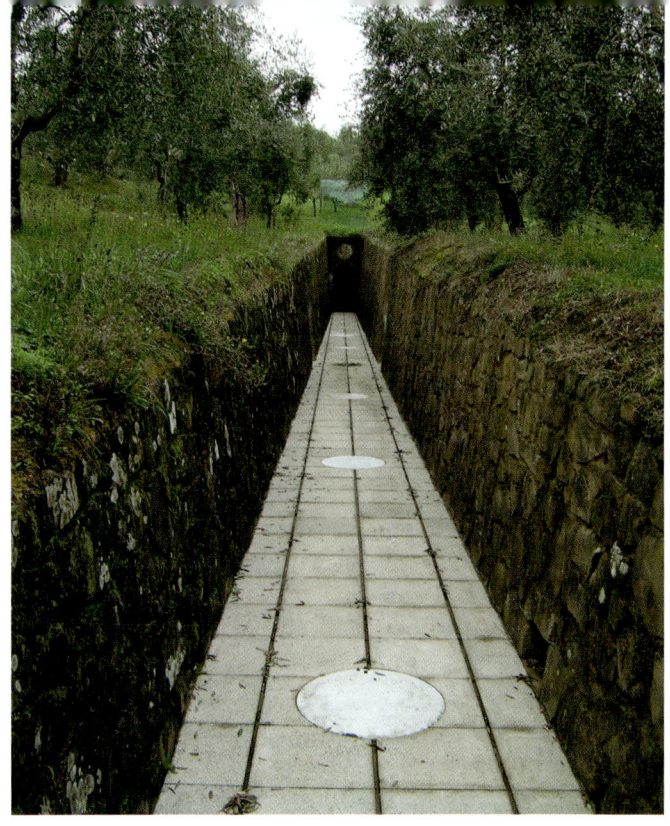

Bukichi Inoue, *My Sky Hole*, 1985–89. Wood, stone, glass, stainless steel, water, and marble, 64 meters long.

In 1981, an advisory committee was assembled, and Amnon Barzel was appointed curator of the project. The question of how working in a specific space might influence artists was addressed from the beginning, as invited participants responded to the site. For each project, the selected artist is invited to visit the park and remain there as long as necessary, discussing the details and difficulties of the work with Gori. The site-specific idea is fundamental for all of the projects carried out at Celle. First, artists choose the place where they want to create their work. Then, together with Gori, they analyze all of the conditions and elements affecting that particular site. This exploratory investigation forms the foundation of each project, so that each work becomes tied to its specific place. For many of the artists, working at Celle also offers a chance to discover connections between their own work and the history and culture of Florence. Gori told me, "Here at Celle we live with the artists and we have to understand their mentality…because they are often renowned personalities. Some of them, after a walk through the site, could tell us, 'I understood everything.' Despite that, we must find the courage to give them advice, to make them realize that creating an installation here is an extremely complicated adventure. It takes a long time before the artist is able to absorb the impact; one must walk around and stay in such an environment on one's own."

Some artists have found their vocation for Land Art at Celle. For instance, Anne and Patrick Poirier, who had never worked in the land before, began their open-space works at Celle. Richard Serra temporarily left steel behind to work in local stone, and Robert Morris transformed himself into an environmental artist. Celle has also introduced some less famous artists to the larger art world.

The permanent collection is housed across more than 3,000 square meters, and outdoor works are sited among rare trees, ponds, and olive groves. Celle also promotes temporary projects and exhibitions, which are usually hosted for one year in the restored farm buildings, the Casa Peppe and Cascina Terrarossa. On these occasions, Beverly Pepper's sculpture/amphitheater (1992) serves as a venue for dance, music, theater, and performance events. The main farm building also includes a large video/conference room for screenings, lectures, and concerts.

In July 2004, Gori invited Sol LeWitt, Christiane Löhr, and Daniel Buren to work at Celle. LeWitt was returning for the third time, with a series of 15 wall drawings made for the Casa Peppe exhibition space. Visitors passing through the 10 rooms find numerous combinations of fine graphite lines drawn—in four directions—on identically sized, black square backgrounds. These works confirmed LeWitt's constancy and persistence as he attempted to visualize all of the possible variations presented by his configurations. In addition to the wall drawings, he also placed a sculpture from the "Structures" series in front of the Casa Peppe. The five-part, white aluminum work follows the numerical combination of 1-2-3-2-1.

Christiane Löhr returned to Celle to present her fragile sculptures in the Poets' Room, inside the Cascina Terrarossa. The German artist uses gathered plant materials, including airborne seeds from reed mace, burrs, thistle, and ivy. With such seemingly impalpable materials she creates microcosms in which nature opens up to a global view. Gori has called her nests and miniature ziggurats "delicate relics, a metaphor of the energy that regulates nature's balance."

Daniel Buren's *La Cabanne Eclatée aux 4 Salles* consists of a roofless structure, its interior divided into four equal sections or rooms. Each room contains two mirrored walls and two colored ones, either red, blue, yellow, or green.

Celle hosts over 60 installations, including works by Alice Aycock, Michelangelo Pistoletto, Richard Long, Magdalena Abakanowicz, and Dennis Oppenheim. In this creative laboratory, artists continuously produce and experiment with new vocabularies in various disciplines of contemporary art.

<www.po-net.prato.it/artestoria/contemp/eng/celle.htm>

Collecting Experience: A Conversation with Steven Oliver

by Donna Brookman

Entering the Oliver Ranch on a narrow climbing road, one suddenly encounters hundreds of white concrete steps cascading down the hill, crossing the road, and continuing below. Bruce Nauman's site-specific sculpture is one of many commissioned works scattered throughout the grounds of Steven Oliver's Alexander Valley ranch. A Fontana sound sculpture rumbles in the hills; wind instruments by Kristin Jones and Andrew Ginzel glint in the trees. Roger Berry's two large steel arcs precisely track the sun at the summer and winter solstices. Other works include sculptures by Martin Puryear, Richard Serra, Ursula von Rydingsvard, and Terry Allen. David Rabinowitch's incised concrete walls for new artists' residences, a collaboration with architect Jim Jennings, and a tower sculpture/performance space by Ann Hamilton, created in collaboration with architect Mark Jensen, were recently completed.

Oliver's unusual approach to collecting has evolved over time, partly through his fascination with artistic process. The owner of a large construction company, he is able to observe, and in many cases facilitate, the realization of each project. Above all, he wants to allow artists time and space to engage intimately with the land.

Donna Brookman: After collecting art for a decade, you commissioned your first site-specific work from Judith Shea in 1985. What got you started?
Steven Oliver: I was really disgusted with the art world. I was tired of reading about art on the financial pages. It was one auction record after another. The world had suddenly discovered contemporary art as commodity. When my wife and I first started out, we collected prints because it was what we could afford. One time I was talking to a friend over dinner, complaining about insurance for a work going to a museum. A grin came over his face (he thought I was crazy up until then), and he said, "You're collecting art as an investment! You're making money on this stuff!" And I said, "No, no, I've never sold anything. It's not that at all."

After that, we decided to commission something. The ranch had been underway five years as a working sheep ranch, we were starting to build this house, and I said to my wife, "Let's do something site-specific, the purest form—I can't sell it, I can't give it away." The truth is, until Richard Serra came, I had a heck of a time getting artists. It was the go-go '80s. Galleries wanted artists in their studios producing stuff to sell. They didn't want them out here mucking around. So we struggled. It all happened by chance. We learned a lot about ourselves and about the process during Judith Shea's project. She had been here a lot, and we found that we missed that, so we said, "Let's do one more."

DB: What got you hooked?

SO: I give Judith all the credit. Our first try could have been a stinker. But she sensed our transition from buying an existing object, when we knew the exact color, shape, and form, to the commissioning process, when it's like a child. If it turns out bad you can't give it back—you're stuck with it. She talked through a lot of issues with us, because she was going through a big transition in her work. Finally she said, "You just have to trust me." It was a magical process. Ellen Driscoll and Roger Berry followed; they both did terrific projects, too.

DB: Could you say something about how the process begins and your insistence on it being a dialogue with this place?

SO: Each artist we invite has to come here three times before making a proposal. They have to come in different times of the year—summer and winter for sure, and they

Bruce Nauman, *Untitled*, 1998–99. Cast concrete, .3 miles long.

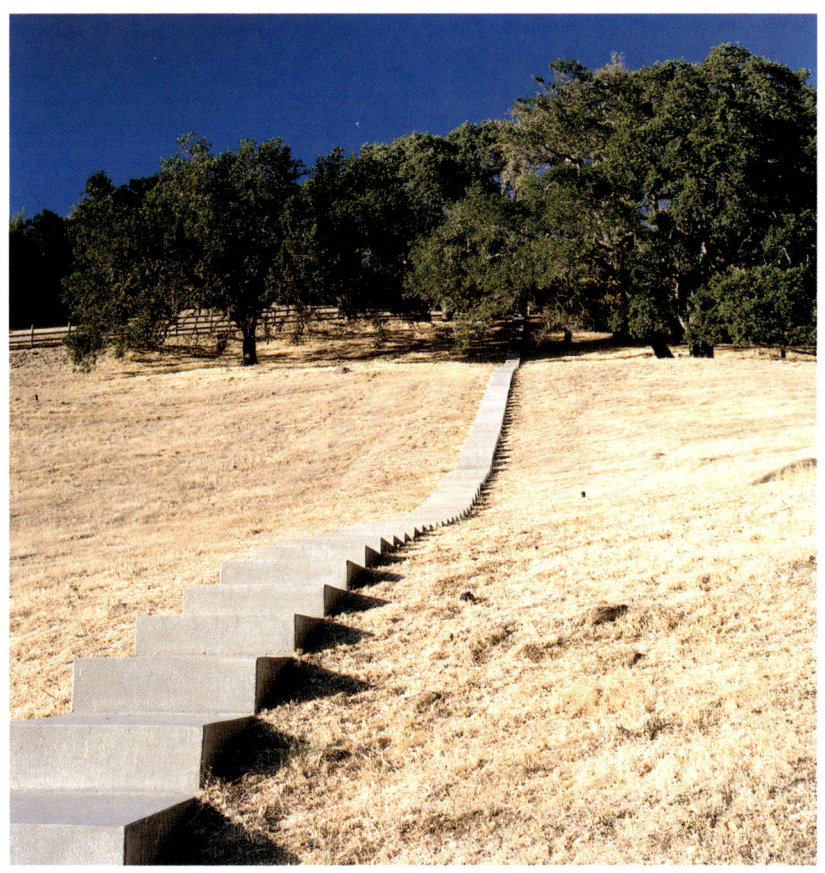

can pick either spring or fall. Early on, we tried to do two works a year, which lasted until 1994. Then, with Dennis Leon and Richard Serra working at the same time, it just became overwhelming. Over the last five years, some projects became drawn out, in some cases a year and a half, and I've become less concerned about it. I always want the next thing cooking. But I don't worry about whether a project takes a year or longer.

DB: Does your involvement vary dramatically depending on the artist?

SO: Yes, and the materials. It's been the same from the beginning. I was very involved with the Rabinowitch because all the carving was done here, but in Judith's case, the bronze and the cast head were done in New York. I went there often and saw them in process. With some, it's just the installation; with others, it's the fabrication. For instance, all of Ursula von Rydingsvard's work was done here.

DB: I was struck by the number of women artists who have completed works here.

SO: Of the first 10, it's about half. We were even with men and women until last year. The women's movement in the '60s freed women to do non-traditional things. I think the outgrowth we saw in the late '70s and early '80s benefited from people such as Eva Hesse. von Rydingsvard was carving with a chain saw, and Shea was casting iron. Ellen Driscoll is the single best welder I've ever seen. I'd have my [construction workers] come up, and I'd say, "I don't know what she's doing, but she's doing it a hell of a lot better than you guys are. Sit here, watch, and learn something."

DB: There is such a variety of work here. Serra and Nauman responded to physical contours; Judith Shea and Ellen Driscoll, to the Arcadian traditions of shepherding and growing grapes. Others, such as Miroslaw Balka and Ursula von Rydingsvard, take it as an opportunity to do something very personal. Somehow this place frees them. The von Rydingsvard is a big project, an important project.

SO: Yes, and it took the longest—13 months of carving, gluing, picking: she was here throughout that time. If an artist is given a supportive environment and essentially no limitations, if they need more time it's no problem, there's no pressure, no deadline. Generally artists who do commissions work in a public process, which is agonizing.

DB: Another piece that I found very moving was the Balka installation, the footprint of his childhood home in Poland.

SO: It's fascinating—two Polish artists, two hundred yards apart, the same sort of angst in their work.

DB: You gave Balka an amazing level of technical support.

SO: It helps when you're in the business. The piece is a single casting of white sand and white cement, so everything came down to one four-hour period. The concrete had to be mixed, moved here, and placed within 40 minutes, and it had to be cured properly, so it was a real logistical problem. We worked about three months to get the

Ann Hamilton, *The Tower*, 2007. Concrete and stainless steel, 78 x 24 ft. diameter.

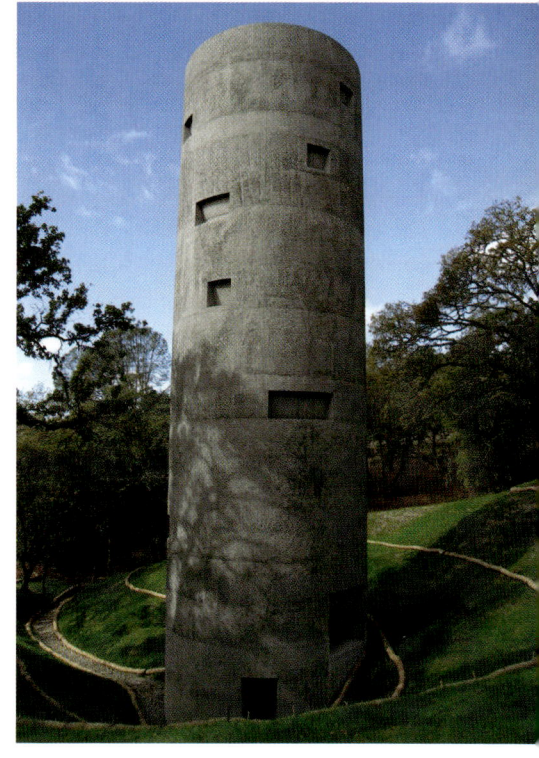

schedule right. A local concrete batch plant allowed us to shut it down for three days while we washed out their bunkers and brought in sand from the Del Monte beaches on 17 Mile Drive, which is the purest white sand, and white cement. If you're doing something serious and interesting, people will go out of their way to help you. They get into it.

DB: What has surprised you about being so closely involved with an artist's process?

SO: I'm constantly surprised. I remember one situation in particular. Roger Berry was talking about the approach to the arch. The road was in a different spot then, and he said, "I really don't like the perspective approaching it this way. I'd rather approach it from over here." And I said, "Well, let's just dig this thing down. We'll get the bulldozers over here." But he said, "No, why don't we just change the path?" That was 15 years ago, and I think in some ways the interaction with artists has changed how I think. It's made me a better person for my clients. I think more creatively. It seems that artists, who are often forced to do more with less, tend to be better problem-solvers because they can't commit unlimited resources.

Having this involvement in art as a life pursuit gives me a reason for my own work, and it enriches my work ethic. This is the only reason I'm still working. I have a lot of wonderful clients and we do a lot of interesting projects, but the brightest people I've ever worked with are artists. They happened to choose this venue for expressing themselves, rather than writing or mixing chemicals in a laboratory.

Someone asked me recently about beauty in sculpture. I don't think beauty has anything to do with it anymore. It's intellect. The intellect may be expressed in a beautiful manner, but I've come to the conclusion that the difference between the very good and the very best artists is this incredible intellect. And I'm not sure that's always recognized. Clearly some of the people who've worked here are more renowned than others. But the ones I find intriguing as personalities agonize over the work, twisting and turning within themselves, and I look over their shoulders while they're doing it, which is what's fun. That's why I'm addicted to the process. And when it ends, it's gut-wrenching in some ways. For instance, when Serra's project ended we talked on the phone once a week for three or four months afterward to try to wean ourselves off the process. That project was a very intense thing to do.

DB: I'm wondering how seeing the artists respond to the landscape has changed your perception of the place.

SO: Immensely. They see things I'd never seen before. My favorite time of year is winter, when there's a grayness, sometimes fog from the valley. You can see the shape and form of the trees. Serra, and Roger Berry too, talked a lot about the shape of the oaks when they're denuded of leaves. You learn from each artist. Each has a different look at it.

DB: What about making ephemeral work? Andy Goldsworthy worked here in 1991. How did you feel about having it all disappear?

SO: It doesn't bother me at all. It's another experience. In some ways I'm not collecting art, I'm collecting experiences now. I find life much more enriching.

DB: What about your project with Ann Hamilton?

SO: We're very excited. Ann and I have been friends for 10 years. I was on the board at Capp Street and helped fund her work there. We became friends, and we've been talking from the late '80s until now, trying to find something to do. Because her work is so ephemeral, making that permanent mark has always been hard for her. [After] she was in the Venice Biennale…she became interested in towers and began to bring me picture books and a lot of books about a particular tower in Italy.

Her project here evolved from the so-called Well of St. Patrick (1527–40), which was built by Clement VII to provide the city with a water supply in case of attack. The well descends more than 60 meters: in order to get enough water to the surface the architect designed a double helix staircase: the mule goes down one staircase, loads up with water, and comes back up the other staircase. The two staircases never touch; the mule never has to turn around and never meets another mule. It's the same form as DNA. Ann proposed a double helix staircase inside the stonework, descending to a water source: into the ground and up out of the ground. It looks rather agricultural in form, like a silo. It is intended as a performance space for poetry readings and concerts of a single voice or a single instrument.

We hired acoustic engineers to do some studies and then realized we didn't really care. Clearly there are going to be reverberations and echoes. The artists will adapt to the space. The nice thing is that the audience and the performers will never be more than a staircase apart, because the audience can all be on the up staircase and the performers on the down staircase. But they're going to be interlaced with each other.

DB: How do you imagine the future of the ranch?

SO: Right now, it's set up to become a public trust with a maintenance endowment. The dilemma is that we played along the edge with a lot of the artists. We've worked with some "acknowledged masters" in recent years, but it hasn't always been that way. So the question is, if you create a trust out of this, how long do you keep works that may not be significant? Artists' careers get rehabilitated. You don't want to decide in one year; but is it 100 years or 20 years? At some point in time, works can be removed if they're not considered significant, and new works can be commissioned. The only other stipulation is that we prefer not to be open to the public with picnic tables and garbage cans, but to have some controlled access for visitors to come in groups. The rest of the time, it will be a residence or retreat center.

Sculpture in the Pines: The NMAC Foundation

by Cécile Bourne-Farrell

The discovery of open-air contemporary art in a region as magnificent as Spain's Costa de la Luz is indeed a unique experience. In 2002, the Fondación Montenmedio Arte Contemporáneo (NMAC) opened its doors to the general public, offering a chance to view works from its collection all year round.

The NMAC Foundation is located in Vejer de la Frontera (Province of Cadiz), in a Mediterranean pine grove. This tremendously scenic setting borders the Parque Natural de las Marismas de Barbate to the south. The Council of Andalusia's guide to natural parks describes these marshes as "a damp area of huge value to indigenous fauna, occupy[ing] a privileged position on the western Atlantic migration routes as a resting and recuperation area for species that arrive...exhausted following their journey from Central and Northern Europe or the African continent." Far from urban centers, the foundation invites artists from all corners of the world to undertake site-specific projects in the form of installations, sculptures, photography, performances, and architecture within nature. Each of the works maintains a close relationship with its surroundings, as the visitor discovers while exploring the Mediterranean forest. To date, more than 40 artists have done projects at NMAC; 20 are represented in the permanent, public part of the collection. Artists in the collection include Marina Abramović, Pilar Albarracin, Maja Bajevic, Maurizio Cattelan, Cristina Lucas, Richard Nonas, Roxy Paine, Ester Partegàs, Santiago Sierra, Susana Solano, Huang Yong Ping, and Shen Yuan. The foundation's main objective is to offer a vision of contemporary art in which natural landscape, social environment, and historical background are determinants in the creative process. From concept through production, each work is undertaken in the province of Cadiz by local technicians and companies under the direction of the artist and curator. In addition to the exhibition program, the NMAC Foundation conducts educational activities such as guided tours and workshops for schools, conferences, publications, generates teaching materials, and in summer months, offers children's courses, nature programs, and open-air concerts.

NMAC's most recent projects situate the spectator as a participant at the intersection of art and life. Some of the works upset banal daily actions, as in the case of Jeppe Hein's *Modified social benches* (2006). Eleven "impossible" benches act as jarring elements in an idyllic landscape that otherwise invites the viewer to contemplation, observation, and meditation. It is impossible to sit down on these "social benches," a situation that creates a sense of displacement: the viewer doesn't know what to do.

In this bucolic atmosphere, Aleksandra Mir's *Love Stories* (2004–07) opens a social process in which we all participate as witnesses and protagonists. She has inter-

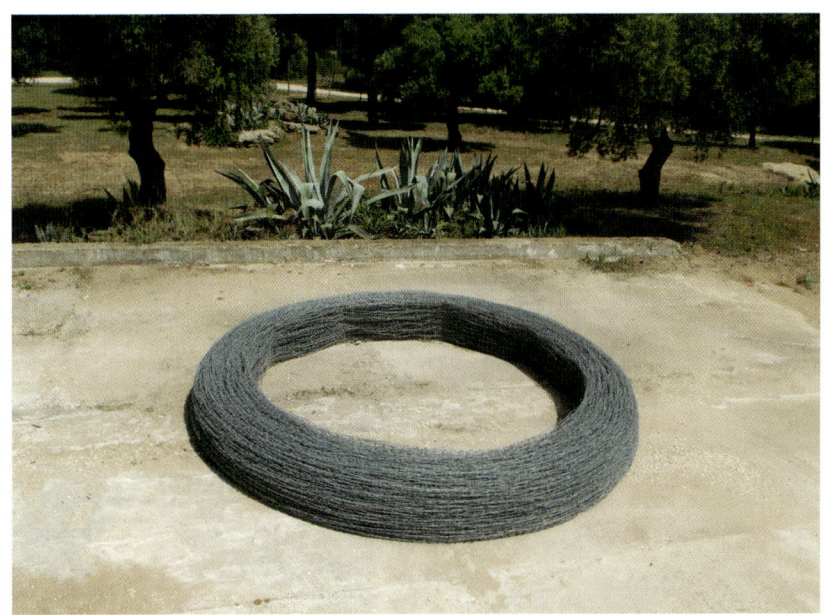

Adel Abdessemed, *Salam Europe!*, 2006. 16 kilometers of barbed wire, 60 x 500 cm.

woven 1,000 love stories from every corner of the planet within the territorial context of a Mediterranean wood, where each testimony has its own tree. Her work attempts to establish ties between the global and the local: the trees act as receptors and guardians of the stories. After compiling the stories and carving the hearts into the pine trees, Mir's next task was to assemble the 1,000 narratives and their accompanying visuals in a book that portrays a multicultural society through emotional experiences. The final stage of *Love Stories* was published in April 2008.

Because NMAC's sculpture park is located at the periphery of Europe, it confronts a unique geographical and cultural situation. Some of the artists, such as Adel Abdessemed, have used their work to address this issue. *Salam Europe!* (2006) consists of rolls of barbed wire in which Abdessemed, with poetic subtlety, lays bare the nightmare experiences of immigrants who try to go over the barbed-wire fence separating Europe from Africa in the city of Melilla. His works, which evoke a strong physical presence, contain an intense spiritual dimension expressing freedom and joy of life as well as violence and death. Jesús Palomino, one of several Spanish artists in the park, contributed a very interesting project, *Antifreeze and 8 Radio Broadcasts* (2006), in which he carved the words "history" (in Spanish) and "friendship" (in Arabic) in ice. He also broadcast eight radio programs in July and August on Radio Vejer, hosting debates on the points where Spain and Africa coincide and differ.

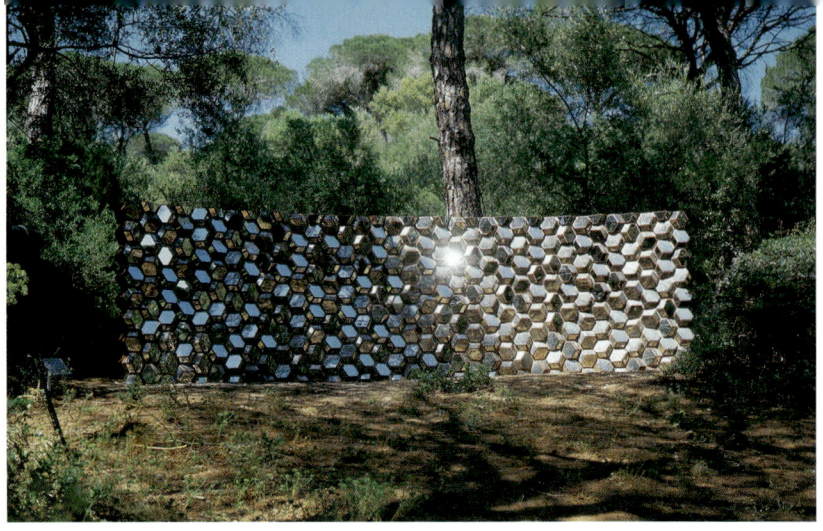

Olafur Eliasson, *Quasi Brick Wall*, 2003. Fired earthenware bricks and polished steel mirrors, 500 x 160 cm.

Due to NMAC's expansion and the scope of its future projects, it has outgrown its current quarters. Architect Alberto Campo Baeza has designed a new space that will not only house a wide range of activities and exhibitions, but will also blend into the landscape as if it were another site-specific artwork. Campo Baeza's design encompasses cultural events and serves as the backbone for articulating and highlighting the surrounding natural scenery. His *White Stripe* is a building with infinite possibilities — nine meters wide and, to begin with, 430 meters long, winding over the Andalusian countryside. The proposal evokes vernacular white-washed architecture, accentuating horizontality and contrasting with the undulating topography of the landscape, with walls running north to south. As is the case with ancient Roman construction, this orientation allows one to walk in the cool shade on the northern side during the summer or warm up on the sunny southern side during the winter. The various expansion projects at NMAC are expected to continue through 2010. *Stupa*, James Turrell's ambitious new project in the park, is an underground installation, invisible from the outside, in which visitors walk through a short tunnel into a pyramid containing the three elements: earth, water, and air. Inside the light-filled room, which is open to the sky, viewers will be able to sit and watch the changing light, testing the limits of perception as Turrell's work blurs the boundaries between light and structure.

<www.fundacionnmac.org>

The World Sculpture Park at Changchun

by Ken Scarlett

The World Sculpture Park at Changchun in northern China has been created on a vast scale. It is an immense park, totaling 92 hectares of undulating hills, with 315 pieces of sculpture by 270 artists from 109 countries. The entrance overlooks a formal and quite symmetrical arrangement: rows of sculptures in extremely diverse styles lead to a fountain, beyond which one can glimpse the towering 23-meter-high granite sculpture dedicated to *Friendship, Peace, Spring*—the theme of the six symposia held since 1997. This focal point was created by five Chinese artists, first as a 2.5-meter maquette, then in clay at full scale, and finally carved in granite by the Chengdu Yilang Sculpture Art Company. Bare-breasted female figures hold aloft flowers and doves as symbols of spring and peace in an ever-upward gesture of confidence. Surrounding this monumental work are five groups of twice life-sized bronze figures representing Asia, Africa, Europe, America, and Oceania—all dancing and playing musical instruments in celebration of peace and friendship.

In the West, we have become strangely uneasy and embarrassed by public expressions of sentiment, but even in translation the concept for the sculpture park comes across as simple yet profoundly poetic: "Highly hold the banner of peace / Powerfully play the note of friendship / Gaily greet the beautiful spring." At the height of the Cold War many people would have dismissed these sentiments as pure propaganda, yet with the relaxation of tensions between China and the West and with the country's strong and rapidly growing economy, China doesn't need propaganda. Certainly the thousands of Chinese visitors to the park appear to appreciate, and to be in tune with, the symbolism.

Beyond the formal entrance, people tend to proceed directly ahead—walking the length of the stone bridge, across the wide lake to the summit of the distant hill—to inspect *Friendship, Peace, Spring*. But it is possible to take the undulating paths that sweep left and right in a series of gentle curves around the lake—and always, every few meters, there is another piece of sculpture. A British sculptor, Lorna Green, wondered if the sculpture-lined pathways would encourage constant walking rather than viewing, though her *Power Flower* is happily sited on a small mound of grass some distance from an asphalt path. It is true that many visitors happily stroll in the sunshine, but every now and then puzzled groups gather to discuss the peculiarities of modern sculpture or stop to have their photographs taken in front of a favorite work.

When I visited for the official opening in 2003, I was able (with an interpreter) to question people at random as they walked in the park. Interestingly, no one criticized works that were outside their experience; rather, the questions were thrown back to me to help explain. Zhan Wang's fascinating *Stainless Steel Artificial Hill and Stone* was more fully appreciated once viewers recognized it as a contemporary version of the traditional Chinese practice of placing stones on pedestals in their gardens. I came across an elderly man gazing at Michael Lyons's *The Dragon Light Series, Spring* — he found this large calligraphic construction in gleaming brass a "comforting abstraction."

The fact that Chinese visitors felt at ease in this new situation reminded me of a previous conversation. When I interviewed Song Chunhua, the former mayor of Changchun, in 1997, he outlined the basis on which the committee had selected works for the park: the sculptor had to be famous and successful in his or her own country, there had to be a variety of styles and media, and the work had to be acceptable to Asian people. Ding Zhenggeng, an art commentator and publisher from Beijing, summed up the range of work as either sculpture of an excellent standard or work that set out to please the public. We may be inclined to think that a sculptor who sets out to please the public is a lesser, inferior artist, but it would seem that Chinese sculptors want to communicate with a wide audience.

John T. Young, Professor of Sculpture and Public Art at the University of Washington and one of the main speakers at the Changchun International Sculpture Conference, succinctly summarized the different attitudes toward public art in the East and the West. The Chinese aim, he said, was to confirm community beliefs; whereas in the West, public art tends to confront the community. Being accustomed

Kim Kwang-Jae, *Childish Heart*, 2001. Marble, 210 x 160 cm.

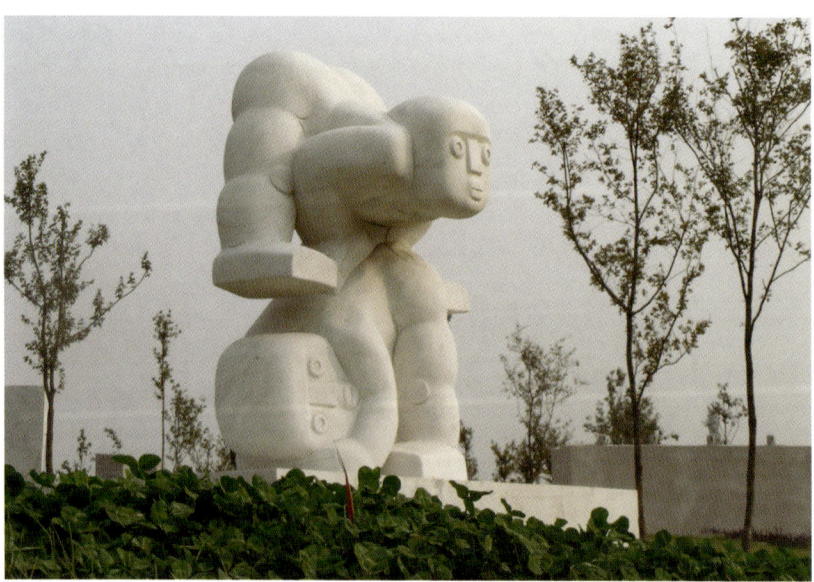

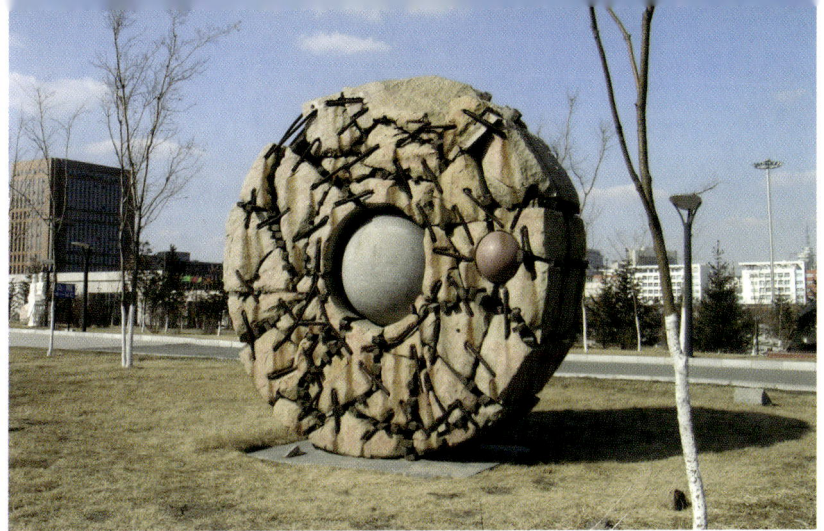

Li Pengcheng, *Tribe Lights*, 2000. Granite, wood, and steel, 300 x 300 x 100 cm.

to art that is often aggressive, critical, and self-oriented, Western viewers may need to adjust in order to fully appreciate the works in the World Sculpture Park. Some of the titles—*The Wings of Spring*, *Song of Springtime*, *Silvery Branches in the Spring Wind*—are indicative of the aims and attitudes. Nevertheless, a few of the works on the theme of spring are unexpectedly experimental: *Spring Stone* by the French sculptor Frederic Oudry is a massive uncut stone with small ceramic buds bursting from its slumbering bulk.

The sculpture park can trace its inception to a sculpture commission for the huge Culture Square. The space lacked a focal point, and eventually a soaring sculpture, *Sun Bird*, was installed. Since then, city authorities have embraced sculpture with extraordinary enthusiasm. Beginning in 1997, six symposia have been held, attended by a total of 270 sculptors from 109 countries and 22 districts in China, including Hong Kong, Macao, and Taiwan. In 1999, I watched the 38 sculptors at work at Shengli Park. It was an impressive sight: two rows of artists and their technical assistants, stone carvers, and welders all hard at work in the brilliant sunshine. For six weeks, each invited sculptor was given air travel, accommodation, materials and equipment, two or three artisans to assist, and a personal interpreter—in return, each sculptor donated one work to the city. It was a well-organized scheme: sculptors could work on a large scale with no financial outlay, and the City of Changchun, in return for its liberal financial support, acquired a great number of sculptures for less than the cost of commissioning them.

During my visit in 1999, I noted that significant changes were occurring in Chinese sculpture, and a survey of the works in the park demonstrates shifting attitudes and new developments. If the established practice of depicting political leaders was already out of favor (and certainly there are no images of Chairman Mao), the influence of what can be called Social Realist Romanticism is still evident. Guo Huaixing's huge bronze *Genesis* shows a muscular heroic figure forging the future with superhuman strength. Wang Ke Ging's *The Idyllic Conception* idealizes creativity, depicting an author in a dramatic pose with pen in outstretched hand. Despite the fact that many of the Western sculptors represented in the park have worked in an abstract or semi-abstract style, there is still an element of symbolic romanticism in a number of their works—as is the case with the Dutch artist Marianne Van Den Heuvel's *Changchun Gate of Peace*.

Changchun's example has been followed by a number of other Chinese cities—Guilin, Hangzhou, Tianjin, and Yanqing—which have also established symposia as a means of acquiring a range of Chinese and international sculpture. The most spectacular is Yuzi Paradise, 26 kilometers from Guilin in southern China, which is financed by an extremely wealthy businessman, Rhy-Chang Tsao, assisted by his art director Shiau Jan-Jen. Yuzi Paradise has a sensational setting of mountains, lakes, and forests, as well as some extraordinarily adventurous architecture.

Changchun, by comparison, is almost completely flat. The sculpture park, however, has been skillfully landscaped to form an impressively large lake and rolling hills. Contrary to our perception of the traditional Chinese garden (which is characteristic of southern rather than northern China), where the visual delights are revealed in a series of carefully calculated, ever-changing views, the World Sculpture Park is more like Versailles, with vistas spreading to the horizon. Undoubtedly it took years for the avenues of trees to grow in France, and the planting is still far from complete at Changchun—though the model shows a densely wooded parkland. Many of the sculptures at present appear too exposed and too regularly distributed along the pathways. In time, however, the citizens of Changchun will have a beautiful park in which to stroll.

The Changchun authorities certainly spent lavishly to establish the World Sculpture Park, and what is more remarkable, it is seen as part of an ongoing process of bringing public sculpture to the city. Wang Xue Zham, Deputy Mayor, spoke at the International Sculpture Conference and outlined plans to develop Changchun as a "city of sculpture." Not only will sculptures be added to the existing collection, but more and more public works will be added to the city—along highways, in squares and parks, at major sites such as the airport, the railway station, and the zoological gardens. It is an ambitious long-range plan. In the space of a few years, Changchun will have undergone an extraordinary transformation, becoming a city distinguished for visionary parklands and sculpture.

The Open-Air Art Museum at Pedvale

by Allison Hunter

Part nature trail, part pagan playground, and part Northern European art hub, the Open-Air Art Museum at Pedvale (or Pedvale, for short) draws international artists as well as a constant flow of tourists to the remote Talsi region of Western Latvia, 75 miles from the capital city of Riga. When founder Ojars Feldbergs spotted the lush rolling hills, forests, and streams of a German country estate abandoned after World War II, he knew instantly that the bucolic setting would be perfect for his museum without walls. In fact, the only walls at Pedvale belong to 200-year-old historic landmarks that house secondary exhibitions. One of the most striking "rooms" at the park is a roofless gallery—the crumbling stone walls reach almost to ceiling height where they meet clouds and blue skies. Inside the walls, Feldbergs's carved stone sculptures rest on pedestals surrounded by red dirt, gravel, and weeds.

Invited artists create work for specific areas of the park, often using stone and wood from Pedvale, during summer workshops that adhere to themes chosen by Feldbergs. The park's thematic programs—2007's was "Stone.Landscape"—attract artists who, like Feldbergs, favor a down-to-earth atmosphere over the ego-circus of a splashy biennial.

Ojars Feldbergs, *51 Heartstones*, 1997. Wood, stone, and paint, 6.5 x 131 x 66 ft.

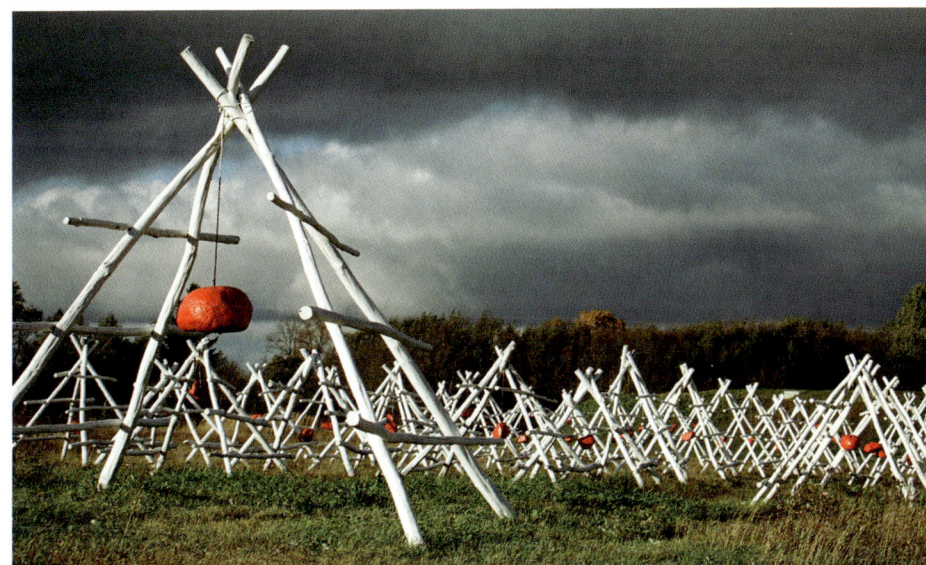

Feldbergs, a renowned artist in Latvia, has exhibited his work throughout Europe, in Japan and South Korea, as well as in nearby countries formerly within the Soviet orbit. Despite his pedigree, he has an elfish sense of humor. In 2002, he served Bloody Marys at the opening of the "Fire" season of that year's "Prime Elements of the World — Fire, Water, Earth, Air" program and vodka at "Water." And when local residents smirk at his eclectic art collection, he laughs right back. In 2001, he allowed artists to erect large white letters spelling PEDVALE, à la Hollywood, on a hill overlooking Sabile.

But the reality of life as an artist in post-Communist Latvia is no joke. Artists have confronted setbacks such as a lack of recognition, material resources, and funding. Feldbergs and his contemporaries endured decades of Soviet censorship only to find independence (in 1991) within a country practically in ruin. Feldbergs says that Latvian traditions, folklore, and imagination sustained creativity during Soviet occupation. Today, however, Latvia must learn from Western capitalist societies, which regularly sponsor artists and art centers.

With little government funding, Feldbergs fosters a dynamic art scene. He promotes artistic practice, experimentation, and the education of emerging Baltic artists at Pedvale. In 2000, he invited U.S. sculptors Kenneth Payne and Carl Billingsly (professors of art at Buffalo State College, State University of New York and East Carolina State University, respectively) to lead an iron-pour workshop, which resulted in their collaborative *Valley Fire*, a 12-foot-tall stone, brick, and cast iron structure with a working fire pit at the base.

Payne and Billingsly enjoyed sharing their expert casting skills with the energetic and appreciative Eastern and Northern European sculptors. After their first foray, they returned to Pedvale, with select college students in tow, to lead additional workshops, despite the lack of basic art supplies and safety materials. Once, instead of using the usual isopropyl alcohol to make a mold wash, they made do with a bottle of moonshine. The hardships, Payne says, are worth it. "In the States, if you tell people you are a sculptor, they hide their children and lock up their wives and close the door and put away their valuables," he jokes. "But over there, it's quite different. Being an artist is considered an honored profession. There's an attempt to understand what you're doing as opposed to the 'Oh well, I don't like that modern art crap' attitude that you can run into here."

Danish artist Erik Schwarzbart, a seasoned professional with a 30-year career, installed *The Cult Place* at Pedvale in 2001. Like Feldbergs, Schwarzbart talks about the magic of the land, claiming a "special energy" where his sculpture rests. "It is obvious that Ojars has a great love for Pedvale, and with his strong energy, he has come far to create an international center of sculpture," says Schwarzbart. His only concern is for the future of the park: "I hope Pedvale does not become a place where artists just put their objects outdoors, but that Ojars will keep the 'site-specific' idea, where the art is made exactly for that place and has a dialogue with the surrounding nature."

Feldbergs keeps the park going with income from modest entrance fees, a restaurant, and a hotel—all of which keep him glued to his cell phone. He manages a small group of hardworking teenagers from Sabile who wait tables, scrub wood floors, and put fresh bouquets in every room. In return, Feldbergs allows them to blast Latvian muzak, which combines tunes by the likes of Elvis and Madonna, sung in Latvian, into the restaurant and the outside seating area. They claim that the "country" people who visit the restaurant love it.

Many native Latvian visitors linger at the restaurant, while their children play on the swings. This is fortunate for visitors who enjoy walking the mile-long trek without the distraction of human voices. The art blends so delicately into its surroundings—nestled in streambeds or tied to tree branches—that you might even miss some of it the first time around. Picking one's way down narrow paths and over mossy streams—more Druid crossing than Disney theme park—it becomes clear that the artworks are not about to overshadow the beauty already "installed" by nature. Feldbergs points out that the path is ancient—he just followed what seemed to have been there for

Mairita and Ivo Folkmans, *Fire Road*, 2000. Wood and sand, 8 x 30 ft.

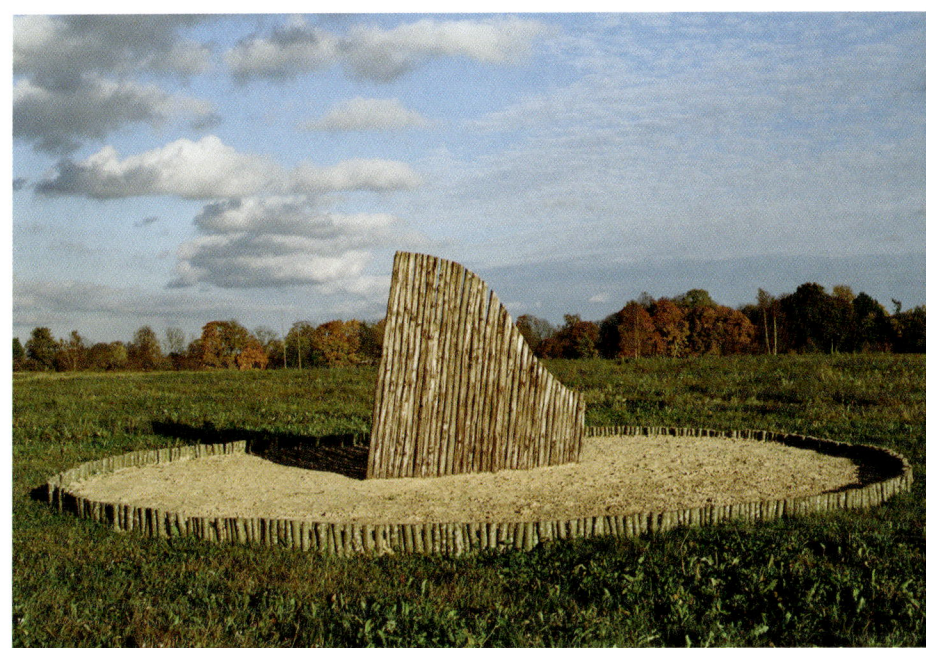

centuries. The 45-minute walk often leaves tourists wanting to bail out after the first half—but there's no way you can cut it short without simply turning back. One Portuguese tourist joked that the endurance factor kept away "fat Americans."

Many park visitors come back year after year. They look forward to revisiting the permanent installations and are eager to catch the latest work by one of Feldbergs's high-quality picks. With the increased interest in his workshops, Feldbergs has decided to dedicate more and more of the virgin land to new art. He sees the growth optimistically. "Pedvale is the convergence of natural landscape, agricultural landscape, cultural heritage, and contemporary art in one entirety," he says, sounding all business. But at sunset, he reveals a different side—the artist who believes "a sculpture is born and needs air—the space of life." Feldbergs quietly excuses himself from a conversation at the tavern, puts his cell phone away, and turns his attention to the sky above the rolling hills of Pedvale, watching the fiery light descend, as though for the first time.

<www.pedvale.lv>

The Cullen Sculpture Garden: A Conversation with Isamu Noguchi

by Tsipi Ben-Haim

In April of 1986, Isamu Noguchi completed the Lillie and Hugh Roy Cullen Sculpture Garden at the Museum of Fine Arts, Houston. "Art is a continuous search," said the artist, then 82. "There is no end to it and that is what makes it so marvelous." This sense of searching and discovery is felt throughout the garden. Geometrically shaped concrete walls, varying in height from two to 14 feet, create intimate spaces and serve as backdrops for human-scale sculptures. Walking paths of red carnelian granite hug rolling, grassy mounds and weave through crepe myrtles, sycamores, and water oak pines. On the day that the garden opened, Noguchi, an enthusiastic guide, explained how the project began and how he felt about its completion.

Tsipi Ben-Haim: Plans for the Cullen Sculpture Garden began nine years ago. What took so long?
Isamu Noguchi: What you see is only a small part of what I originally planned. At first I thought to plan an island because there had just been a flood. Then I thought the garden might be depressed (sunken), but they said that it would collect water. I put up walls because of the traffic; they said, "No walls." There were many contradictions

The Lillie and Hugh Roy Cullen Sculpture Garden, aerial view.

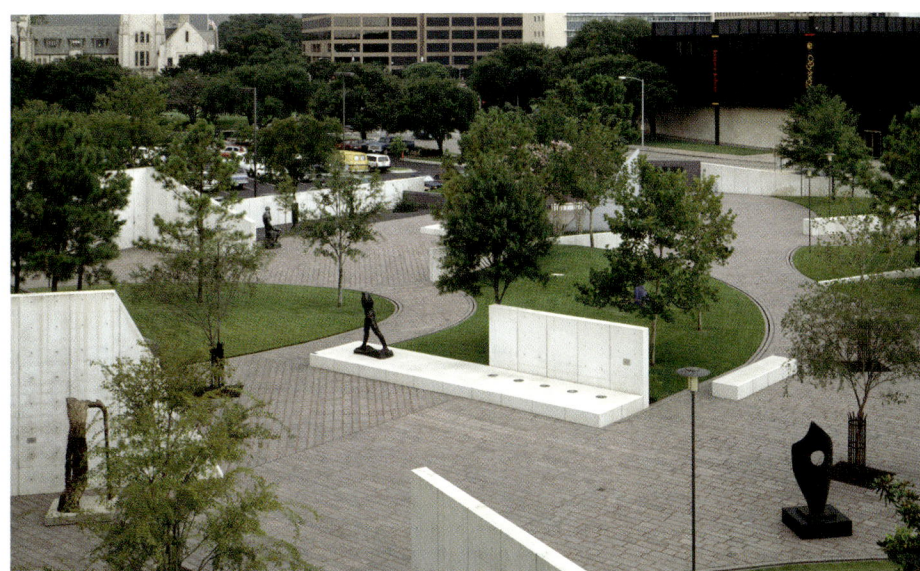

to resolve. But if you can read the problem planted before you, you may latch onto a higher truth and achieve what is correct.

TB: Did you achieve your goals in the final creation of the garden?

IN: I am pleased, especially with the contradictions within the garden. It is not exactly a walled site, although there are walls. It's not exactly open, and yet everyone can walk in from almost any direction. I feel that there is a kind of conversation going on between the trees, walls, spaces, people, and sculptures. It is an alive place.

TB: This type of project normally requires constant collaboration. Is that the case here?

IN: My collaborations are of a different sort. I don't collaborate on the design. I collaborate on the use. The architect—in this case, Shoji Sadao—works out the best way to fabricate and assemble all the elements. An artist may work with others, and for others, yet he must finally do it for himself or he will not gain confidence.

TB: How would you like people to see and treat the garden?

IN: I hope that the open feeling of the garden breaks down the boundaries between people and sculpture. The sculptures should not be confined to the garden like possessions. I want people to enjoy the garden, to sit, walk, look, discover, play music, and constantly experience something new while adopting the garden as their own environment. When people walk through the garden, I hope they will hear a conversation between the walls and spaces, people and sculpture.

TB: The garden is a piece of sculpture in itself.

IN: There are many kinds of sculpture. A garden is a living sculpture. A sculpture on a pedestal is a thing on a pedestal. Monumental sculpture goes outside the realm of art into architecture. Then we have the human-scale sculpture, one rooted in the ground where you are. It's a matter of scale.

TB: Through the years you have created many gardens—in Paris, Detroit, Los Angeles, and Jerusalem. Is the Cullen Sculpture Garden different?

IN: Gardens for me are sculptures made with nature, yet each one is different from the others. The Billy Rose Sculpture Garden (Jerusalem) is closest to the Cullen Garden. They were made to accommodate sculptures by other sculptors. However, they are very different from each other because of the nature of the location. The Cullen Sculpture Garden is located in an urban environment on only an acre of land. I wanted it to be connected to the outside world, yet isolated. All of the sculptures in the garden will be human scale, more or less.

TB: Once you finish designing a sculpture garden, do you ever go back and assist in placing new sculpture or give advice on maintenance?

IN: No, absolutely not. I do not interfere. Choosing the sculptures, placing them, taking care of the trees and the grass are all up to the owners, the museum. Peter Marzio and Alison Green are deciding what to put in and where.

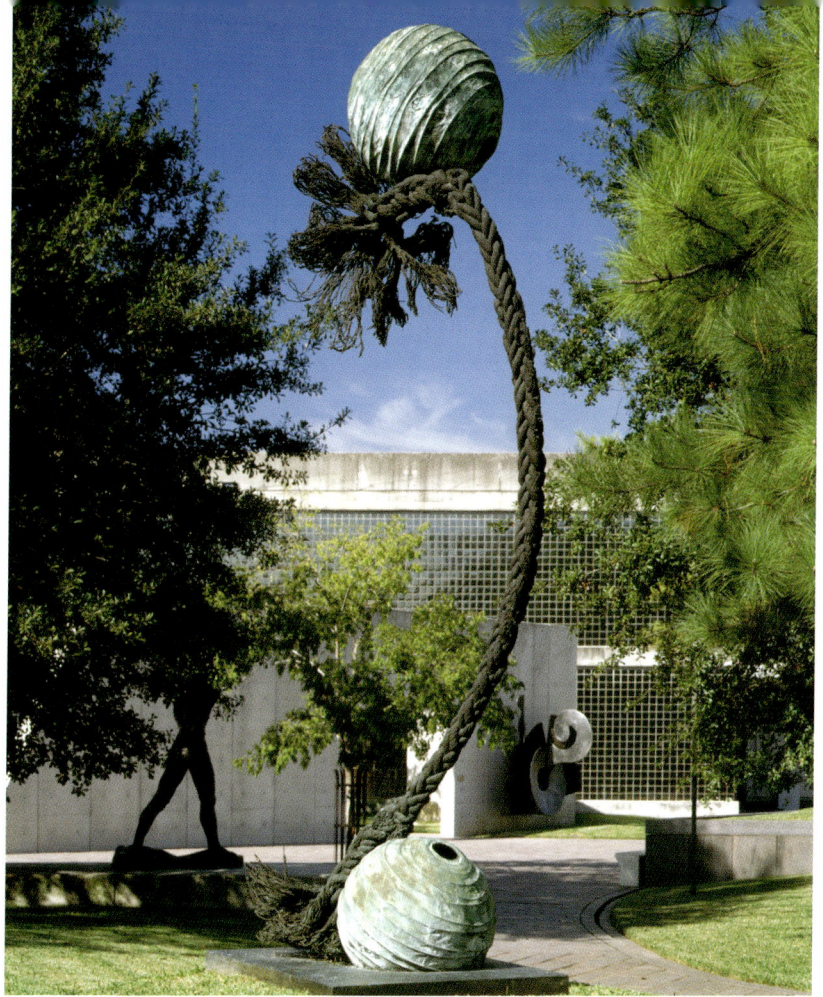

Joseph Havel, *Exhaling Pearls*, 1993. Patinated bronze, 130 x 55 x 33 in.

I recently revisited my garden at UNESCO in Paris. It was overgrown with weeds, jabbering away and having a wonderful time. The garden is all on its own with nobody taking care of it. I've never seen it look so beautiful. I hope that time will also play with this garden as it grows older.

TB: Do you have any regrets about the finished project?

IN: There are things I would like to change. I would like the light boxes changed. This corner is too crowded. The stone bench here should be lower.

TB: What do you wish for the garden, now that it's on its own?

IN: Not to be a repository of gifts.

<www.mfah.org/sculpturegarden>

Hic Terminus Haeret: Daniel Spoerri's Garden

by John O'Brien

I first encountered Daniel Spoerri's work through one of his "snare-paintings." This object (actually, a set of objects) consisted of a wall-mounted tabletop onto which the remains of a meal had been fixed: drinking glasses, cigarette butts, an ashtray, cutlery, dishes, and some residual food all clung to the wooden surface, sealed within transparent glue. Peeling labels, the fading colors of the ordinary objects, and the effects of time seemed to contradict the scene's air of recent abandonment. The tabletop itself was quite fascinating, both in how it defeated gravity with its unusual verticality and in how its collection of residual objects hovered precisely between the determination of a sculptural composition and the haphazardness of found debris. It was hard for me as a viewer to determine just how to situate my own body in relation to this displacement of the everyday. It felt like everything was becoming topsy-turvy. It was likewise weird to imagine just how Spoerri selected the moment to freeze the meal. Why stop there and not after a few more bites?

Later, I read more about Spoerri's "Tableaux Piège" ("Trap Pictures," "picture-traps," "snare-pictures," or "booby-trapped paintings"; although none of these translations works entirely, all are acceptable) and how he and other artists in the Nouveau Réalisme movement were intent on making cast-offs, residuals, and detritus from the

Daniel Spoerri, *Labyrinthic mural path*, 1996/98. Stone and grass, 60 x 40 meters.

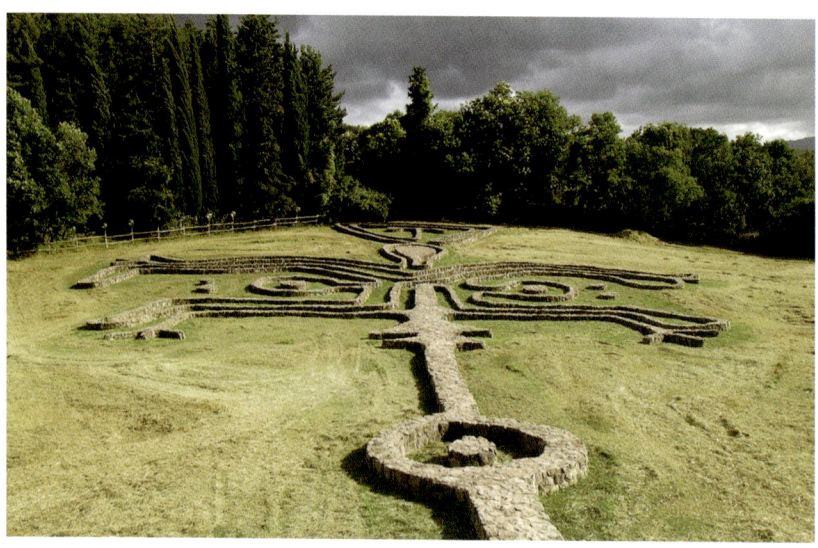

world into the core of their poetics. Still later, I read about the ephemeral qualities of Spoerri's work with food and his longstanding investigations of coincidence, randomness, and chance. With this memory of the relatively anarchical nature of his work, I was surprised to discover that he had established a permanent sculpture garden in the hills near Siena. Aside from wondering what Spoerri, who is often associated with Fluxus, would make within the parameters of permanence, I wanted to explore Tuscany, an area known for its natural beauty and graceful landscapes. So, I set off to visit the Hic Terminus Haeret garden and, from there, I was able to speak with Spoerri by phone about his work.*

Spoerri's interest in the idea of a park for sculpture can be traced to the Sacro Bosco at Bomarzo. This extravagant garden, which features topiary monsters and grotesque stone carvings (<www.parcodeimostri.com>), was commissioned in the 16th century by Pier Francesco Orsini. Small, but powerful and haunting, Bomarzo has fascinated Spoerri since he first discovered it in 1964. The property he turned into his own park is more expansive, and it is now home to 87 permanent works by 42 artists, including Spoerri, Dani Karavan, Meret Oppenheim, Not Vital, and Jean Tinguely. Spoerri describes the park as a kind of "album di poesie" or chapbook, in which he has annotated the passage of his time with his closest peers through a physical transformation of the land.

What is immediately striking about Hic Terminus Haeret is the relationship between the artworks and the natural environment. Unlike conventional sculpture gardens in which the sculptures stand away from the neutral framing device of surrounding trees and plants, Hic Terminus Haeret allows the park's natural features to envelop the work. The extensive walk that constitutes a visit is chock-full of unexpected appearances. The interplay between natural elements in the garden and the metal and stone works accentuates their reciprocal differences, heightening awareness of both.

Rounding the corner on an uphill path, viewers suddenly find themselves above a field dotted with sculptures in a sort of oasis (*Eight Skinny Nightmares*, 2003). A nearby tower features a telescope mounted on the railing (*Voyeur*, 1996/98). The scope can be trained on three sculptures mounted on raised pedestals in the distance (*Bullock's head*, *Snow Angel*, *Dreifuß*). Typical of the programmatic changes in viewing conditions within the garden, *Voyeur* can only be seen "clearly" at a distance, since the sculptures are raised too far above the ground to be seen from the field itself. *Eight Skinny Nightmares* seems more accessible, but the tall plants surrounding this oasis/thicket make any approach daunting. The gathered nightmares leer out at the viewer from the tangled brambles.

Elsewhere, pushing through a row of trees, viewers come upon a vast petroglyph walkway, which cover half the expanse of a meadow. *Labyrinthic mural path* (1996/98) is based on a pre-Columbian image of the sun god meeting the first woman. Off to the right, an Arman fountain made of ploughs and reaper blades rises from the water (*Monument for Settlers*, 1999/2000). An especially beautiful and moving sculpture hides within a glade of bushes and trees. Here, Spoerri re-created the room in Paris where he began his work in the visual arts (*Chamber No. 13, Hotel Carcasonne, Rue Mouffetard 24, Paris 1959–1965*, 1998; this is the second version, the first was made in wood). The strangeness of the cast metal room is accentuated by the tilt of the floor (an homage to the "The Hanging House" built on an inclined rock at Bomarzo). Each element of the room was painstakingly reconstructed: the table with leftovers, the rumpled bed, the small gas stove, some elementary carving tools. The degree of detail is fascinating, like a miniature painting enlarged. The mortality that *Chamber* frames in its role as a memento mori is mitigated by the softness of the surrounding nature. Like many works in the garden, opposites seem to be reconciled in context.

During his life in the arts, Spoerri has sought to create situations that dislocate viewers' certainties and expectations. He privileges internal poetic coherence over stylistic continuity, oscillating freely between traditional and unusual materials. This approach to art-making gives his work a particular dynamism and accords it a degree of difficulty for the viewer. In his garden, the visitor is offered a view of his eclectic

Daniel Spoerri, *Circle of Unicorns*, 1991. Bronze, 9 elements, 250 x 40 x 50 cm.

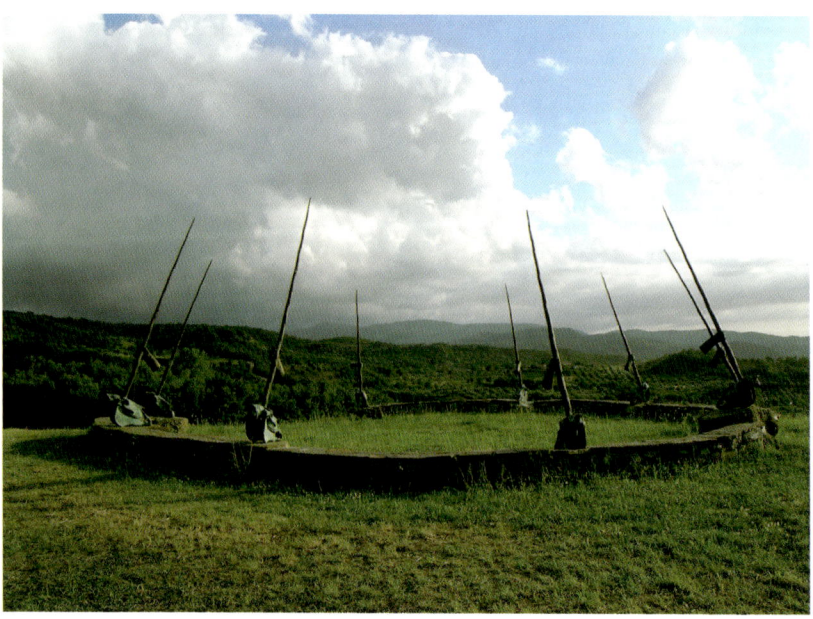

approach in its entirety. Without a doubt, Spoerri's profound intention is to set visitors off on a path of initiation and awakening. On the way, they can discover how the "raw" and the "cooked" can be united (even in antithesis or conflict) and how art can transform the most disparate of materials. The Hic Terminus Haeret garden is a subtle, liminal study in the overturning of things. After a visit, objects and ideas of the everyday world no longer appear as they did before.

Note

* Special thanks to Daniel Spoerri for speaking with me from Vienna on July 18, 2007. Thanks also to Susanne Neumann, artist and cultural manager of the garden, for her time and photographs. All references are derived from those conversations and from *Il Giardino di Daniel Spoerri*, edited by Anna Mazzanti, (Siena: maschietto&musolino, 1998–99).

<www.danielspoerri.org>

Little Sparta: Ian Hamilton Finlay's Garden

by Anne Barclay Morgan

In the uplands of southern Scotland, Ian Hamilton Finlay gradually created one of the most impressive contemporary sites integrating sculpture and environment: the garden surrounding his house. A poet and artist, with works in sculpture gardens and public spaces throughout Europe, Finlay also devoted over 25 years to planning, building, and expanding his neoclassical garden, which he named Little Sparta. In transforming four acres of desolate moorland into an intricate series of landscaped spaces, he selected shrubs, trees, and other natural elements to complement his sculptures, revealing a refined sense of spatial rhythm. Set at the considerable altitude of 1,000 feet, the garden only really exists in the summer, though Finlay considered the foliage as much a part of the site as the sculpture. Before his death, he gave ownership of the garden and its sculpture to the Little Sparta Trust, and the foundation has managed the site since 2006.

    Finlay's home was originally an abandoned croft outside Edinburgh, remote enough to daunt all but the most determined art enthusiast. Through his own intense physical labor and uncompromisingly challenging designs, the land on all four sides of the original house has been transformed into carefully planned areas, each highly distinctive and bearing a title. A map identifies 36 sites, and a minimum of two hours is needed to obtain a general overview of the layout. In order to read the inscriptions on Finlay's sculptures and walkways, and appreciate the subtleties of his ideas, a visitor could easily spend days wandering through the landscape.

    The gate in front of the house bears the name, "Little Sparta." Finlay originally called the house Stonypath, but that was before his 1978 "five-year hellenization plan." Once inside, the visitor comes across a Roman garden, a sunken garden, stone walkways, paths, small intimate places, and, behind the house, numerous ponds as well as large open spaces that embrace the sky and merge into the windswept moor.

    On the ground, hanging from branches, or nestled among the bushes and trees, Finlay's poetic sculptures are often surprising in location, material, and content. Some embody emblematic metaphors, blending a motto or an idyllic poem with the visual element. Others make statements about war and social order. To reflect the crisis of values in the modern age, Finlay elaborated on the concept of a neoclassical re-armament, in which Greek and Roman deities are reincarnated as war machines. His evaluation of cultural forces, particularly their interaction with destructive elements, is dominant. Materials range from stone to bronze, brightly painted metal, resin, and brick. Along with the classicizing statues that one would expect in such a garden, objects such as sundials, posts, and pillars are juxtaposed with vessels, aircraft carriers, and other emblems of war, in addition to miniaturized obelisk- and pyramid-shaped monuments. Inscriptions often combine textual and visual references to artists such as Albrecht Dürer.

Outbuildings also form part of Finlay's design. The Garden Temple, with its inscriptions "To Apollo," "His Music," "His Missiles," and "His Muses" across the façade, has been the focus of many disputes with regional authorities. In 1983, in what was then called the "First Battle of Little Sparta," the sheriff tried to confiscate works from the Garden Temple; he was stopped by a group of Finlay's supporters. A month later, however, the sheriff removed the works, some of which belonged to private collectors and institutions; many were never returned to their owners. As a result, "Little Sparta" remained closed to visitors for a year. Ironically perhaps, the temple overlooks the beautifully serene Temple Pond, beyond which lies the Temple of Philemon and Baucis.

About two-thirds of Little Sparta is intricate and intimate, with many hidden surprises and great compositional variety within a very small space. Beyond the Claudi Bridge (referring to Claude Lorrain), the garden expands, stretching out into the vastness of the moor. Overlooking Loch Eck, the largest body of water, various structures and sculptures show the diversity of Finlay's designs. On one edge of the water, a

Ian Hamilton Finlay with Nicholas Sloan, *The Present Order*, 1983. Purbeck and Whitsum stone, installation view.

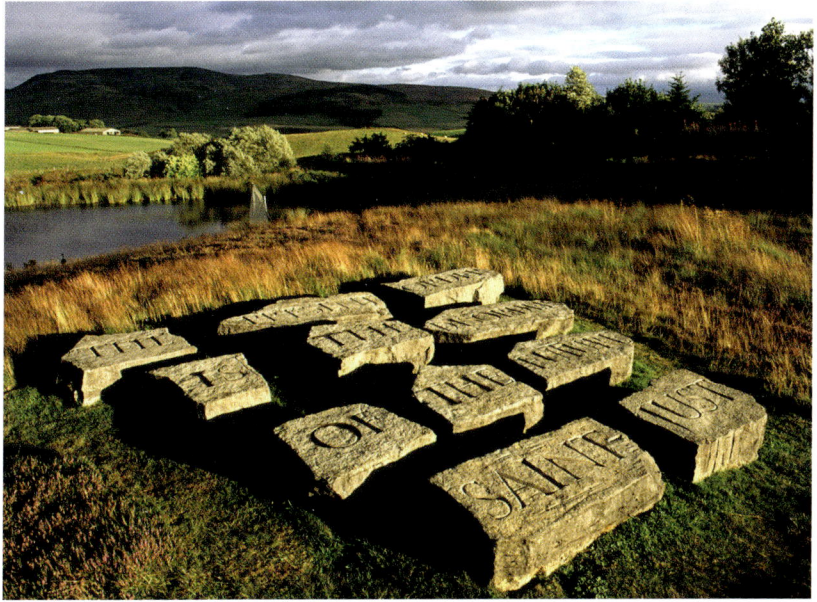

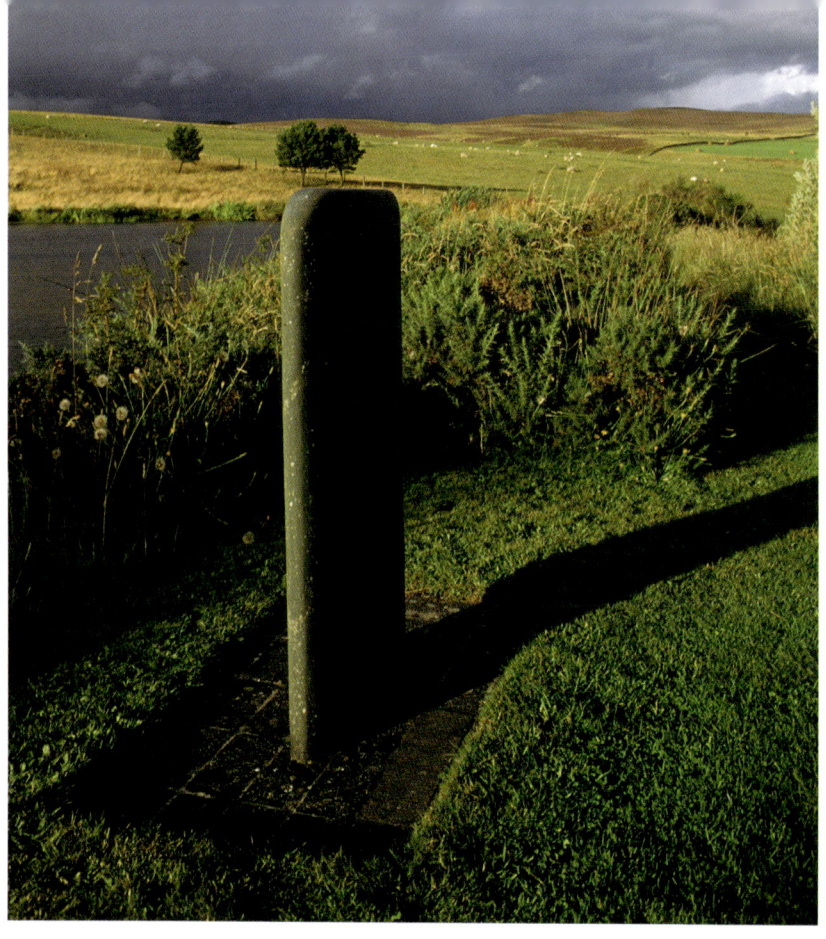

Ian Hamilton Finlay with John Andrew, *Nuclear Sail*, 1974. Slate, installation view.

solitary column, inscribed with a quotation from the French revolutionary Saint-Just, makes its stand against the barren hills and ominous sky. *Nuclear Sail*, a tall slate sculpture, rises on the other side. On the hill above squats *Little Goose Hut* (1982), and nearby, a huge work made from mammoth blocks of stone aligned in four rows, each inscribed with a word from the phrase "The Present Order, Is The Disorder, Of The Future, Saint-Just," would be best read from an airplane.

Finlay did not originally plan for a public garden. Inspired in part by the garden of William Shenstone, an 18th-century English poet, Finlay viewed his garden as a process, and process had become an ideology for him. The very fact of working with nature gave the notion of permanence a different meaning. Flowers, plants, trees, and sculptures all became integral parts of his design. Following these organic principles, Finlay felt that he was restoring a world and a culture largely lost at the beginning of World War II.

Finlay's designs show the workings of a meticulous mind. He primarily employed craftspeople from England, who carved the inscriptions and fabricated his sculptures to his designs. In all of his work, there was a purity of thought, of concept, a certain objectivity, and the absence of personal psychology.

Although Finlay didn't like Little Sparta to be considered as his chef d'oeuvre, he tested ideas here that he later used in larger, more public locations. For *Sacred Grove*, one of Finlay's favorite works (it stands at the heart of the Kröller-Müller Museum's sculpture garden in the Netherlands), he first experimented with the stone tree-columns in Little Sparta. "I couldn't really have done [*Sacred Grove*] without doing it first here, in order to understand how to put the stone in front of the trees, what happens with the roots of the trees, what problems there are likely to be and also how it would actually look," he explained.

At Little Sparta, as well as in his commissioned outdoor work and published proposals for new gardens and landscape improvements, Finlay emphasized the integration of sculpture with landscape. To concentrate on the sculpture in Little Sparta was not his intent: he disapproved of focusing a camera on the objects. In contrast to the contemporary sculpture garden, which Finlay considered a "deplorable manifestation," every element in his garden is a crucial part of larger whole.

<www.littlesparta.org>

Robert Irwin's *Central Garden* at the Getty

by Collette Chattopadhyay

Robert Irwin's *Central Garden* (1997), inaugurated with the Getty Center in Los Angeles, is like a slow overture. Comparable to the first movement of a four-part symphony, it needed time and the seasons to unfold its full orchestration of colors, textures, patterns, fragrances, sounds, and flora. Lodged between the museum pavilions and the Research Institute, the garden is, as Irwin puts it, "a sculpture in the form of a garden that's aspiring to be art."* Transforming with the seasons and over time, it challenges the conventional concept of sculpture as an immutable, cast, chiseled, or fabricated work. By its second year, for example, the London plane trees, which border a cascading stream that descends into a reflecting pool, had nearly reached their full height, offering shade for the seasonal plants clustered around their trunks.

Central Garden's themes of light, space, ephemerality, and transformation are the same leitmotifs that brought Irwin to prominence as a founder of the Light and Space movement in the mid-1960s. This dematerialized work emphasizes sensory perception as the essence of art. Precedents for *Central Garden* include Irwin's *Filigreed Line* (1979–80) at Wellesley College in Massachusetts, *Two Running Violet V Forms* (1981–83) at the University of California in San Diego, and *Sentinel Plaza* (1989–90) at the Pasadena Police Department Building in California. Like these pieces, *Central Garden* creates intriguing dialogues with earthworks by artists such as Robert Smithson and Andy Goldsworthy, using the elements of nature and time in conjunction with light and space.

Five years in the making, Irwin's garden is located on a 134,000-square-foot plot of land, formerly a rugged, arid canyon. He faced at least two formidable site challenges. First, there are the spectacular city and ocean views that fall to the left and right as visitors enter the complex. For some, these views alone will justify the trip. With such phenomena vying for viewer attention, Irwin was up against nothing less than the power of nature itself. Simultaneously, Richard Meier's imposing, travertine buildings frame and encircle *Central Garden* with their massive Modernist cadences of monumentality. Indeed, from the elevated location to the marble buildings that echo with memories of Greek antiquity, to the pilgrimage of ascent required for reaching the complex, the Getty Center is laden with the parlance of power.

Creating a counter-fugue to this dialogue, Irwin's work plays in a knowing and sophisticated manner with the rubrics of authority. Emphasizing variable, transitory, and ephemeral elements, his work physically and theoretically inverts the emphases of power and permanence established elsewhere on the Getty campus. Extending such themes spatially, Irwin created a sunken garden, conceptually reversing the journey of ascent inherent in arriving at the Getty. Suggesting that a wild yet cultivated garden can be construed as art, Irwin challenges the assumption that art is an extraordinary and uncommon experience. *Central Garden* is thus constructed around a motif borrowed from nature: a ravine with a stream that leads to a waterfall and ends in a reflecting pool.

As one descends into *Central Garden*, city, sea, and architecture slowly disappear from view. The pathway to the bottom is divided into four sections, perhaps echoing the seasons. Moving from the plaza level through a myriad of small, irregular stairs or by means of a single processional staircase, visitors arrive at a circular plateau. This leads to a Zen-like, zig-zagging garden path that slows descent and encourages the observation of a rambling manmade creek that echoes a mountain stream set with roughly cut California and Montana boulders. As the brook disappears beneath a second dais, the viewer enters a tier embellished with six steel armatures, which in winter resemble barren trees. In spring these appear as exotic flowering bougainvillea palms, though nature herself knows no such species. Circling this platform to the left or right, the viewer glimpses the stream transformed into a waterfall. A second zig-zagging trail defined by 2.5-foot-high Cor-ten steel walls leads to a closer vantage point. The garden's climax is an elegant reflecting pool graced with a floating maze of azaleas. The cadence of the descent moderates the viewer's accustomed city pace while putting a spin on the concept of art as something rarefied.

Robert Irwin, *Central Garden* (detail), **134,000 sq. ft.**

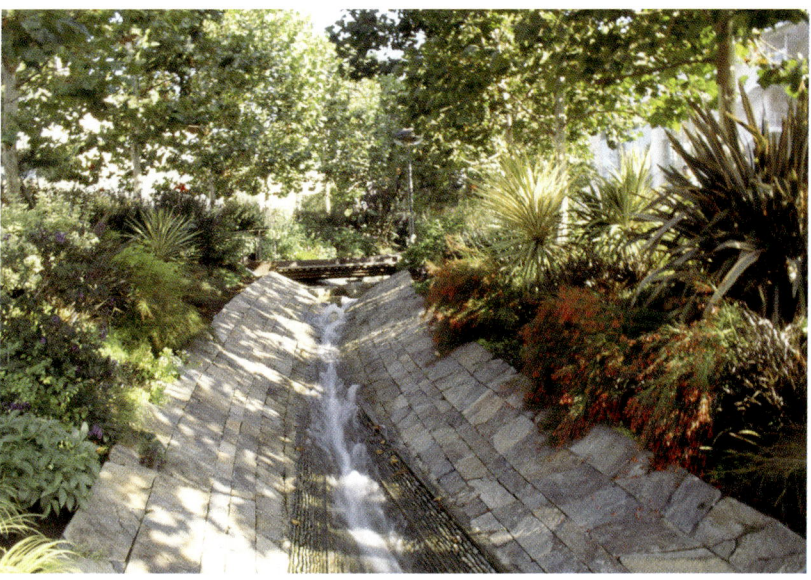

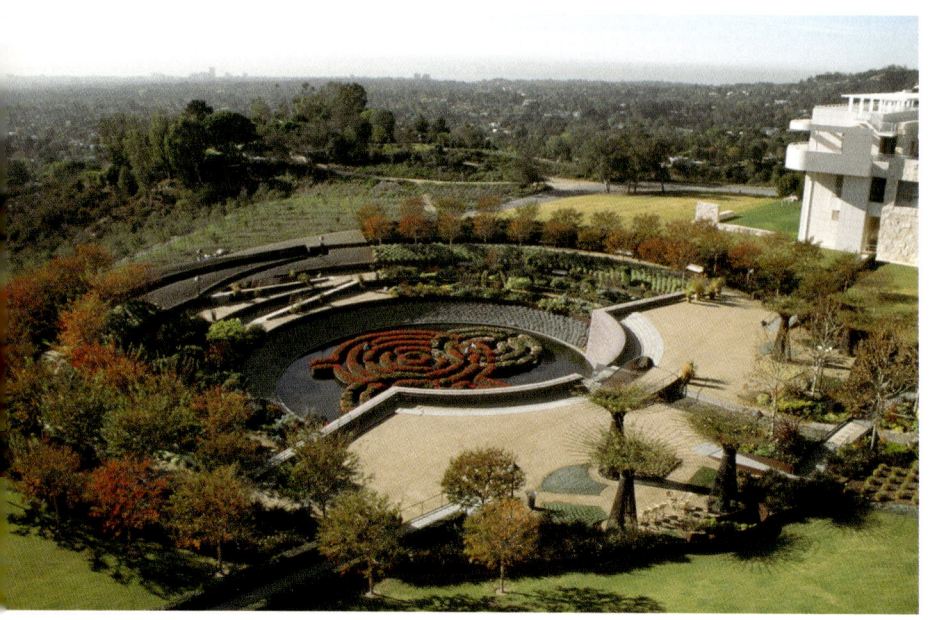

Robert Irwin, *Central Garden*, 134,000 sq. ft.

Irwin wittily calls this location the power point of the complex. An upward glance offers a panoramic view of the garden and Getty buildings, establishing the symbiotic dichotomies that interrelate *Central Garden* to the architecture above. In configuration, *Central Garden* mirrors the circular geometry of the Research Institute; but where the institute enunciates space as positive, solid, and convex, the garden presents space as negative, open, and concave. Setting a temporal palette of plants, light, and space against the securely moored edifices of marble, mass, and mountain, Irwin plays the ephemeral against the permanent, the ordinary against the rarefied, and nature against culture. Alluding directly to the Getty's role as an art mecca, *Central Garden* suggests that art and beauty reside as much in the enjoyment of ordinary nature as in any extraordinary place or thing.

Thus, perhaps nowhere better than in *Central Garden* is Los Angeles' metaphoric struggle between nature and culture more fittingly addressed. Physically, Irwin has constructed the garden as a canyon, echoing the original configuration of the land and thus paying homage to the history of the site. In addition, the dichotomy of art understood as ordinary as opposed to extraordinary reverberates with relevance in a city celebrated for its spectacular natural vistas and plagued with manmade problems. Juxtaposing nature with culture, *Central Garden* locates artistic experience in coastal bluff grasses, native plants, and regional stones.

For over a decade, *Central Garden* stood as the pre-eminent outdoor sculpture at the Getty, its spaces usually filled with visitors walking the paths, relaxing under the trees, drawing and photographing, and studying its plants. In June 2007, however, it was joined by five new sculpture oases on the campus. These spaces, designed by Richard Meier and Partners and the Olin Partnership, showcase a gift of modern and contemporary sculptures donated by the late film producer Ray Stark and his wife, Fran. The 28 predominantly figural works enhance Meier's austere and pristinely structured space and supply a historical foundation for Irwin's very contemporary vision of sculpture.

Note

* Irwin, quoted in Kristine McKenna, "Welcome to Eden (Circa 1997)," *Los Angeles Times Magazine*, December 7, 1997: p. 40.

<www.getty.edu/visit/see_do/gardens.html>

Nek Chand's *Rock Garden*

by Minhazz Majumdar

I stood surrounded by hundreds of strange beings, fantastical creatures arrayed around me in every direction. Where was I? Lost in a world of dreams or hallucinations? Actually, this was no flight of fancy, but a world created by Nek Chand Saini, better known as Nek Chand. I was standing in his magnificent *Rock Garden* located in India's famed city of Chandigarh, designed by Swiss architect Le Corbusier. The *Rock Garden*, paradoxically, is both the antithesis of the city's detailed planning and an embodiment of the spirit of creativity that defines Chandigarh. An awe-inspiring site spread over 40 acres, this manmade environment of twisting canyons, magnificent waterfalls, and high fortresses is filled with thousands of unusual natural rock forms and sculptures fashioned from waste and found objects. More than just a repository of unusual statues and figurines, the *Rock Garden* is, itself, one giant sculpture, the result of Chand's skillful manipulation of space and scrap.

Chand is a self-taught artist who refuses to be neatly slotted. Sculptor, visionary landscape designer, installation artist, mystic, and master builder, he works with a variety of materials to create new spaces. He is a purveyor of dreamscapes so monumental and so original that they defy conventional categories. Nothing prepares you for the dramatic impact of the environment that he created single-handedly—made even more amazing by the fact that he did not set out to be an acclaimed artist but was simply following the dictates of his heart, trying to translate a vision (literally in his case) into a concrete reality.

Chand's artistic journey is made more extraordinary by the fact that he toiled for nearly 20 years in absolute secrecy, creating the most fantastic of sculptures with the most humble of materials—all kinds of discarded urban and industrial waste. The story of Chand's foray into sculpture is a wonderful saga in itself, a tribute to humanity's innate sense of beauty and a testimony to the universal search for meaning and creativity. Born in 1924, he came to Chandigarh in 1951, leaving behind his native village after the violent Partition of India in 1947 to seek employment on the massive building project. Appointed a roads inspector with the Chandigarh Public Works Department, Chand found himself captivated by the beautiful rock forms he encountered in the course of his work. Chandigarh is nestled in the foothills of the Shivalik range, one of the oldest mountain ranges in India and a treasure house of ancient eroded stone. As he cycled along on inspection tours, Chand's attention was also caught by the great amounts of waste material generated in the course of clearing scores of villages to build the city. From 1958 to 1965, he collected rocks and waste materials, carrying them little by little on the back of his cycle to his secret place deep inside a jungle on the outskirts of the city.

A deeply spiritual man, Chand created his garden as a meditation and a prayer. For him, it has always been a sacred place, ideal for the kingdom of his imagination. At first, he built a small hut by the side of a stream and began creating sculptures of animals, birds, and people from the waste gathered there. At this point, he had collected over 20,000 unique rock forms. These rocks were not inanimate objects for him; as he often claims, they spoke to him. Working on his garden became a major obsession—every evening, at the end of an arduous day at his job, he cycled to the mosquito- and snake-infested jungle where he worked by the light of burning tires to create his fantastical creatures, not one but hundreds of the same kind. He began carving a whole new topography, creating his "sculpted spaces," each one different from the others; then he slowly filled these spaces with the denizens of his imagination. Nature's agents of change, such as wind, weather, water, birds and animals, and plants were (and continue to be) his allies in the process of creation.

In 1973, a government survey team accidentally discovered the hidden garden and was astounded by its size and beauty. Since the garden was unauthorized, illegally occupying government land, by law, it should have been demolished. Fortunately,

Nek Chand, *Rock Garden* (detail), 1950s–present, ongoing project in Chandigarh, India.

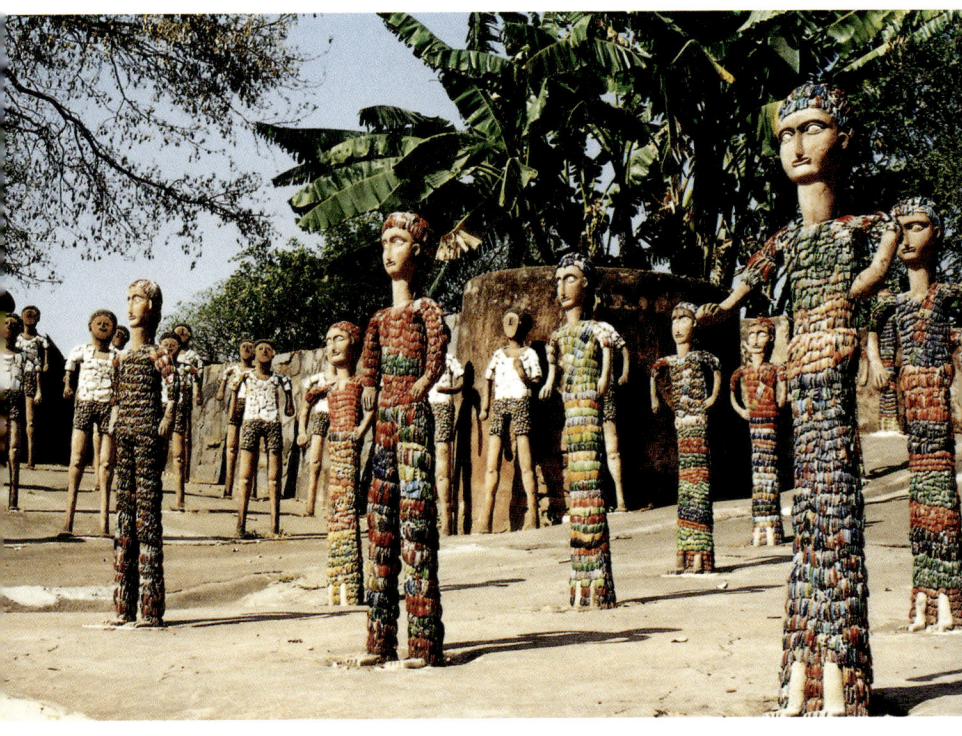

many in the local administration realized its uniqueness and permitted Chand to carry on with his endeavors, even providing him with a salary, workmen, and a truck to transport material. Named the *Rock Garden*, this exceptional visionary art environment was formally opened to the public in 1976, and since then, it has seen more than one million visitors. However, it has not always been smooth sailing. Chand has had to face opposition from jealous local bureaucrats and lawyers bent on preventing the garden's continued existence and expansion. His battles included a court case, which in 1989 was finally decided in his favor, allowing for the expansion and protection of the *Rock Garden*.

Chand's genius lies in the soulful way that he transforms waste into art on a monumental scale. For him, discarded objects are not redundant: they retain an aesthetic worth and possess the magical capacity to transform environments. They are not simply inanimate objects; instead, they possess a force and energy of their own. Following this belief, Chand bestows aesthetic value on all manner of industrial and household junk. Whatever the raw material—old drums, discarded electrical fixtures, bottle caps, fluorescent light tubes, cycle parts, broken pots and crockery, foundry slag, even human hair collected from barber shop floors—Chand's vision enables him to engage in a creative dialogue with it and to create a new form of beauty. Over the years, he has established one of the largest recycling programs in Asia in the *Rock Garden*. According to him, just as nature recycles constantly, so should man learn to use the waste that he generates. He firmly believes that "any conflict between nature's will and man's design is bound to lead to overall destruction." The *Rock Garden* is his effort to explore "the aesthetic dimension" of the essential harmony between man and nature.

As an artist-builder, Chand was inspired by the skillful use of concrete in Le Corbusier's buildings. Concrete appeared magical to him—a fluid paste that could take any shape given to it. It also lent itself to his innovative techniques of embellishment and his innate desire to re-use and recycle since it could be covered with different materials to create diverse and dazzling effects. His control over this medium is tremendous: the concrete forms in the garden are tactile and organic, seeming to spring from the earth itself, especially in the gigantic walls of the manmade canyons and waterfalls. He has used wet sackcloth to give an interesting texture to the concrete pillars and walls, the fine criss-cross of lines on the surface adding a new dimension to the smooth gray surfaces. So masterful is his use of concrete in creating topographical features and so skillfully has he enmeshed nature's creative forces with his own that it is very difficult to tell where the natural finishes and the manmade begins. Is that a real tree trunk or a concrete one? Was this waterfall always there or are Nek Chand's hands behind it? The lines are blurred, everything natural and artificial fusing into a seamless whole.

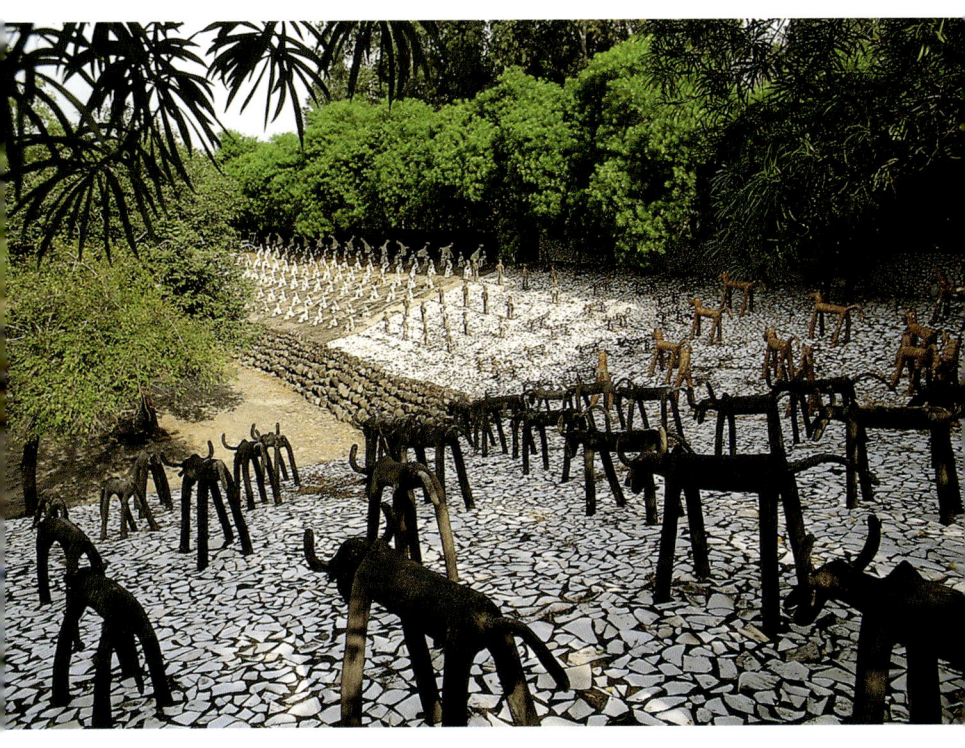

Nek Chand, *Rock Garden* (detail), 1950s–present, ongoing project in Chandigarh, India.

The statues of men and women, birds and beasts, also reveal Chand's mastery of concrete. They consist of metal armatures, often made from discarded bicycle parts over which concrete bodies are molded: bicycle seats become faces, and the forks are turned into legs. Each figure is given a different mosaic skin — an outer layer of broken bangles, bottle caps, pottery shards, and other found objects embedded onto the concrete surface. Most of the animal and human forms are life-sized, though some are smaller or larger than life. Among his noteworthy characters are the bangle ladies, every inch covered in colorful stripes of broken bangles. Their heads are topped with human hair, and their faces wear different expressions. Then there are the crockery figures, whimsical creatures encrusted with ceramic shards, wearing tea cups and teapots for hats, some holding trays in the manner of butlers. Tipsy drunks with their bottles of beer; village belles with their swirling skirts, carrying water-pots on their heads and standing under the streaming waterfalls; flamboyant peacocks — Chand captures the inner essence of these different beings with grace and skill. Most enigmatic are the figurines made of small bits of clinker, their concrete faces smooth in contrast, their beady eyes staring hard into the distance. Giant sculptures made from waste cloth are another of Chand's specialties. Enormous amounts of cloth are twisted around metal frames to create solid forms, the tremendous variety of recycled fabric adding vibrancy to these village folk and animals. Chand's recycling also extends beyond the statues: entire walls of the various chambers have been sculpted out of waste, be it the striking wall of electrical plug molds, discarded tube lights, clinker, or what seems to be the contents of an entire bathroom.

Chand did not stop at creating one sculpture of each kind; instead, he has made entire series of the same sculptures, assembling large groups of beings to create a feeling of abundance and togetherness. The impact of seeing row upon row of a particular kind of sculpture is tremendous—one instinctively revels in the profusion. Within the *Rock Garden*, the visitor is just as much on display as the sculptures. Most of the figures are set in rows on sloping platforms surrounding the viewer. Walking along, it is not hard to imagine that the animal and human figures are looking at you, rather than the other way around.

Inspired by intuition and designed as a kingdom, the *Rock Garden* is divided into three distinct phases, each completed over a different time period. Chand has imbued each phase with its own character, creating distinct enclosures to delight and surprise. The various chambers include the King's Court, the Queen's bathing complex, and a place for musicians to perform, as well as scenes from village life. The earlier parts of the garden, Phases I and II, have been fashioned as a labyrinth, filled with idiosyncratic details at every turn. The chambers, each one colorfully embellished, have high walls and small doorways so that one has to bow low to pass through. The path twists and turns, moves up and down through narrow mysterious gorges where visitors walk single file, and then opens into broad avenues to reveal grand waterfalls. Everywhere there is a sense of discovering the unexpected: the deeper you enter, the keener your expectation becomes. Phase III is the most spectacular part of the garden—there are over 50 gigantic concrete arches winding along, each arch holding a huge family-sized swing. Old or young, people cannot resist these swings, something about them frees the child inside.

Chand is not a "producer" making art for sale or consumption. He wants to offer "a different kind of relationship—one in which the creator and his creations engage the viewer in heightening his inspirational awareness of his environment, his sense of wonder, his playfulness, and his own spirit of creativity." Walking around the *Rock Garden* is definitely not just a stroll in a park—it is akin to a spiritual pilgrimage, a preview of the journey of life. In Phases I and II, you are mostly alone on the narrow twisting pathways. The doorways connecting the various chambers force you to bend down in humility before you are admitted into the presence of the otherworldly beings. Many paths lead nowhere, forcing you to turn around and challenging you to make decisions. You are absorbed in solitary contemplation of both your inner and outer environments. Phase III offers a contrasting sense of openness, of coming out of the wilderness, of companionship. The avenues are broader, with spaces that afford a collective experience: you are now part of a large group. Chand's environments are not only physically attractive, but also spiritually stimulating.

An extremely unassuming man, indeed a man of great spiritual depth and humility, Chand has no time to pontificate about his art. He has been feted the world over, with exhibitions in Berlin, Paris, London, Madrid, the U.S., and Holland. In Paris, he was given the Grande Medaille de Vermeil, and in India, he was awarded the prestigious Padam Shri in 1984. The *Rock Garden* has also been featured on an Indian postage stamp. Several of his sculptures have been placed in museums and art centers across the world, including the John Michael Kohler Arts Center in Sheboygan, Wisconsin, and the National Children's Museum in Washington, DC. However, all this acclaim and attention have not altered the simplicity of his nature or his devotion to his art. Past the age of 80, he is still passionate about his work, eager to realize in three dimensions all the creatures that inhabit his dream world, beings from another realm brought to earth by his artful labor. He is at the *Rock Garden* every day, at home among his creations, working his magic to create more delightful experiences and objects. Thanks to the transformative visionary art of Nek Chand, the debris of one group of people has become the aesthetic experience of a multitude.

<www.nekchand.com>

Alternative Outdoor Spaces: Socrates Sculpture Park as a Case Study

by Alyson Baker

Sculpture parks have been founded for many reasons: to exhibit and expand an existing collection, to create a landscape where art and nature can co-exist or interact, to energize or revitalize a community or public space, and to establish a collection of permanently placed or temporarily installed large-scale sculpture. By definition, a sculpture park requires monumental artistic production and acres, not square feet, of land. The scale alone demands vast resources, and to institute and maintain a sculpture park can be a considerable undertaking. There are as many methods and models for the development and management of sculpture parks as there are sculpture parks. Many of the best known and most highly regarded were initiated by collectors and benefactors who donated land and artworks, or by museums venturing beyond the walls of their institutions, or by municipalities, universities, and corporations that recognized the myriad benefits of making art an integral part of their communities.

A less common paradigm is that of the artist-centered and production-oriented sculpture park. This alternative model, which is often specific to a place, but can also be transient, opportunistic, and mobile, focuses on commissioning and exhibiting pieces that respond to a particular location and set of circumstances. Whereas traditional outdoor sculpture venues present works from past art historical periods and disparate places of origin, these spaces are established for the creation and exhibition of art that is born of the present moment and immediate location. Carved out of city lots, reclaimed land, or repurposed, disused, or abandoned space, these are often grass-roots initiatives run on a tight budget through the generosity of small foundations, businesses, landowners, townships, and city agencies.

Many of the earliest artist-initiated and artist-run sculpture parks developed as opportunities to make and show large sculptures that operated outside institutional parameters. In the 1970s, artists increasingly wanted to work beyond the scope of museums and galleries by inserting and integrating sculpture into the landscape. Later, this artist-driven model continued to evolve in response to the needs of sculptors working with dimensions and materials that could not be accommodated by the confines of interior spaces. Over time, as artists have continued to challenge notions of what sculpture can be and do in a public context, innovative and responsive outdoor venues for their work have continued to develop. Driven by the unusual requirements and expanding parameters of current artistic enterprise, in addition to a desire to redefine the meaning and presence of public art, this alternate model is, by necessity, adaptable and resourceful.

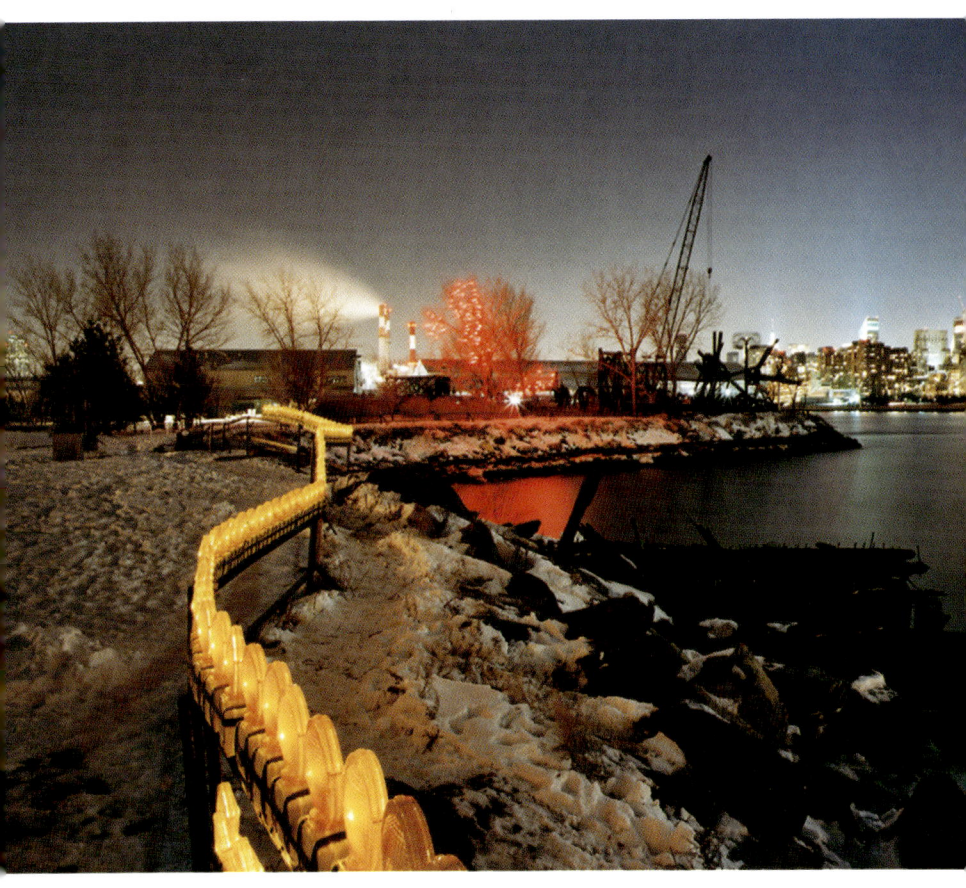

View of Socrates Sculpture Park with (foreground) Jude Tallichet, *Flash Park*, 2004, 200 emergency barricade lights and police and firetruck light bars, and (background) Matthew McCaslin, *Roots of the Nightshade Family*, 2004, 100 red light bulbs.

Some of today's most inventive new sculpture parks are dynamic environments created by groups of artists who emphasize the creative process, production, and the role of the artist in shaping how the public interacts with the artwork. Such an approach relies on partnerships, public participation, and volunteerism; it is often used as a (successful) method for galvanizing and empowering low-income neighborhoods or under-served constituencies. Approaching the sculpture park as a center for creative activity, artists can work in concert with their community to create pieces that bring together many voices.

Alternative open-air sculpture spaces also differ from more traditional sculpture gardens in the fact that they are based on a studio model that focuses on

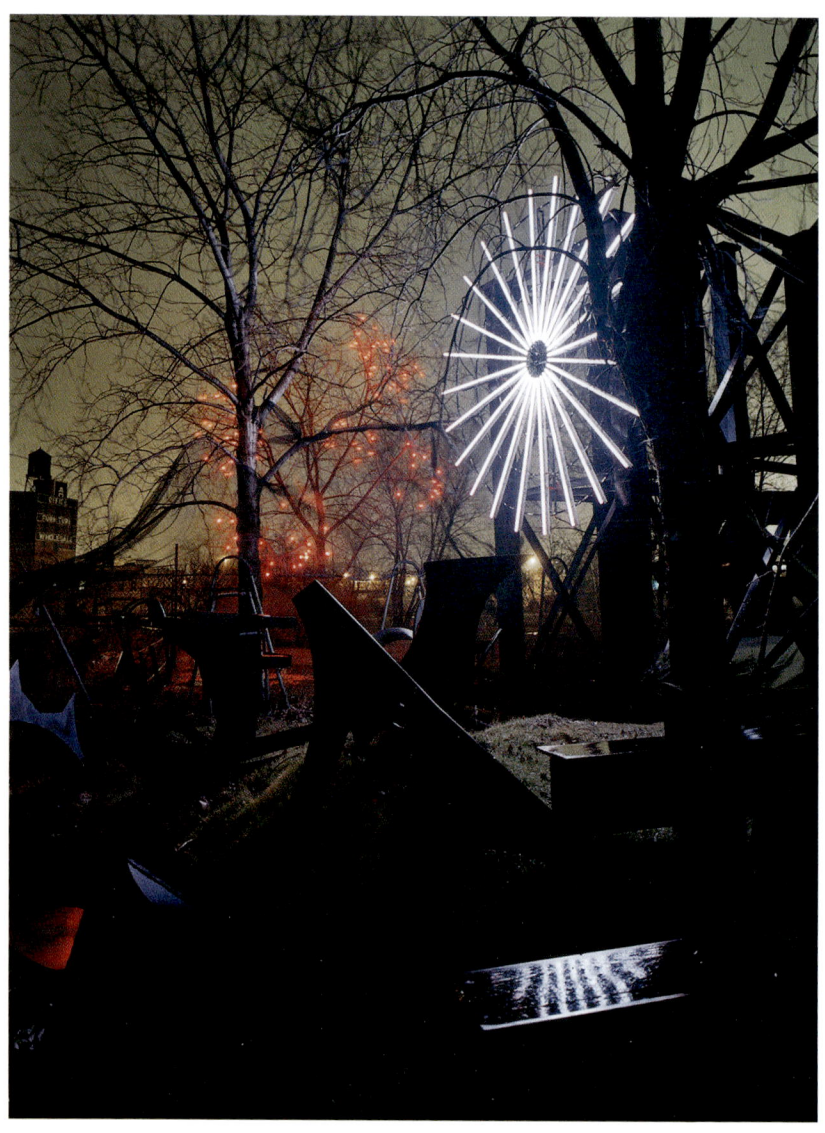

View of Socrates Sculpture Park with (foreground) Leo Villareal, *Star*, 2003, 24 LED tubes, color sequencer, and metal frame, and (background) Matthew McCaslin, *Roots of the Nightshade Family*, 2004, 100 red light bulbs.

process, rather than a collection or museum model that prioritizes the presentation and preservation of existing works and seeks to collect and exhibit works of high quality and proven significance. In a studio-style sculpture park, artists make their work on site, and because this work often incorporates materials and methods that are untested or pushed past their intended applications, the new model must accommodate experimentation, trial and error, and—at times—failure. Not all sculptures produced in this context are successful. Artists need to have a place and an opportunity to take risks, unrestrained by the pressures of the art market or the rarefied exhibition hall.

Socrates Sculpture Park in Long Island City, New York, is a pioneer in the field of contemporary sculpture parks and a remarkable case study in the development of an artist-driven institution that fosters innovative outdoor sculptural practice while serving a local community as well as national and international art audiences. Socrates, where I serve as executive director, was founded in 1986 by Mark di Suvero. The site was an abandoned city lot located a few hundred feet south of his riverside studio and just north of Isamu Noguchi's studio and newly founded museum. Although this spectacular location directly on the East River offered panoramic views of the Manhattan skyline, it had become an illegal dumpsite filled with rubble, construction debris, and junked cars. di Suvero saw potential here that few could have imagined, and his vision, energy, and perseverance were so strong and compelling that he was able to rally a group of artists, community members, and elected officials to transform this derelict 4.5-acre site into an open studio and exhibition space for artists and a neighborhood park for local residents.

Through his Athena Foundation, di Suvero had been offering studio space and financial resources to artists who needed space and funding to create sculptures that they could not undertake in small, expensive New York City studios. Socrates became an extension of this initiative, expanding the Athena Foundation's scope to include more artists and an even greater amount of space—these artists not only needed the opportunity to build their work, but also a chance to exhibit it and make it publicly accessible. di Suvero was clear about the park's purpose—young artists were to have their own space to build and show their sculptures, working all the while with the community.

di Suvero deeply believes in the power of art to transform. He established Socrates Sculpture Park in this unlikely place—at the time, a low-income, neglected, crime-ridden, and unprepossessing urban district—knowing that it would benefit not only the artists who worked there, but also the surrounding community. In order to make the park welcoming and accessible to a diverse and broad audience, Socrates hosts many free activities and programs that compliment the exhibitions, including concerts, performances, film and video screenings, fitness classes, special events and festivals, and children's art-making workshops. The inclusive and democratic spirit in which the park was founded, and the belief that creative expression must be shared as well as nurtured, still drives Socrates' mission.

Today, Socrates flourishes as a unique New York City park, an internationally acclaimed open-air contemporary art venue, and source of inspiration and civic pride in a gentler, cleaner, and safer neighborhood. Many young artists are attracted by the neighborhood's relatively cheap rent; in addition to the Isamu Noguchi Museum two blocks away, P.S.1 is just two miles from the park. Socrates remains the only site in New York City that provides artists with opportunities to create and exhibit outdoor sculpture and multimedia installations in an open environment encouraging interaction among artists, artworks, and the public. To date, Socrates has hosted over 700 artists. Local residents use the park to take in the skyline, fish, walk their dogs, and, of course, to enjoy the art. Other visitors include busloads of children, tourists, and high school and college students on internships and apprenticeships. In keeping with its tradition of local involvement, the park also employs people who live close by. It is a shining example of how a disparate community can organize to reclaim land and create an ever-evolving natural landscape and an urban oasis for the presentation of public art.

For over 20 years, Socrates has remained at the forefront of new artistic practice because it is responsive to the aspirations of artists and has found ways to accommodate innovative and experimental artistic practice. In addition to the two major exhibitions that the park has produced every year since its founding, programming has expanded to include additional exhibition opportunities that allow for more ephemeral, performance-based, temporary, and interactive works. The park's major endeavor is the emerging artist fellowship program, which supports successful applicants with grants. An outdoor studio program is open to artists from all over the world. And a third program enables artists to propose already constructed works for installation. These new opportunities respond to artists who want to create and present pieces that do not conform to the requirements of longer term installations and who continue to reinvent and redefine the tradition of art in public spaces.

Socrates' growth has been slow and measured, keeping pace with its surrounding neighborhood while striving to meet the needs of its artists and audiences. It is a work in progress, and, while it now boasts impressive flowering gardens and fruit trees, it also retains much of its original gritty, urban character. As Jonathan Goodman discovered during his visit a few years ago, "Socrates Sculpture Park is far more than the sum of its parts. As a community center, it works democratically for the propagation of sculpture among people who have not had much experience with art. As a center for emerging artists, it shows and helps young sculptors who are just beginning to be recognized. And as a functioning site for the construction of large pieces, it offers a laboratory for those interested in the mechanics of joining together big pieces of steel, as well as other materials."* A great deal of perseverance and a resolute belief in the transformative power of creative expression have allowed a tremendously dedicated family of artists, patrons, volunteers, neighbors, and government leaders to forge a common ground. Setting a standard for ways in which artists and communities can work together while remaining relevant in the larger context of a rapidly expanding international art world is one of Socrates' greatest achievements.

Note

* Jonathan Goodman, "Socrates Sculpture Park: A Blend of Art and Community," *Sculpture*, April 2001: p. 43.

<www.socratessculpturepark.org>

Europos Parkas

by Joyce Ellen Weinstein

Gintaras Karosas first conceived of Europos Parkas, Open-Air Museum of the Center of Europe, when he was a 22-year-old student at the Vilnius Art Academy in Lithuania. He chafed at the highly structured Soviet-style classes in studio art, but lectures in contemporary art and Eastern philosophy deeply influenced him. They became the driving aesthetic for the design of Europos Parkas and the placement of more than 90 sculptures by artists from 24 countries in a sculpture park that spans 55 hectares.

To Karosas, the park is an ever-evolving personal work of art, a place "where everything exists in unity as a whole entity, where some places are empty and some places are full, where the placement of sculpture is sometimes unexpected, where some things are hidden, where there are often surprises, and where the happiness of discovery is paramount." From the beginning, he rejected the idea of conventional landscape architecture. Only the main road into the park is formal. He never draws or plans, saying that he intuitively feels the "right placement of objects in the right place."

To start the park, Karosas needed permission from the authorities—a formidable challenge under Soviet regulations. After endless attempts, he succeeded in 1988 and began searching for land commensurate with his criteria—fully grown forest devoid of buildings. "Life is too short for planting," he says. The land had to be close to Vilnius and have a "good feeling."

Karosas finally selected a deep forest with fallen trees lying on top of one another—"a mountain of trees like Siberia." For four years, he worked alone, clearing the land with a chain saw sent by Canadian relatives. During the initial work, he began to think about the ideal placement of the first sculpture. "In the beginning," he says, "it was difficult to feel where to place the sculptures, but it has become easier over time." By 1992, a year after the fall of communism, there was a park, a house, and a sculpture by Karosas himself but no way for people to enter—no road yet existed. Karosas and two men from a nearby village worked in all weather, and after two years they had a one-kilometer dirt road. Eventually the municipality laid asphalt.

Still attending the art academy, Karosas planned the First International Sculpture Symposium in Lithuania for his sixth-year final project. But the school authorities considered his idea as an impossible undertaking, one that would make Lithuania look foolish in the eyes of the world. Karosas was dismissed by the academy. Undaunted, he continued. One of the first people in Lithuania to take advantage of a new law establishing nonprofit institutions, he sought sponsorship. Lithuanian UNESCO and the Soros Foundation gave materials, tools, and organizational supplies. With their

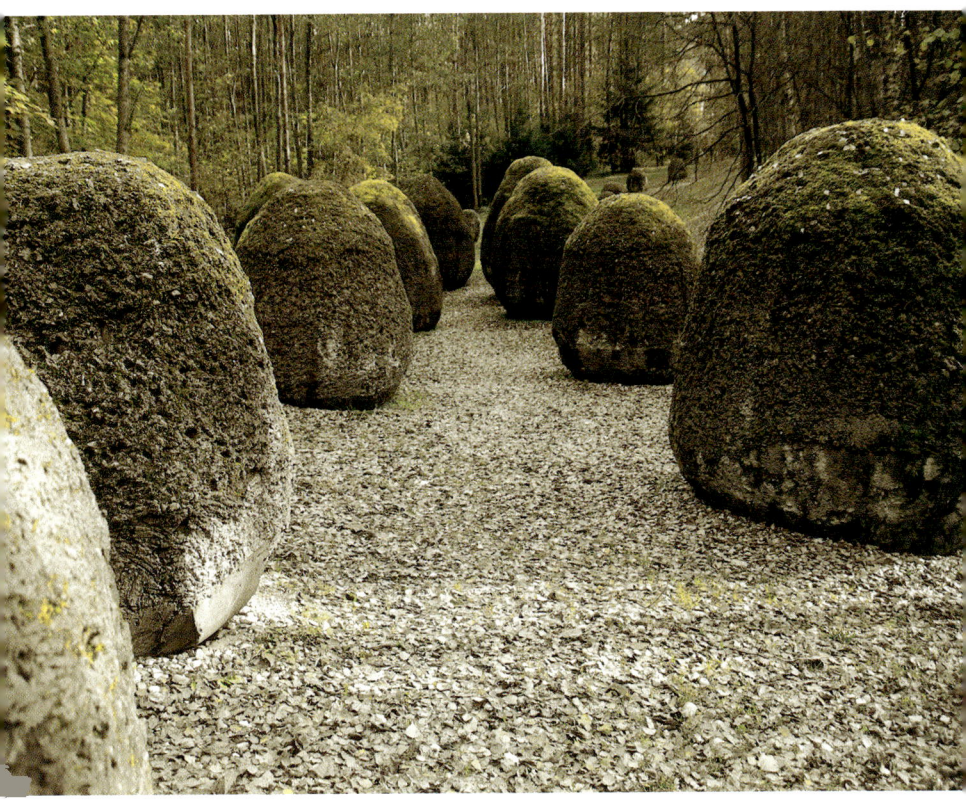

Magdalena Abakanowicz, *Space of Unknown Growth*, 1998. Steel framework, concrete, and stone boulders, dimensions variable.

help, letters and invitations were sent to artists' unions and academies in many countries. In spite of the organizational difficulties, 10 sculptors from Hungary, Greece, Finland, Lithuania, and the U.S. participated. They worked in wood and stone, and their pieces remain on the grounds today.

To everyone's surprise, the event was a success, and it received tremendous publicity. Planning the second symposium was easier. An old factory with serviceable machinery was rented to build Irish sculptor Laurent Mellet's *Requiem for a Dead Pony*, a rusted steel structure resembling a horse whose leg is a wheel that turns to create a crying sound. Three other pieces were created that summer.

Today, sculptors can attend the symposium, create work over time, donate completed work, or participate in events for young artists from Central and Eastern Europe. There is also an artist's residency program. Admission fees account for about one third of the park's financial resources. The rest comes from membership and funding.

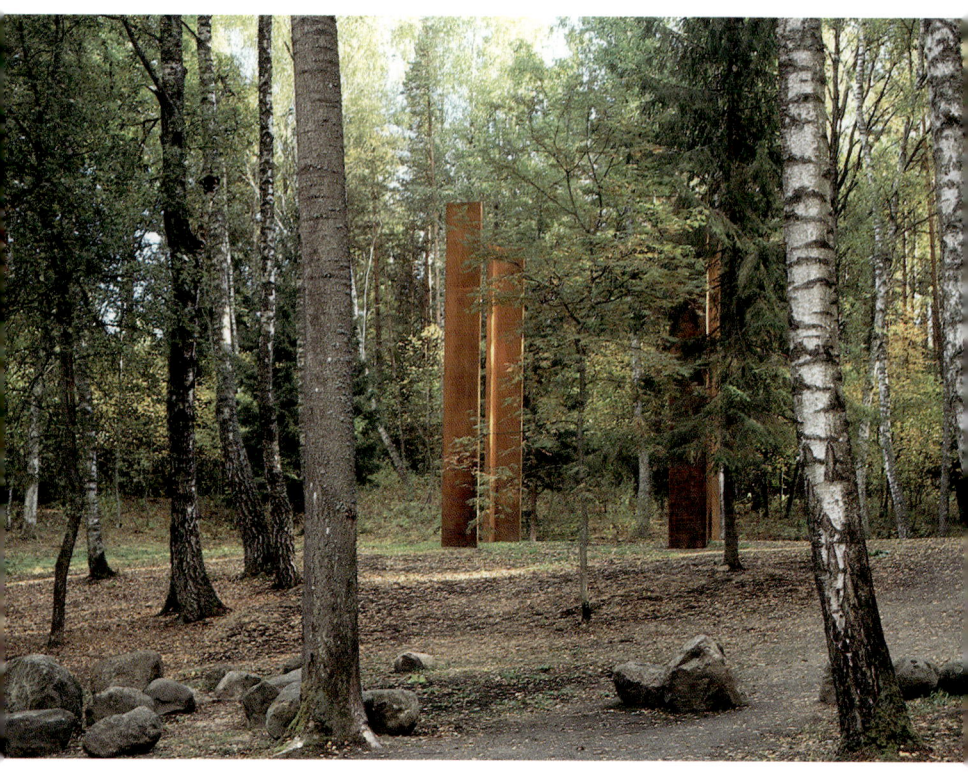

Gintaras Karosas, *The Place*, 2001. Steel and stone boulders, 770 x 84 x 84 cm.

In 1996, the first large-scale project was planned. Although skeptical at first, Dennis Oppenheim agreed to build *Chair Pool* at the park, with the understanding that it must be completed in three weeks. After many conversations between Karosas and Oppenheim, money was raised for the construction. Sending an exact model, specifications, and his assistant to supervise the construction in a local factory, Oppenheim saw the sculpture built on schedule. A second piece by Oppenheim, *Drinking Structure with Exposed Kidney Pool*, also graces the landscape. Shaped like a house with corrugated roofing, the structure rests on two parallel welded steel tunnels, which form arcs that theoretically allow it to rock and the front portion to dip down steeply to reach the water. Leaning toward one side, the structure seems to embody contemporary feelings of instability.

In 1997, Magdalena Abakanowicz visited the park to consider space for a small-scale sculpture. After seeing the fantastic possibilities, she planned a large-scale project. Karosas says that, like him, Abakanowicz seeks the right placement of objects in the right surroundings. The result is *Space of Unknown Growth*, which spans an area of over 2,000 square meters. A range of massive concrete boulders, in 22 variously sized forms, creates a majestic landscape, a space for deep personal experience. "Abakanowicz," says Karosas, "feels the park work is one of her best."

In 1998, after Karosas had made his park a success, the Vilnius Art Academy invited him to complete his studies. His final project, *For Your Convenience*, consists of various chair-like granite forms. Creating its own landscape in a tucked-away grove, the Minimalist-style work invites people to rest and contemplate their surroundings. Karosas's other works in the park include *Monument of the Centre of Europe*, *LNK Info Tree*, and *The Place*, another Minimalist work set in a space adjoining a pond. The pond gradually narrows into a stream that flows down a slight hill partially surrounding the sculpture. Four steel beams, each eight meters high, are angled into a shape that almost creates a square. Slowly moving the structure, Karosas intuitively found the most satisfying space: "I create objects called landscape sculptures. They only belong to a particular space; they do not speak too much. I cleanse them of unnecessary coatings and idle words. Those things and phenomena, which look simple at first sight yet reflect an essence, are meaningful to me." Through technology that pressed metal granules into the steel, the construction was evenly covered with bright, burnt-sienna/orange rust, the same color as the top half of the weathered, surrounding pines. The softness of the landscape acts as a foil for the hardness of the steel, producing an awe-inspiring place and "joining nature with human intelligence." *The Place* evokes British dolmen or menhirs, without resembling them in form or placement, conjuring an ancient site of veneration.

Massimo Ghiotti and Mindaugas Tendziagolskis have installed recent additions to the park. Perfectly placed in a semi-secluded meadow, Ghiotti's 10 monumental steel sculptures pay homage to a post-industrial age. Made from gigantic springs, pistons, crane claws, chains, and leaf springs, each piece is framed so as to inhibit the natural movement of its parts. Except for the polished steel pistons, the objects are coated with a dark red-brown industrial paint, which creates a uniform look across the works. The geometric symmetry evokes Bauhaus purity of form while suggesting the Futurist love of the device. A native of Turin, Italy, Ghiotti reminisces about that once-mighty industrial city. The push/pull of the chains linked to the enormous hooks, and screwed onto the frames with even larger screws and bolts, speaks to the tension between the past and present. Elegant in their quiet, classical beauty, these pieces create nostalgia for machinery. In time, the weather will cover the surfaces with a patina, bringing the system closer to nature.

Tendziagolskis drew inspiration from the ancient games played by shepherds in Lithuania. *Mobile Games*, installed adjacent to the café and made primarily of stainless steel and synthetic rope, is based on the circle and the triangle. Five distinct objects form sculptures/toys/games. In one, 10 bars create a ladder large enough for an adult to climb. The ladder is built into the shape of a triangle whose point is fixed into the ground, and the triangle is set into a large wheel, at least seven feet in diameter. The entire mechanism can be pushed or pulled; someone on the ladder rotates in space as the wheel moves across the ground. These beautiful objects are meant to be enjoyed both visually and physically. The details placed at specific intervals within each toy are meant to encourage involvement, stretching the possibilities of bodily movement. One's natural inclination toward invention or self-preservation extends or limits the range of play.

As art critic Michael Brenson says, "Europos Parkas is a bridge between different cultures." Karosas does not think that it matters whether those who come to the park like the art or not. What is important is what they come away with—the experience that nature, art, and people are all connected, one unified whole.

<www.europosparkas.lt>

Franconia Sculpture Park

by Ann Klefstad

Both adventurous and populist, Franconia Sculpture Park is first and foremost a sculptor's paradise: it's a great place to visit if you like sculptors along with your sculpture. All work is done on site, by artists in residence at the park, so visitors can engage the makers in conversation while the works are being created. People seize this opportunity. The sign at the park entrance reads, "Open dawn to dusk, 365 days of the year." Of course, this being Minnesota, subject to snow and ice and other insults to mammalian life, the sculptors are only in residence during the temperate season: largely May through September.

Franconia is a child of both Wave Hill and Socrates. Like its parents, it strives not only for a beautiful presentation of sculpture in the landscape, but also for an experimental aesthetic in which noble failures are accepted along with radiant successes. Each year, Franconia hosts 40 artists at all levels, with residencies varying from three days to six months, depending on the artist's need. Participants are provided with room and board, outdoor studio space, machinery, tools, staff support, and, as funds

Aaron Dysart, *1963 Black Walnut*, 2007. Black walnut and paint, 25 x 18 x 15 ft.

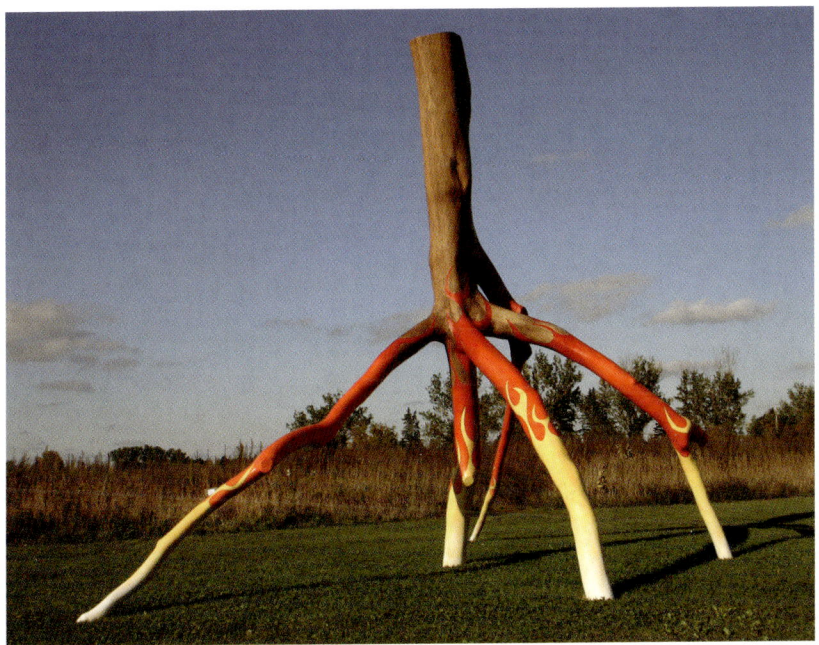

permit, materials and stipends. Time spent in residence also allows artists to develop a network among their peers and helps create a nationwide community of artists. Some artists return many times: Jon Isherwood, Su-Chen Hung, Rico Gatson, and Michael Bigger are among the many who have done beautiful works at the park. Mark di Suvero has also lent works to Franconia.

Founded by John Hock (a sculptor who has worked with Anthony Caro and Mark di Suvero), with the help of artists Fuller Cowles and Tasha McNutt (now Hock), Franconia arose from a communitarian ethos. It carries on in the spirit of its founders, who met at Skowhegan. John Hock is still director of the park. After 10 years, it's well established in the hearts of artists, visitors, and educators and hosts frequent visits, both planned and impromptu, to its site along a heavily traveled tourist route leading from Minneapolis to the scenic towns along the St. Croix River.

Franconia relocated in 2006, trading its original 14-acre rental for a new 20-acre setting, purchased on a shoestring but filling with sculpture nonetheless. The summer 2007 session marked the first full season in the new location. There are great plans for this facility: the building program has begun with a 10-bedroom house for resident sculptors, a small studio for two-dimensional work for future residence programs, refitted and beautifully grafittied trailers for intern housing, and several fully equipped work areas with gantries, welding equipment, a 10-ton forklift (painted pink), and two cranes. An interpretive center and outdoor eating areas are also finished. Hock notes that the new park wants to "reinvent the relationship between artists, audience, and the land." The plans call for green architecture and openness to rural lifestyles.

Franconia is not a park for permanent sculptural installations. It solicits sculpture, mostly built on site, in several ways. Potential resident artists apply, and are accepted, to make work at the site, using the help of park staff (who are endlessly hardworking and ingenious in the service of resident artists). Jerome Fellowship artists apply to a jury made up of critics, sculptors, and curators. They are given a stipend and also make work in residence at the park. Interns are also chosen through a competitive process and spend each morning helping the resident pros and each afternoon working on pieces of their own.

The climate in the middle of southern Minnesota farm country can be punishing in July and August, peak season for Franconia, but the nearness of the lovely St. Croix River (designated a Wild and Scenic Waterway) means that relief is always close at hand. Sculptors work all day in the sun, then gather for a festive dinner after sunset, prepared by each artist-in-residence in turn (sculptors, for some reason, are almost always good cooks). On really grueling days, a contingent sets off for a dip in the river before dinner, often riding the park's big F250, its cab decorated with a pair of steer horns.

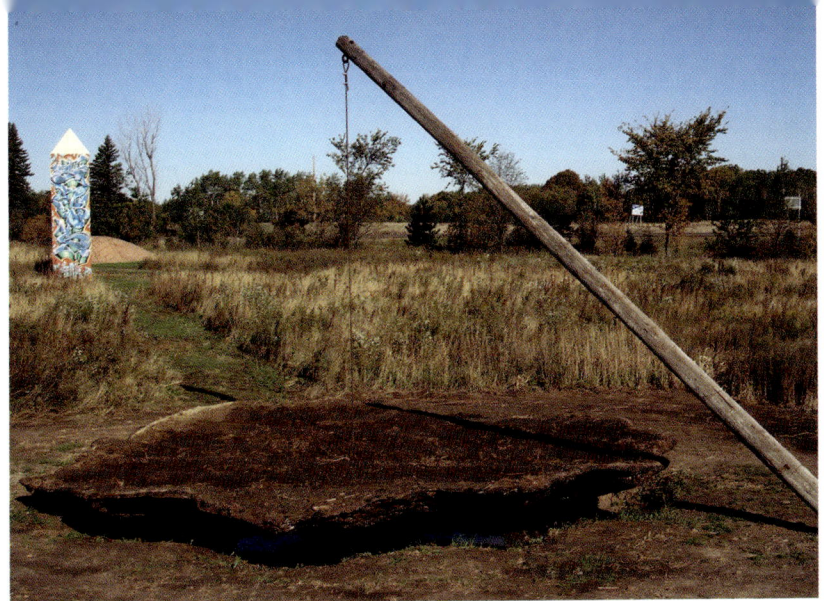

Su-Chen Hung, *Lift*, 2007. Cast stone, wood pole, cable, and earth, 18.6 x 33.75 x 24.9 ft.

As part of its commitment to community, Franconia offers outreach programs for at-risk youth and workshops for young children to learn to handle tools and make sculpture. The park also maintains connections with schools in the region. For the artistic community, it runs a regular season of public critiques, cooperating with the Visual Arts Critics Union of Minnesota (VACUM) to host six monthly talks by sculptors in residence at the park. Two attendant VACUM critics moderate and engage the (usually vociferous) crowd of sculptors, interns, and fans—who then stay to continue the talk over barbecue.

The park also plays host to other organizations of sculptors, such as the roving nomads who do iron pours. Every year, the English sculptor Coral Lambert returns to Franconia with her cupolette and gathers a crew of regulars and some newcomers for a week-long residency to build sand molds and pour iron sculptures. The same group of iron sculptors hosts a symposium in the U.K. in alternate years—the US–UK Iron Symposium.

Franconia truly expands the world of sculpture in terms of audience and in terms of the skills and techniques of sculptors. Interns and professionals alike learn new ways to work, new materials, and new ways of relating to landscape. It's an amazingly generative place that still retains its artist-founded ethos, despite the increasingly uptown look of its plans. It's working to hold on to both ends of its nature.

<www.franconia.org>

Salem Art Works

by Jacqueline Keren

Peter Lundberg sits atop his 20-ton sculpture *Freya* as the flatbed truck on which it rests backs into place. Descending from his perch, he watches as a crane lifts the massive form and places it on the ground. On its back, the sculpture appears lifeless, a mass of poured concrete and steel. But as the crane sets it upright on the lawn, it awakens, primal yet graceful, and takes its place within the landscape.

And so goes another day at Salem Art Works (SAW), a sculpture park and arts center coming to life on the grounds of a former dairy farm in Salem, New York, an agricultural community east of Saratoga Springs. Founded in 2005 by sculptor Anthony Cafritz, SAW has already begun to build an impressive collection of outdoor sculpture by international and regional artists. In addition to Lundberg, who is well known for his monumental concrete and steel forms, the sculpture park includes works by Mark di Suvero, Serbian-born Zoran Mojsilov, and Nora Simon of Greenwich, New York, with new pieces added as more sculptors come to work at SAW.

Cafritz, whose work transforms ordinary objects by recasting them in new materials and juxtaposing them in unexpected ways, began envisioning an interdisciplinary arts center over 20 years ago. In designing SAW, he looked to Black Mountain College, an experimental college that redefined the boundaries between teacher and student and encouraged collaboration. With similar goals in mind, Cafritz set out to assemble an arts community that would plan, build, and program activities to foster artistic expression and appreciation.

In 2003, he began working with artist and arts administrator Barbara Carris and installation artist Ciaran Cooper, and the three started to plan more concretely. After many months spent searching for a location, Cafritz found the former Carlos Cary Farm in Salem. Work began in February 2005 with the clearing of the grounds and outbuildings for the sculpture park and the construction of studio space for an artist residency program. In late spring, the first resident artists arrived, a group of more than 20 sculptors. Their pieces were displayed at the North Bennington Art Park, in an annual outdoor sculpture exhibition curated by Cafritz in western Vermont.

Sculpture, Cafritz believes, is enriched by the presence of other arts, and he is committed to keeping the center open to all disciplines to assure a "progression of thought and dialogue enriched by diversity." This diversity, Cafritz hopes, will prevent "artistic myopia" and help SAW steer clear of the limiting effect of a single voice or vision.

Cafritz and a core group of artists oversee the operations and maintenance of the organization and physical plant. Many in the group have known each other for 20 years or more, while some have arrived through other channels. Leif Johnson, a sculptor who works with glass and steel and whose imaginative pieces have been exhibited nationally, exemplifies the type of person behind SAW. As overseer of the physical plant, he is helping to build multi-use spaces for workshops, performances, and exhibitions, in addition to a forge and glass-working shop for resident artists that he also plans to use himself. "There's an energy here," he says, "Everyone knows what to do and does it. Things fall together well."

Cafritz is determined to connect SAW and its participating artists to the local community. His intention is to weave art into the life of the village in a myriad of ways. To this end, he is keeping some of Salem Art Works' land open to agricultural use by local farmers. Internships create opportunities for high school students to take part in the building of SAW and to take a closer look at sculpture as it is made. Workshops, presentations, and performances have been held or are in the works. But most important is making sculpture an everyday experience for local residents, rather than something they have to seek out. This connection to the community, Cafritz hopes, will enrich both the town and SAW.

With over 72 sculptures, including site-specific works, installed on 120 acres, the sculpture park is very much a reflection of the artists working at or in residence

Chris Duncan, *Hey Joe*, 2007. Steel and concrete, 100 x 74 x 60 in.

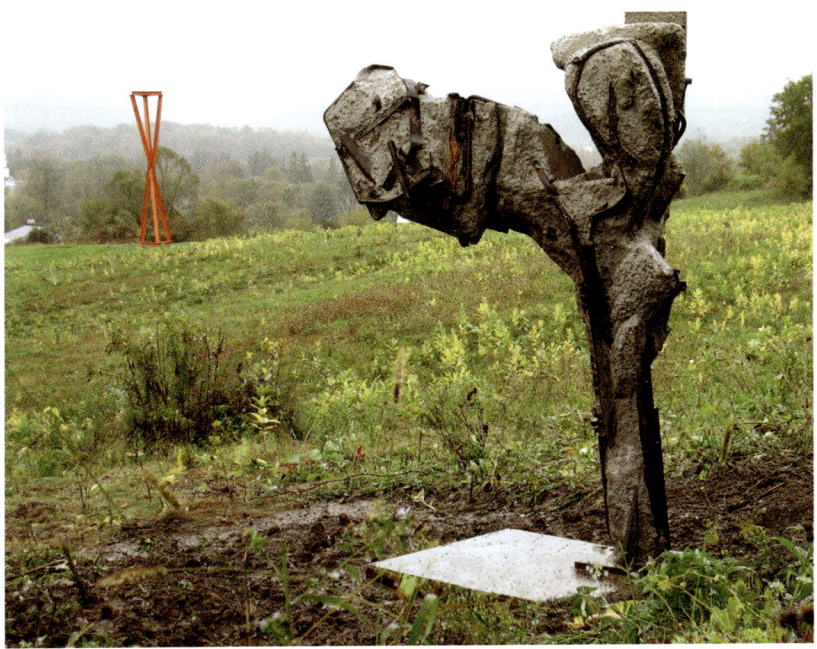

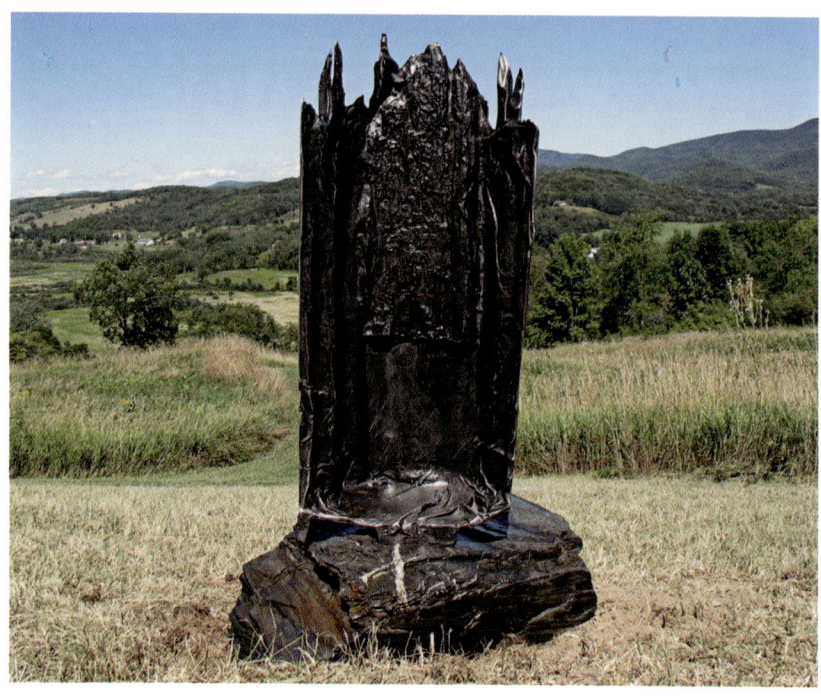

Felicia Glidden, *Matris Fe*, 2007. Cast iron and slate, 119 x 68 x 40 cm.

at SAW. While some pieces, including two monumental works by Mark di Suvero, are here indefinitely, others will rotate in and out of the collection. Indoor space includes a barn for special exhibitions and a building that currently displays work by Cafritz and Carris.

    Past the entrance where *Freya* rests solidly on the ground, lawns and gardens surround what was once the main farmhouse. Nestled in the greenery, sculptures are sited to complement and contrast with the landscape. Situated beneath a low hanging tree, Leif Johnson's *Chair* uses slate and iron to transform a school desk into an artifact, a piece both weighty and fluid, nostalgic in its emptiness. Nora Simon's *Weeping Willow* stands before a small stream in a bucolic corner, a gaunt steel sculpture cascading into the grass, reminiscent of a carving on an old headstone. *South African Violet*, by Gary Humphreys from Bennington, Vermont, takes a different approach: the charismatic piece jumps out of the landscape with a springy nest of petals in bright, emphatic steel.

    Walking through the grounds, vestiges of the old life of the farm can still be seen, as chickens roam near the main house. Outside one of the barns, Zoran Mojsilov's *Aladdin*, a bird-like composition of wood and steel, dominates a small picnic area. Beyond the house, a path leads past exhibition and work space to a natural amphitheater. Sculptures are tucked into the hills or on the slopes that line the walkway. Mark di Suvero's *Double Tetrahedron* rises around the corner, relocated from New York City's Madison Square Park. di Suvero, who describes Cafritz as a "brilliant young art activist," moved two sculptures to SAW "with the hope that the energy of these works, shown before in a New York City park and an art gallery, would underline the joyousness and openness of making art together for a bright and beautiful, brave new world."

The path climbs to the top of Cary Hill where the second di Suvero, *For Euler*, affords a view of the village and a green-clad ridgeline in nearby Vermont. With its uplift and simplicity, the piece draws the viewer into its open interior, where a swinging centerpiece becomes a touchstone, a resting place from which to connect with the surrounding hills. In the same way, Salem Art Works has drawn art and energy from near and far to build a sculpture park that dynamically reflects the many hands involved in its creation.

<www.salemartworks.com>

Toronto Sculpture Garden

by Gil McElroy

On the east side of Toronto's downtown core lies a sliver of land, 80 feet wide by 100 feet long, squeezed between two mid-19th-century, Georgian-style buildings that frame an impressive view of the Cathedral of St. James directly across the street. The building that once stood on this site was demolished in 1938 to make room for a 22-car parking lot. Since 1981, the cars have been displaced by objects and structures that include a lighthouse, a log cabin, a UFO, and even a row of vending machines dispensing bottled water, for this is now the site of the Toronto Sculpture Garden (TSG).

In 1974, Louis Odette, a prominent Canadian art patron and collector, was inspired to develop a sculpture park in downtown Toronto after a visit to a sculpture garden just outside of Rome. He spent five years searching for an appropriate site, and

Liz Magor, *Messenger*, 1996–97. Log cabin, trees, bushes, flagstone, and mixed media, approximately 50 x 100 ft.

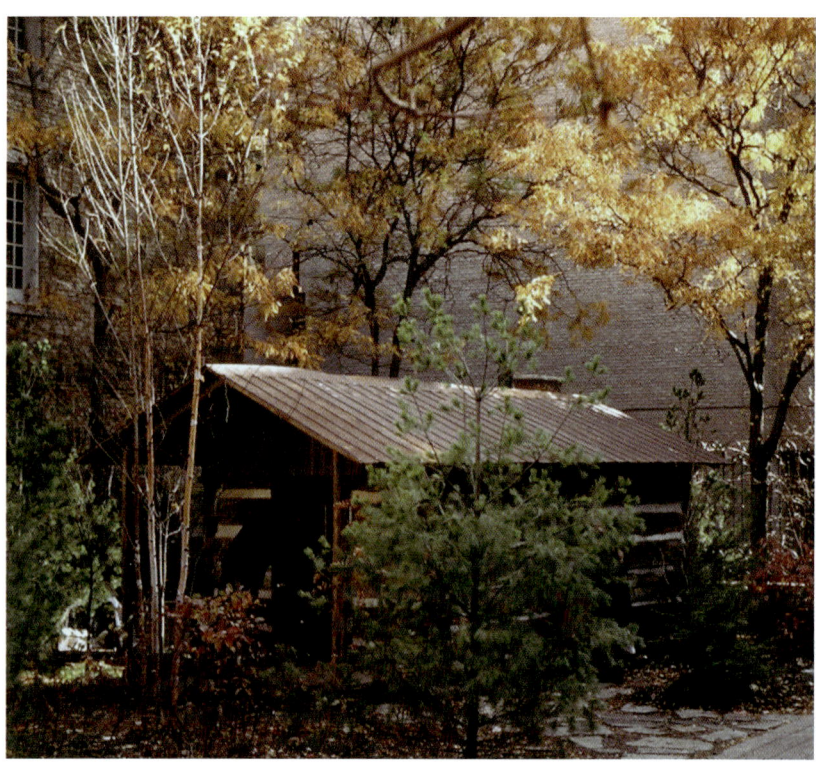

in 1979, this narrow parking lot on King Street East was finally chosen. Odette formed the L.L.O. Sculpture Garden Foundation to fund TSG's annual operating expenses (the city, which actually owns the property, looks after its maintenance) and hired Rina Greer, an independent art consultant, to serve as director, a position she has held since the garden opened. Two exhibitions are mounted each year—58 to date, showing the work of over 80 artists—selected by the 10-member Art Advisory Board, each of whom serves a three-year term.

Eric Glavin's *Sprawl* (installed in October 2000) saw the site through the winter months when the patio of the restaurant bordering the garden on the east side was closed and the waterfall on the wall of the building to the west was shut off. Amid the relatively upscale gentrification in this part of Toronto, and the grass, trees, and wrought iron fencing of the garden itself, Glavin's ground-hugging, industrial-looking work—all aluminum siding, steel tubing, roofing paper, and concrete—was visually jarring, a cross between a Judd-like Minimalist sculpture and a building component escaped from some manufacturing plant or suburban mall. A quiet, pleasant park in the downtown seemingly became nothing more than a despoiled piece of real estate.

This suits Odette, Greer, and the members of the board just fine: the Toronto Sculpture Garden may be characterized by its changeability and adaptability, but it is hardly about becoming part of the neighborhood status quo. According to Greer, the site "serves as a testing ground for artists to experiment with public space and to address issues of architectural scale, materials, and context." Artists seeking to work at the garden are encouraged—indeed, expected—to regard the site as more than just a bit of grass and trees on which to plunk a sculpture and to respond to the setting as both an architectural and social environment.

For instance, Liz Magor's sculptural installation *Messenger* (1996–97) involved a complete reworking of the garden's landscape, including the planting of trees and shrubs and the construction of a small log cabin, à la Lincoln or Thoreau, in the midst of it all. Like Glavin's piece, Magor's work made for a jarring visual juxtaposition, frontier rusticity running headlong into upscale urban. *Messenger* evoked the function of a park or garden as a place of solace and escape in an area of Toronto with far too little green space, while messing about with the caricaturish idea of the pioneer log cabin as an isolated bastion in the wilderness, a safe haven in the midst of nature red in tooth and claw. In the transposition of these ideas to a highly urban setting, Magor showed the soft white underbelly of such myth-making—so very much a part of the construction of Canadian (and, for that matter, American) history.

In contrast, Ben Smits's *Craft, From Outer Space to You* (1999) invoked a kind of sci-fi myth-making that, for all its techno-futurism, was firmly rooted in the scary geo-politics of the Cold War. Here was the clichéd flying saucer of '50s B-movie fantasy and conspiracy theory nestled quietly on the sculpture garden lawn, its

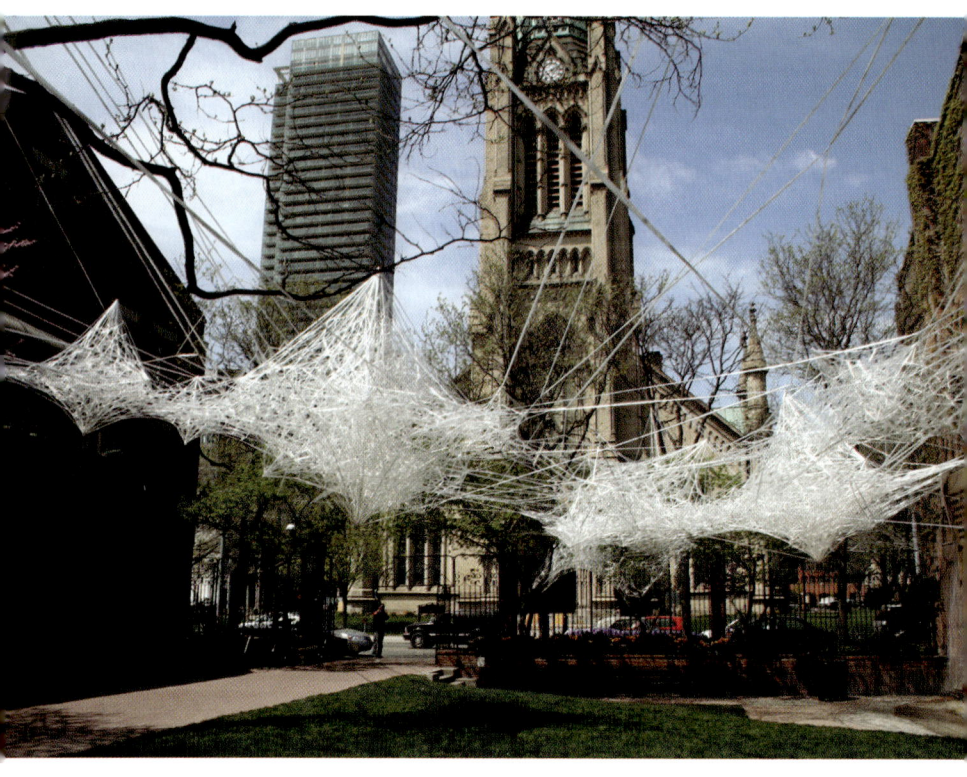

Ludwika Ogorzelec, *Mist: from the Space Crystallization Cycle*, 2007. Plastic film, bamboo, and steel wire, 80 x 100 ft.

metal hull gleaming in the sunlight and lit by neon at night. Reportedly Smits discovered a bullet hole in the work when dismantling it, and an absurd, iconic bit of 20th-century pop culture regained its former footing as a threat. But this time, to whom?

Such a cultural shift was also part of James Carl's *fountain* (1997), a work consisting of nine vending machines set in an arc across TSG's lawn, each dispensing bottled water and proffering an image of part of a waterfall (in place of the usual advertising) that cumulatively made for a curving, panoramic photograph of Niagara Falls (or, more accurately, the Horseshoe Falls on the Canadian side). While the Falls were a fearsome and threatening force in 17th-century minds, their harnessing as a source of hydro-electric power in the late 19th century and coeval transformation into a tourist destination changed all of that forever. Structurally aping the curving arc of the Horseshoe Falls, *fountain* evinces its use value today as both image and commodity.

Finland's Pirkkala Sculpture Park

by Allison Hunter

The Pirkkala Sculpture Park, which has no gate, no entrance fee, not even a sign, spills out from the center of town into the backyards and sidewalks of Pirkkala, 47 miles north of Helsinki, Finland. "We're putting this town on the map," says one of the artists invited by curator and local art hero, Villu Jaanisoo. The 40-year-old Estonian artist lured 20 international artists to participate in the 2003 Sculpture Symposium and Iron Pour, a three-week residency and workshop that generated the inaugural collection.

Without an office, much less a board of directors, Jaanisoo convinced the municipal government to invest in his curatorial debut—the creation of a "border-less" sculpture park. Having participated in numerous sculpture symposia throughout the world, Jaanisoo knew that he could populate the park almost instantly by staging a symposium and iron pour, with room, board, and materials provided for participating artists. However, he refused to limit the range of work by medium (cast iron), and he actively recruited artists whose approaches to sculpture go beyond the boundaries of tradition: "At first, sculpture was bronze, stone, and wood, and now it can be sugar cubes, shit, signs, or things we haven't seen yet. Sculpture has changed more than anything and that's exciting."

The resulting collection includes a modest range (given the three-week time limit) of three-dimensional work, including thousand-pound metal forms on pedestals, as well as a decaying cow horn installation, a site-specific work involving a Finnish shed, and a 40-foot-high sculpture made of steel fencing and twist ties.

The iron pour, which started late in the endless "Midsummer night," drew local townspeople, foundry workers, and news media, all fascinated by the cupola, a miniature blast furnace based on a medieval model. The cupola design, introduced to Jaanisoo by American sculptors, was handmade from contemporary materials (think metal barrels and duct tape). The pour introduced this rogue casting method to local art students and foundry workers who watched in awe. Indeed, the furnace stole the show as volunteers (mostly art students from the symposium), draped in full-body leather gear, collected the spewing molten iron into a heavy bucket carried by two people who poured the fiery red liquid into dozens of black sand molds.

Most of the molds, which ranged from five to 50 pounds, belonged to the art students whose works were exhibited at the end of the symposium. Larger works by symposium artists were cast off-site at local foundries. This alone was a coup for Jaanisoo, who deftly talked his way into gaining access and free labor from the pristine industrial factories. According to the wily artist, "It's about personal connections

In keeping with its experimental mandate, in summer 2001, the Toronto Sculpture Garden featured *Desire*, a work by senior Canadian artist Tom Dean involving a flock of bronze swans and a gathering of baby cherubs. And in the fall, to complete the 20th-anniversary celebration that year, a commissioned work by New York-based artist Micah Lexier was installed. After 20 years behind the urbane façade of its wrought iron fencing, TSG was showing no signs of trying to blend in. Since then, artists showing works in the park have included Ludwika Ogorzelec, Jennifer Marman and Daniel Borins, Luis Jacob, Maura Doyle, Jiang Jie, Charles Goldman, and Stephen Scofield.

<www.torontosculpturegarden.com>

(talking, joking, and explaining the art). It's not so much about money. It's about how particular factories want something else, maybe a piece from me."

Despite the odd hours of access to the factories, sometimes at three or five in the morning, a handful of artists jumped at the chance to cast their molds (in bronze, steel, or aluminum), a process worth thousands of dollars. Coral Lambert, a New Orleans-based British artist, cast her 1.5-ton steel *Isolammi (Big Water)* at "one of the biggest steel factories in that part of the world," one normally used for casting submarine parts: "Due to insurance reasons, I was only able to do a minimum amount of labor at the factory; I could be there as a director. This involved a different set of artistic skills. For example, my foam pattern was unconventional, and, as the sand was packed onto it during the sand mold process, it was designed to compress so that the form would become more pronounced through the process. The workers had not done this before so they had to feel they could trust me. Even with the language differences, a mutual respect built up. When the translator had to run off, sign language worked. We also had the same steel-toe sandals, which helped."

Other artists felt strongly that the cost to the municipality was minimal compared to the value of the artworks, which were donated or loaned to the town. According to John Ruppert, "It certainly has cost an awful lot of money and effort and time and hours from the city for all this to happen. But they also got a hugely valuable product. They couldn't buy this stuff. There's labor from the artist, but that's not really the value. The value is in the concepts and the years of profession behind the work."

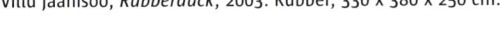

Villu Jaanisoo, *Rubberduck*, 2003. Rubber, 330 x 380 x 250 cm.

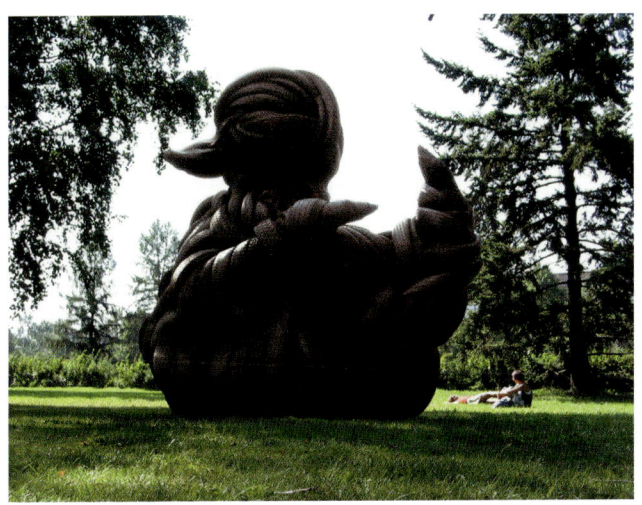

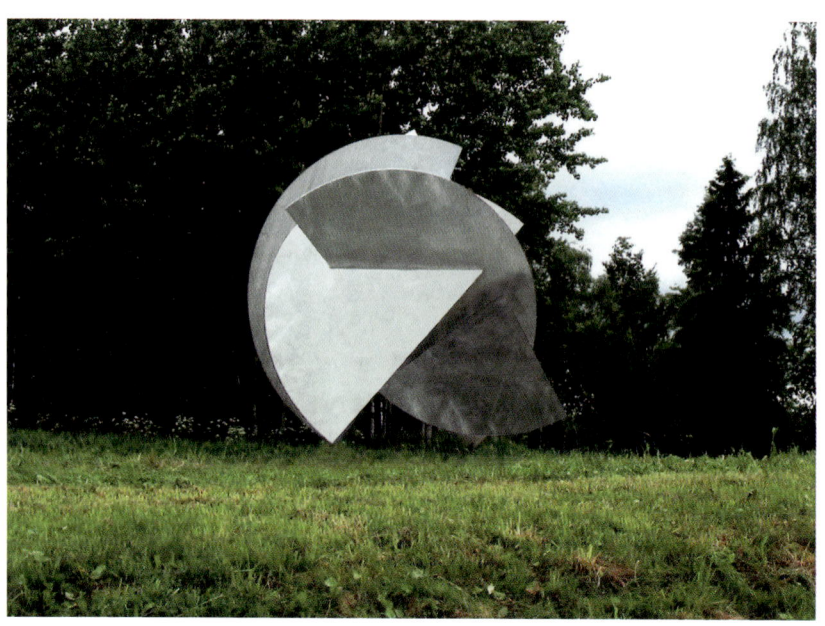

Jack Soans, *Whirl*, 2003. Steel, 400 x 400 x 400 cm.

Jaanisoo and his wife, artist Hanna Vihriälä, view the symposium as a micro-community where artists network, philosophize, and mentor younger art students. "Most of the time as an artist, you're alone. It's really lonely work, and the whole idea of a symposium is to come together," says Vihriälä. The artists and the dozen students lived, worked, and ate at the Nouliala Elementary School, where even the largest egos had to crouch gingerly on tiny plastic chairs in the children's cafeteria. "We think it's important that students learn how to do their own casting and how to do it cheaply. It's one of the reasons we started doing these workshops, and it grew into this symposium," Jaanisoo explains.

And now, after the flurry of artistic activity, the town of Pirkkala plans to continue producing a sculpture symposium every two years and to establish a yearly residency program with one or two artists at a time, either with Jaanisoo or another curator. According to Jouni Salonen, Pirkkala Secretary of Cultural Affairs, the town was not always so supportive: "A few years ago, some really opposed the idea of cast iron sculptures in nature." Perhaps overcoming that battle gave Jaanisoo the desire to show the town more than just cast iron. At the end of the day, the Pirkkala Sculpture Park is Jaanisoo's lesson, "to show people what sculpture is, what sculpture can be."

<www2.pirkkala.fi/sculpture>

Buffalo Bayou ArtPark and Community

by Kevin Jeffries

What does a sculpture park mean to a community? If I had been asked this question in 1999 when I was first tapped to take over as director of the Buffalo Bayou ArtPark (BBAP), I could have given you a clear, precise, and uplifting answer. Seven years later, and a year after I stepped down and have had time for reflection, I must admit that I have no idea. Not because the park lacks meaning to the community, but because the park deals with multiple stakeholders, all of whom have their own needs, all of whom place a unique meaning on the park, be it positive, negative, or neutral.

What a sculpture park means to one community may compromise what it means to another, which can cause conflict. Funders, who see the park as a way to raise the profile of the city and make it more attractive to potential employers and employees, ascribe a meaning that repels the sculptor, who sees the park as a way to raise awareness of social problems that the funders would rather see swept under the rug.

When I became director, I was advised by one board member not to forget that BBAP existed to be a thorn in the side of the city administration. It's tough to reconcile that mandate with the requirement that the park work with city agencies and demonstrate that it is improving the city's quality of life, or increasing tourism to the city, or whatever the arts are expected to do for the city this year.

With hindsight, I can see now that many of the problems I faced as director were due to conflicts between the different communities we dealt with and that those conflicts arose from the various meanings they placed, or imposed, on us. This may have been inevitable, but it is ironic considering our beginnings. BBAP, at least at one time, was close to being the ideal artist-run sculpture park. Its founding event was a temporary exhibition of sculptures on the publicly owned site of an old farmers market on the banks of Buffalo Bayou in downtown Houston during the summer of 1987.

The show had been organized to take the place of the Bayou Show, an annual display of sculpture sponsored by the city, which was cancelled because the city had blown a bundle of money on a concert by Jean-Michel Jarre the year before. A crisis for some, this situation provided an opportunity for an emerging group of local artists.

The Watermelon Flats Show of 1987, which featured work by about 25 artists, was organized with the support of downtown organizations, the Houston parks department, and various arts organizations. It was a unique event, lightning caught in a bottle. The Houston *Chronicle*'s art critic called it "an enthusiastic, multi-artist revelry full of energy and imagination." It wasn't necessarily an artistic success since the pieces were uneven, but that was part of the magic. The uniqueness of the setting was central to the show's appeal. The works' "very hiddenness

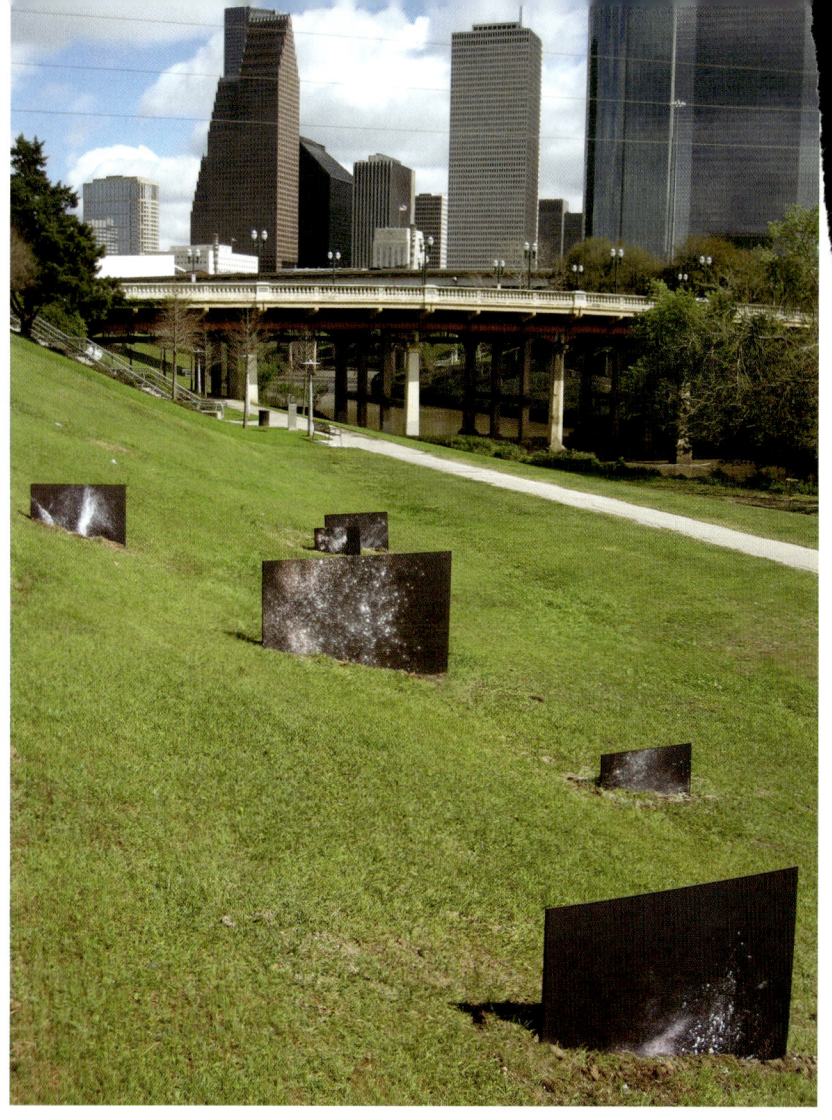

Barry Stone, *Decking the Path to Blessedness*, 2008. Photographs printed on vinyl and mounted on Sintra, 28 x 72 in., 30 x 45 in., and 20 x 30 in.

is part of the exhibition's concept, and coming upon an unexpected object is intrinsic to the visual experience."

Looking back, one can detect, between the lines, a "meaning" then that was impossible to reproduce later. The show's "unexpectedness," the fact that objects were hidden in an area where art had never been placed before, was exciting and unique. The coming together of the community in a new location, with new possibilities, created a camaraderie that can only happen once. It was important that these were young, emerging artists anxious to develop their careers. A collective urgency fueled them. This common sense of purpose—the response to the crisis when the Bayou Show was cancelled, the use of a new location for the exhibition, and the shared desire to establish artistic careers—created an intense community among these artists. It was a pure manifestation of the artistic impulse. At that moment, it was easy to say what a sculpture park meant to a community—it was all about the incessant need to create. We could make such a clear statement because we knew who the community was, and what the exhibition was intended to accomplish.

Everything was in place, except that there was no park at the time, only a one-time show. And there were other supporters of the exhibition motivated by other considerations. The publicly owned site was important to many other communities for many other reasons. But the success of the Watermelon Flats Show led to additional shows and spurred the desire to bureaucratize the process of installing temporary work by creating an organization to handle it. The Buffalo Bayou ArtPark is that organization. It was deliberately designed to be run by volunteer artists, and it was funded on a shoe-string budget of roughly $10,000 a year. These parameters were intended to keep the park closely connected to the local arts community and tied into the original artistic impulse that shaped the Watermelon Flats Show.

This expectation, of course, is unrealistic: artists grow older and careers evolve. Once established, an artist turns to other goals and objectives. As these objectives lead people in different directions, the nucleus of a single community falls apart. The original meaning of the park becomes lost, at least to its founders. Others step in to take their places, but their objectives differ and the meanings they attach to the park are not the meanings that created it. The lightning caught in the bottle dissipates and cannot be replaced.

What's more, the very creation of a formal organization adds new meaning to the park. The chief goal of an organization is to preserve the organization. Organizations need funds and supporters, each of whom has his or her own unique reason for working with the park. To preserve itself, the organization has to bend to the requirements placed on it by its supporters.

As an example, Houston's cultural arts council used three separate criteria over the course of my directorship to judge the merit of applications for funding: community-building, quality of life, and whether an organization increased tourism. These shifts were not deliberately capricious, they were simply the result of changes in how the council received and allocated revenue. In order to qualify for funding, and then justify it in a final report, we had to change our story three times. At first, BBAP meant stronger communities, then we meant a more livable city, finally we meant heads in beds. An organization forced to reinvent itself every time its funding mechanism changes is constantly in flux, its meaning subject to shifts in the political environment. In our case, the meaning that had once been sought purely in the art placed in the park, and the artistic spirit that guided it, was lost.

It is worth noting that BBAP is not a city organization. It does not receive designated funds from the city for the work installed, aside from the grants available to all arts organizations through the cultural arts council. The bulk of the funds spent on the installed work was raised primarily through local foundations and supporters. It is also important to point out that the city's arts organizations have no authority over city property. Their approval of a piece does not mean that it can be installed. A variety of city departments have jurisdiction over different parts of the park, and they are responsible for issuing the permits that allow work to be installed.

Each department has its own mission and is often engaged in turf wars with other departments. Small organizations like BBAP can sometimes become pawns in battles between various groups. Since each department has its own mission, each one tends to see the park in terms of that mission. The park may mean one thing to the parks department, which has jurisdiction over one segment, and another to the public works department, which has jurisdiction over another. At last count, six separate city, county, and state agencies had some type of jurisdiction over some part of the land occupied by BBAP. Each agency has to be dealt with at different times, in different ways. And each has to be approached in terms of the meaning it places on the park.

Then there is the matter of competing organizations. Some nonprofit groups were and are interested in the park's land for reasons unconnected to the art. Artists were not the only people involved in organizing the Watermelon Flats Show. One of the supporters of the original show, Central Houston, is a group composed primarily of businesses located in downtown Houston and devoted to the "redevelopment and revitalization of downtown." Like many American downtowns in the mid-20th century, central Houston was neglected as residents moved to the suburbs. Other areas, edge cities, emerged and began to draw business from the downtown area. Central Houston's interest in the exhibition was conditional on its ability to help redevelop downtown. Artists are the vanguard, and if they become interested in an area, others will follow. Watermelon Flats was one of a handful of downtown locations where artists were gravitating, so their interest could be expected to bring others along. To a degree it did. For Central Houston, and the business sector in general, BBAP means the creation of an environment conducive to profit.

Other organizations are also stakeholders, if not in BBAP, at least in the environmental or historical aspects of its location. The site of the Watermelon Flats Show is a quarter-mile upstream from Allen's Landing, where Houston's founders, a couple of land speculators from Brooklyn, stepped off a steam boat in 1837 and decided to make a fortune. The town grew in fits and starts, and the area served as the city's port until

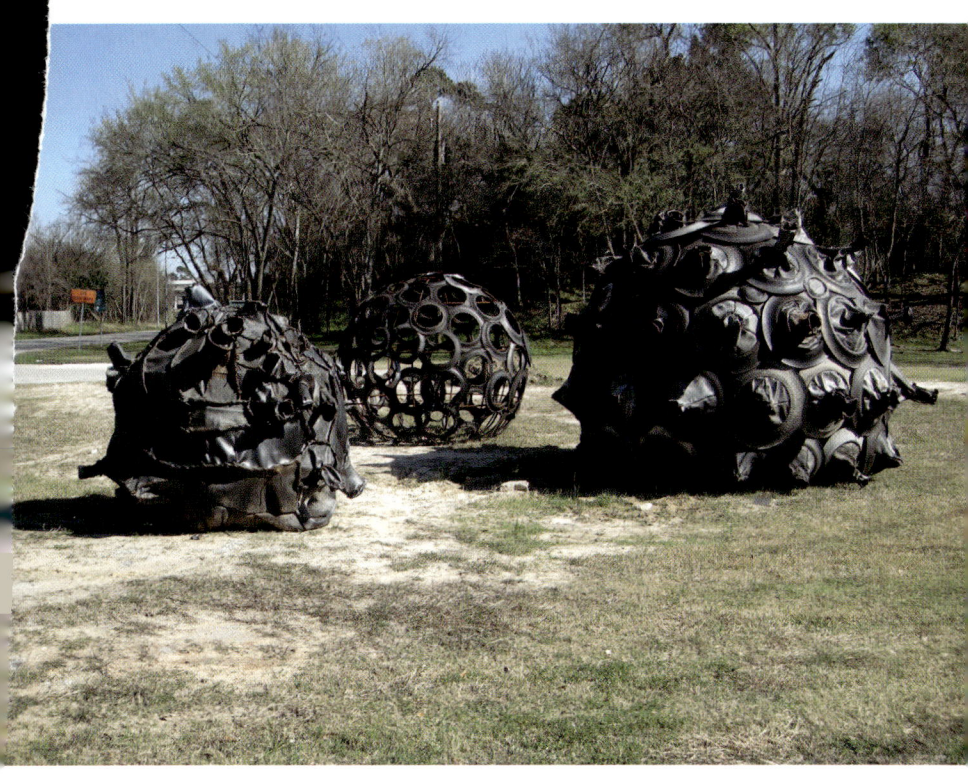

Kathy Kelley, *Suckling is Continuous*, 2008. Found tire elements mounted to rebar frames, 6–10 ft. diameter.

the current port, several miles further downstream, was dredged in 1909. The bayou was neglected for much of the rest of the century. Many downtown buildings backed up into it, including the farmers market whose foundation would host the Watermelon Flats show. Several city streets and a major interstate are constructed over it. In the 1960s, its banks were almost replaced with concrete embankments.

Despite periodic efforts to make it appealing, by the 1980s the bayou was unkempt, overgrown, and popular with the area's homeless population. The construction of several roadways decades before had created a barrier between the bayou and nearby residential areas, so there was little sense of connection between the bayou and all but a small handful of Houston residents. About the time of the Watermelon Flats Show, other organizations began to take the area seriously and sought to revitalize it for their own purposes, according to their own visions. Some of these purposes were based on the area's history, others on its environmental importance, and others on potential recreational uses.

The location of the park is loaded with multiple meanings, each with its own constituency with a connection to a particular group dedicated to that meaning. The bayou as a natural feature had a meaning to each of these groups, which had nothing to do with BBAP or the idea of public art. Environmental groups will pursue actions to preserve the area's ecosystem, historical groups will push for the creation of markers to remind passersby of what happened here or there, and so on. Each can provide opportunities for collaboration, but collaboration requires compromise, which not everyone is willing to do.

As we know, temporary public art, as much as it might seem valuable to us, is not necessarily valuable to others. If the construction projects developed by other organizations force us to relocate work, we comply. If a well-connected local attorney can write a seven-figure check to build a nearby skateboard park because his grandson likes to skateboard, we make adjustments. If board members of competing organizations want to try their hand at organizing a separate arts event, or even develop a public art master plan without our involvement, we determine the best way to fight for our interests. Again, everyone has his or her own attitude toward the park, which accordingly conditions their relationship to it.

The question then becomes whether such organizations will continue their support of the park if they no longer believe that it revitalizes downtown, or if a different type of sculpture park can do the job better. BBAP has always focused on local emerging artists, but as downtown's arts infrastructure has evolved, efforts have been made by some organizations to focus efforts on established artists with national reputations. Projects with these individuals can swamp the financial and organizational capabilities of a small group like BBAP. What began as a park dedicated to the local community can then become—though fortunately this hasn't happened yet—redefined in a way that shuts out the very population that started it all. There's some irony.

This all may be part of the natural growth cycle of any artistic endeavor. After the clarity that embodies an initial period of euphoria, the realities of survival and the individual directions that artists take lead to a period of compromise and detachment from the original mission. The founders then grow detached, and the park becomes something different, something shaped by competing forces that tries to make too many people happy and therefore, of course, makes no one happy. At least that's what I think on gloomier days.

I was never able to reconcile these competing forces with one another and have left it to others. This decision was driven more by exhaustion than a lack of ideas about how to address the issue. Since I want to conclude on a hopeful note, I'll offer two possible approaches.

The first is to embrace these multiple meanings and make them the subject matter of exhibitions, and to do so boldly. When Steven Siegel toured the site while developing ideas for a project, he remarked that a particular area overgrown with weeds, beneath a highway overpass, near a homeless man's camp, and across the bayou from pristine glass towers, was "charged." The intersection of man/nature, wealth/poverty, order/disorder was exciting on multiple levels. The multiple meanings active in the area ought to be embraced. Ignore the very possibility that a single meaning exists. Invite controversy: make it central to the park's mission. This makes some people unhappy and can cause some to withdraw support for future events. Fundraising can suffer, but that may have to be accepted. In the case of BBAP, such an approach may come closest to retaining the maverick spirit that made the Watermelon Flats Show a success.

The second possibility is to acknowledge that the Watermelon Flats Show was in fact lightning in a bottle and can never be recaptured, pulling up the stakes and replanting them elsewhere. You can only do something unexpected once. When you replicate it, you repeat yourself and start to become predictable, which is boring. That's the worst thing art can be.

Houston covers over 600 square miles. And none of it is zoned. The resulting juxtapositions are amazing, and sometimes horrifying. Chemical plants next to residential areas, businesses, and churches, ragged strip centers, 50-story condos jutting out of an empty field, neighborhoods of all conceivable types (each with its own aesthetic), a wooded east end that belongs in the 1950s, a Galleria area that might as well be Dubai, and all of those bayous, everywhere. Only the most mindless booster will tell you it's all pretty, but it is practically all "charged." And that creates opportunities, which is what the Watermelon Flats Show was all about to begin with. To embrace these opportunities would be jump into the void, but that's what it's all about isn't it?

<www.buffalobayou.org/artpark.html>

Photo credits

cover	Tony Cragg, *Bulb*, [Courtesy the artist and Cass Sculpture Foundation]
p. 11	Henry Moore, *Reclining Figure*, [Christina Ali]
p. 12	Henry Moore, *Locking Piece*, [Christina Ali]
p. 17	Richard Deacon, *Like a Bird*, [David Heald, Courtesy the artist]
p. 18	Anish Kapoor, *Cloud Gate*, [Walter Mitchell, Courtesy City of Chicago]
p. 23	Barbara Kruger, Henry Smith-Miller, Laurie Hawkinson, and Nicholas Quennell, *PICTURE THIS*, [Courtesy North Carolina Museum of Art]
p. 24	Thomas Sayre, *Gyre*, [© Thomas H. Sayre, Courtesy North Carolina Museum of Art]
p. 29	Scott Burton, *Six-Part Seating*, [Courtesy National Gallery of Art, Washington, DC]
p. 31	Louise Bourgeois, *Spider*, [Courtesy National Gallery of Art, Washington, DC]
p. 34	Dan Graham, *Two-way Punched Steel Hedge Labyrinth*, [Courtesy Walker Art Center, Minneapolis]
p. 37	David Nash, *Standing Frame*, [Courtesy Walker Art Center, Minneapolis]
p. 40	Carlos Luna, *War-Giro*, [Courtesy Museum of Latin American Sculpture]
p. 41	Noé Katz, *The Secret Voyage*, [Courtesy Museum of Latin American Sculpture]
p. 43	Ilan Averbuch, *Skirts and Pants (after Duchamp)*, [Mark Wilson]
p. 44	Chakaia Booker, *No More Milk and Cookies* and *The Conversationalist*, [Mark Wilson, Courtesy Marlborough Gallery, NY]
p. 47	Arman, *Pablo Casal's Obelisk*, [Judy Cooper, Courtesy New Orleans Museum of Art]
p. 49	Arnaldo Pomodoro, *Una Battaglia*, [Judy Cooper, Courtesy New Orleans Museum of Art]
p. 53	Alexander Calder, *Eagle*, [Paul Macapia, Courtesy Seattle Art Museum]
p. 54	Anthony Caro, *Riviera*, [Paul Macapia, Courtesy Seattle Art Museum]
p. 57	Mark di Suvero, *Pyramidian*, [Jerry L. Thompson, © Storm King Art Center, Courtesy Mark di Suvero and Storm King Art Center, Mountainville, NY]
p. 58	Aerial view of OSP, [Paul Warchol, Courtesy Seattle Art Museum]
p. 61	Magdalena Abakanowicz, *Negev*, [© The Israel Museum, Jerusalem]
p. 62	Margaret Evangeline, *Gunshot Landscape*, [Courtesy The Fields Sculpture Park at Omi International Arts Center]
p. 65	John Ruppert, *Pumpkins*, [Malgorzata Mosiek, Courtesy The Sculpture Foundation, Inc.]
p. 69	Andy Goldsworthy, *Storm King Wall*, [Jerry L. Thompson, © Andy Goldsworthy, Courtesy Galerie Lelong, NY]
p. 70	Alice Aycock, *Three-Fold Manifestation II*, [Jerry L. Thompson, © Storm King Art Center]
p. 73	Patricia Piccinini, *Nest*, [Courtesy Middelheimmuseum]
p. 74	Corey McCorkle, *Yayoi*, [Courtesy Middelheimmuseum]
p. 78	Henry Moore, *Reclining Figure: Arch Leg*, [Ken Scarlett]
p. 81	Andy Goldsworthy, *Hanging Trees. Oxley Bank. Yorkshire Sculpture Park*, [Jonty Wilde]
p. 82	James Turrell, *Deer Shelter*, [Jonty Wilde]
p. 85	Marta Pan, *Floating Sculpture, Otterlo*, [Courtesy Kröller-Müller Museum, Otterlo, the Netherlands]
p. 87	Barbara Hepworth, *Squares with Two Circles*, [Courtesy Kröller-Müller Museum, Otterlo, the Netherlands]
p. 90	View of Laumeier Sculpture Park, [Ray Marklin, Courtesy Laumeier Sculpture Park]
p. 91	Vito Acconci, *Face of the Earth #3*, [Mike Venso, Courtesy Laumeier Sculpture Park]
p. 93	Kahn/Selesnick, *Apollo Lunar Rover Crash Site*, [Courtesy the artists and The Fields Sculpture Park at Omi International Arts Center]
p. 94	Mikala Dwyer, *Empty Sculpture*, [Courtesy The Fields Sculpture Park at Omi International Arts Center]
p. 97	Carlos Dorrien, *The Nine Muses*, [David Steele, Courtesy The Sculpture Foundation, Inc.]
p. 98	Isaac Witkin, *Eolith*, [David Steele, Courtesy Nadine Witkin, Estate of Isaac Witkin]
p. 103	Bill Woodrow, *Regardless of History*, [Courtesy the artist and Cass Sculpture Foundation]

p. 104 Abigail Fallis, *DNA DL90*, [Courtesy the artist and Cass Sculpture Foundation]
p. 107 Alexander Liberman, *Aria*, [Bill Hebert, Courtesy Frederik Meijer Gardens & Sculpture Park]
p. 108 Juan Muñoz, *Broken Nose Carrying Bottle Number One*, [Chuck Heiney, Courtesy Frederik Meijer Gardens & Sculpture Park]
p. 115 Nils-Udo, *Clemson Clay Nest*, [Courtesy South Carolina Botanical Garden]
p. 117 Fatu Feu'u, *Guardian of the Planting*, [Sally Tagg]
p. 118 Igor Antic, *Paysage multiplié*, [© Le Vent des Forêts]
p. 121 Alfio Bonanno, *Between copper beech and oak*, [Courtesy TICKON]
p. 123 Alan Sonfist, *Maze of great oak of Denmark within stone ship—1001 young trees*, [Courtesy TICKON]
p. 127 Anne O'Callaghan, *Relic of Memory*, [Isaac Applebaum]
p. 128 Lois Andison and Simone Jones, *Tidal Pool: Ode to Tom Thomson*, [E.J. Lightman]
p. 132 Michael Warren, *Antaeus*, [Courtesy the artist]
p. 133 Kat O'Brien, *Seven Shrines—Na Seachta Scrinta*, [Courtesy the artist]
p. 136 Roberley Bell, *Arcadia Bell*, [Stefan Hagen, Courtesy the artist]
p. 137 Luis Castro, *Ese Botero es mio (recordando Felipe Pirela)*, [Eva Heyd, Courtesy the artist]
p. 144 Antony Gormley, *Together and Apart*, [Courtesy Wanås Foundation]
p. 147 Maya Lin, *11 Minute Line*, [Anders Norrsell, Courtesy Wanås Foundation]
p. 149 Sol LeWitt, *1-2-3-2-1*, [Courtesy Gori Collecton—Fattoria di Celle, Pistoia, Italy]
p. 150 Bukichi Inoue, *My Sky Hole*, [Courtesy Gori Collecton—Fattoria di Celle, Pistoia, Italy]
p. 153 Bruce Nauman, *Untitled*, [Wardell Photography]
p. 155 Ann Hamilton, *The Tower*, [Mark Jensen]
p. 159 Adel Abdessemed, *Salam Europe!*, [Francis Billet]
p. 165 Ojars Feldbergs, *51 Heartstones*, [Courtesy Open-Air Museum at Pedvale]
p. 167 Mairita and Ivo Folkmans, *Fire Road*, [Courtesy Open-Air Museum at Pedvale]
p. 169 Aerial view of Cullen Sculpture Garden, [Courtesy Museum of Fine Arts, Houston]
p. 171 Joseph Havel, *Exhaling Pearls*, [Courtesy Museum of Fine Arts, Houston]
p. 172 Daniel Spoerri, *Labyrinthic mural path*, [Susanne Neumann]
p. 174 Daniel Spoerri, *Circle of Unicorns*, [Susanne Neumann]
p. 177 Ian Hamilton Finlay with Nicholas Sloan, *The Present Order*, [Andrew Lawson]
p. 178 Ian Hamilton Finlay with John Andrew, *Nuclear Sail*, [Andrew Lawson]
p. 181 Robert Irwin, *Central Garden*, [Jim Duggan, © 2006 J. Paul Getty Trust]
p. 182 Robert Irwin, *Central Garden*, [Jim Duggan, © 2006 J. Paul Getty Trust]
p. 185 Nek Chand, *Rock Garden*, [Courtesy Nek Chand Foundation]
p. 187 Nek Chand, *Rock Garden*, [Courtesy Nek Chand Foundation]
p. 191 Jude Tallichet, *Flash Park*, and Matthew McCaslin, *Roots of the Nightshade Family*, [Steven L. Cohen, Courtesy Socrates Sculpture Park, McCaslin: Gering & López Gallery, Tallichet: Sara Meltzer Gallery]
p. 192 Leo Villareal, *Star*, and Matthew McCaslin, *Roots of the Nightshade Family*, [Steven L. Cohen, Courtesy Socrates Sculpture Park and Gering & López Gallery]
p. 197 Magdalena Abakanowicz, *Space of Unknown Growth*, [Gintaras Karosas, Courtesy Europos Parkas]
p. 198 Gintaras Karosas, *The Place*, [Courtesy the artist and Europos Parkas]
p. 201 Aaron Dysart, *1963 Black Walnut*, [Courtesy Franconia Sculpture Park]
p. 203 Su-Chen Hung, *Lift*, [Courtesy Franconia Sculpture Park]
p. 205 Chris Duncan, *Hey Joe*, [Courtesy Salem Art Works]
p. 206 Felicia Glidden, *Matris Fe*, [Courtesy Salem Art Works]
p. 208 Liz Magor, *Messenger*, [W.N. Greer, Courtesy Toronto Sculpture Garden]
p. 210 Ludwika Ogorzelec, *Mist: from the Space Crystallization Cycle*, [W.N. Greer, Courtesy Toronto Sculpture Garden]
p. 216 Barry Stone, *Decking the Path to Blessedness*, [Elaine Bradford, Courtesy Buffalo Bayou ArtPark]
p. 219 Kathy Kelley, *Suckling is Continuous*, [Elaine Bradford, Courtesy Buffalo Bayou ArtPark]